The *Confederados*

The *Confederados*

Old South Immigrants in Brazil

Edited by
Cyrus B. Dawsey
James M. Dawsey

The University of Alabama Press
Tuscaloosa

∞

The paper on which this book is printed meets
the minimum requirements of American National
Standard for Information Science–Permanence of
Paper for Printed Library Materials,
ANSI Z39.48–1984.

Library of Congress Cataloging-in-Publication Data

The Confederados : Old South immigrants in Brazil / edited by Cyrus B.
Dawsey [and] James M. Dawsey.
p.   cm.
Includes bibliographical references and index.
ISBN 0-8173-0944-6 (alk. paper)
1. American Confederate voluntary exiles—Brazil—History.
2. United States—History—Civil War, 1861–1865—Refugees.
3. Brazil—History—Empire, 1822–1889.   4. Immigrants—Brazil
—History—19th century.   I. Dawsey, Cyrus B., d. 1976.   II. Dawsey,
James M.
F2659.A5C66   1995
981'.00413—dc20
94-9461

British Library Cataloguing-in-
Publication Data available
First Paperback Printing 1998
1 2 3 4 5 • 02 01 00 99 98

To Judith MacKnight Jones

Confederado historian

Contents

Contents

Foreword

Michael L. Conniff

Every book has a history, including this one. Sinewy lines of causality stretch like vines into the foliage of the past. The Dawsey brothers who have contributed so much to this book spent their childhoods in the interior of the state of São Paulo, Brazil, where their parents served as missionaries in the Brazilian Methodist Church. Their grandparents were also missionaries who, responding to the religious fervor of the early twentieth century, moved to Brazil where they remained most of their years. Grandfather Dawsey preached his first sermon in Brazil at the *Campo* chapel of the *confederados* near Santa Bárbara, and Grandmother Dawsey was later buried near the tomb of Prudente de Moraes in the nearby city of Piracicaba.

Auburn University, located in central Alabama, has also played a role in the development of this book. One of its important functions as a land-grant institution has been to promote agricultural and educational development overseas—just as the Southern emigrants from Alabama and neighboring states did over a century ago. The university's main library is compiling a special collection of documents for research into this remarkable episode in American history. Thus, it was no accident that thirty to forty people who follow the story of the *confederados* gathered here for several days in July 1992 to share research findings and map out new directions.

Nor was it an accident that the Southern émigrés wound up in Brazil. That country had always fascinated observers and invited comparisons with the United States. The English writer Robert Southey, who lived in Rio de Janeiro in the early nineteenth century, predicted in his magisterial *History of Brazil* that the country would surpass the United States in virtually all forms of endeavor. A hundred years later, Theodore Roosevelt pointed out the similarities between the two countries and predicted that they would become great powers and allies. Both countries featured a plantation economy dependent on slaves imported from Africa, and students of race relations have created a small industry devoted to comparisons between the different ways racial groups have interacted. Thus Brazil has always fascinated and attracted Americans.

The cataclysmic U.S. Civil War drove the timing of the Southern emigration: followers of the defeated Confederacy could not wait to leave, as Wayne Flynt's chapter makes clear. From the standpoint of the receiving

Conniff

country, however, the timing was unpropitious. In 1865 Brazil plunged into the War of the Triple Alliance, the slave question began to heat up, and soon an economic depression deflated the boom of preceding decades. The emperor, Dom Pedro II, had done much to encourage the migration; yet by the time the Southerners arrived he was overwhelmed with the war, domestic problems, and eventually his own failing health. The *confederados* largely had to fend for themselves. In consolation, however, they did not have to face a hostile government, as did Southern émigrés in Mexico after the execution of Maximilian.

Seen in the long term, though, Brazil and Latin America as a whole were beginning to seize control of their destinies in the years of the Southern out-migration. Argentina, Brazil, Chile, and Mexico (after a few years) consolidated their nationhood and entered a period of dramatic export-led growth. They rapidly replaced the Iberian mercantilism of colonial times with industrial capitalism and became engaged in the world economy. It was a good time for Americans to get in on the ground floor, so to speak. This may account for the unusual effect that the *confederados* had in Brazil: their impact was amplified by the effects of rapid modernization.

As Laura Jarnagin makes clear, the Southern emigration to Brazil took place within a framework of world-wide proportions. Industrialism and the transportation revolution made anything seem possible, even taming the mighty Andes mountains and Amazon jungle. Science, new technologies, educational advances, and the rise of international trade made it seem that progress was inevitable. Indeed, the positivism of the age became a faith of sorts, at least for those in the core regions. No matter that the Southerners were moving from one periphery to another, they could dream of using the system for their own advancement.

The emigrants did not operate in a social vacuum either. Personal acquaintances, family networks, Freemasonry, business contracts, churches, and other associations constituted a dense web of relations that encouraged emigrants to leave the United States and sustained them in Brazil. Because prominent families in both countries—like the Calhouns and Yanceys and Campos Sales—promoted the emigration, its eventual success was favored. It would not stretch the point to say that those networks embrace Auburn University even today, through family ties, agreements with foreign universities, academic exchanges, and friendships.

The reader needn't be Alabamian, or Southern, or Brazilian, to enjoy this book. These pages contain fascinating portraits of individuals who took great risks and led adventurous lives—for example, Lansford Warren Hastings, Sara Bellona Smith Ferguson, Frank McMullan, and E. H.

Quillin—and their writings have the power to transport us back into the past. Some of the accounts are classic—such as the spinach revolt in Henry Ford's Santarém plantation. These people and dramas belong among the great stories of human existence.

Is the world a different place because of the Southern migration to Brazil? Some things would have happened anyway—the arrival of the mold-board plow and watermelon, for example—but others would almost certainly not have. The educational contributions of people like Annie Newman, for example, bore fruit that nobody could have predicted. The early Baptist and Methodist missionaries would be astonished to see the present day robust churches and schools founded over a century ago. And it may even be true that Brazil's rank as one of the world's greatest exporters of agricultural commodities would not have come to pass without the timely contributions of the Southern farmers.

A look at the other large body of Americans in the hemisphere—the Canal Zonians of Panama—offers a contrasting vision. The Southerners in Brazil exchanged culture and lifestyles with the Brazilians, becoming a truly hybrid community today. The Zonians, meanwhile, resisted contact with and adoption of Panamanian ways. They remained aloof and behaved as if superior to the natives, an attitude that led to harsh feelings and resentment. The canal was an exclusive American operation in their eyes, not a shared responsibility. In the end, the Zonians left Panama, and little remains of their handiwork except the canal. The cultural, intellectual, and social possibilities of coexistence were never realized. As this volume points out, the *confederados* in Brazil were different. They eventually became part of the local social fabric, and their contributions left a profound impression on the host country.

It has been a great pleasure for me to be associated with this book and the people who made it. I expect it to find a wide and appreciative audience, here and in Brazil.

Introduction
The *Confederados*

Cyrus B. Dawsey and James M. Dawsey

A curious event occurs at a site a few miles outside of the town of Santa Bárbara, Brazil. As often as four times a year, people from throughout the country gather at a small chapel and cemetery situated amid the sugarcane fields, where, dressed in costumes of nineteenth-century America, they sing old Protestant revival hymns and listen to a sermon. After the worship service, the people share a traditional dinner on the grounds, which includes biscuits, gravy, and Southern fried chicken. Some of those eating do not look Brazilian. They have red hair, freckles, and blue eyes. The older ones spend the afternoon in conversation, catching up with news of family and friends. They talk, not in Portuguese, but in a quaint English dialect. The younger ones dance, play, and listen to the oft-told stories of their elders.

The periodic gatherings are reunions of the *confederados*, descendants of Americans from the South of the United States who, dissatisfied with the outcome of the Civil War, packed or sold their belongings and moved to Brazil in the 1860s and 1870s. Although the saga of discontented Confederates sailing to new homes across the seas has been told before, there is much concerning this event that remains obscure. Details of the story have faded with time, and some aspects are clouded by romantic attachment to the Southerners or by misperceptions concerning the emigrants' motives.

Oftentimes, American and Brazilian visitors to the *Campo* (field) cemetery at Santa Bárbara search for familiar names among the tombstones. Among those buried there are Carltons, Cobbs, Greens, Moores, Norrises, Owens, Smiths, Steagalls, and scores more—all common names in Alabama, Georgia, Mississippi, South Carolina, and Texas. Inscribed on the headstone of one of the founders of the community are the words "Soldier rest! Thy warfare o'er. Sleep the sleep that knows no breaking, Days of toil or nights of waking." Nearby, another marker claims that an early settler "died in perfect peace."

Who were the ancestors of these people who still speak English and gather periodically near Santa Bárbara? Where did they come from? Why did they leave the United States? And what led them to settle in that particular region of Brazil?

C. B. Dawsey & J. M. Dawsey

Tombstone of a Member of the Steagall Family at Campo, Santa Bárbara
(*Photograph by Cyrus B. Dawsey*)

Certainly, the pride, courage, and stamina of the rebel emigrants and the adventure of their quest have done much to stimulate both fanciful imagination and scholarly curiosity. Novels, magazine articles, newspaper accounts, historical papers, and referenced academic publications, with varying degrees of accuracy, have recounted elements of the story. And yet, there is much about the nineteenth-century migration and settlement that has not been fully examined.

Although there are many questions to be answered concerning the historical context and the event of the migration itself, two topics related to the Southerners who moved to Brazil stand largely unexplored by the academic community. One concerns the cultural impact that the *confederados*, as they came to be called, exerted on their host country. Many descendants of the Americans state that their ancestors, though a tiny fraction of all those who immigrated to Brazil in the late nineteenth century, introduced innovations that transformed the rural economy. More important, the Americans are said to have marked educational and religious institutions in Brazil with an influence that has persisted to the present.

A second topic that remains virtually unexamined by scholars concerns the ways in which the original settlers and their descendants fit into the larger Brazilian society. Most immigrant nationalities that arrived in Brazil were quickly absorbed by the surrounding culture. Though they numbered but a few thousand and appeared earlier than most of the groups from other nations, the Americans maintained very distinctive traits, and some descendants still speak English as a first language. Why has this group held on to many of its ways while others, though larger, have not?

This volume explores these and other topics related to the notable fact that descendants of Southerners who have lived in Brazil for approximately 125 years continue to see themselves as a distinct people. The book consists primarily of essays written by some of the principal scholars working in this area. The genesis of the book took place at a special conference held at Auburn University, Alabama, in July 1992, sponsored by the university's Institute for Latin American Studies and the Alabama Humanities Foundation. The conference introduced an important firsthand account of the Alfred I. Smith family's emigration to Brazil and explored four interrelated themes concerning the post–Civil War migration and settlement of Americans in Brazil: (1) the social, economic, and historical context in the United States and in Brazil at the end of the Civil War; (2) the events of the nineteenth-century migration and settlement; (3) the initial and continuing influence of the Americans and their descendants on Brazilian society; and (4) the persistence and preservation in Brazil of elements of the American, Old South heritage.

Similar to the conference, this volume also is organized around these themes and the Smith narrative. It should be noted, however, that not all of the oral presentations from the conference are represented in this book and that, conversely, a substantial amount of material in the book was not presented at the conference.[1] Rather, the essays included herein express the current status of research by important scholars who are examining questions related to one or more of the above themes. Most of the contributors have already published significant related work, so their essays are often extensions of efforts that have been under way for some time.

Tracing the Story

The scholarly quest for information concerning emigration from the American South began in earnest during the first half of the twentieth century. After reading Ballard Dunn's *Brazil, the Home for Southerners* (1866), Daniel P. Kidder's *Sketches of Residence and Travels in Brazil* (1845), Lansford Warren Hastings's *The Emigrant's Guide to Brazil* (1867), and many old issues of the *New Orleans Times* and *De Bow's Review,* Lawrence Hill wrote an article entitled "Confederate Exiles to Brazil" which appeared in the *Hispanic American Historical Review* in May 1927. He followed that article with a three-part series for the *Southwestern Historical Quarterly* entitled "The Confederate Exodus to Latin America." In the first installment, subtitled "Romance and Strife" (1935), Hill examined the conditions in the South that led to emigration; the formation of colonization associations; the activities of agents such as William Wallace Wood and colony organizers such as Hastings; governmental migration policies in Latin America, especially in Brazil; and the selection of sites for colonies in Latin America. In the second part, "Dixielands in South America" (1936), he described the colonizing efforts in Paraná, at Juquiá, Santa Bárbara, Rio Doce, Santarém, in Rio de Janeiro, and on the Orinoco. And in the third part, "Confederates in Middle America" (1936), Hill looked at colonies in British Honduras and Mexico.[2]

A small group of Hill's contemporaries also contributed in important ways to the beginning of scholarly study of Southern emigration to Latin America. In 1928 Mark Jefferson published "An American Colony in Brazil" in the *Geographical Review* and predicted impending doom for the inhabitants of the colony. Peter Brannon, editor of the *Alabama Historical Quarterly,* conducted research concerning Confederate emigration and published articles in the *Quarterly* in the summer and fall of 1930. And soon after, Blanche Henry Clark began her efforts, while still a graduate student, to find new information about the Southern diaspora. She mailed letters to everyone she could locate who might have information about emigration, including dozens of persons in Brazil and in the United States. As a result of her research, Clark (by that time, "Weaver") published two very important studies in the *Journal of Southern History,* "Confederate Immigrants and Evangelical Churches in Brazil" (1952) and "Confederate Emigration to Brazil" (1961).[3]

Additional articles appeared in scholarly as well as popular literature of the mid-twentieth century. In 1940 Desmond Holdridge published "Toledo: A Tropical Refugee Settlement in British Honduras" in the *Geographical Review;* James E. Edmonds wrote "They've Gone—Back Home!" for the *Saturday Evening Post* (1941); and Jose Arthur Rios published "Assimilation of Emigrants from the Old South in Brazil" in *Social Forces* (1947).[4]

Hamilton Basso's "Last Confederate" appeared in the *New Yorker* in 1953. That same year, Frank A. Knapp, Jr., published the more scholarly "A New Source on the Confederate Exodus to Mexico: The Two Republics" for the *Journal of Southern History.* In 1956 W. C. Nunn completed the first in-depth study of emigration to Mexico. His book *Escape from Reconstruction* included interesting detail but with limited documentation.[5]

Several other book-length studies followed in the 1960s. Alfred Jackson Hanna and Kathryn Abbey Hanna's book *Confederate Exiles in Venezuela* appeared in 1960, and Andrew F. Rolle's *Lost Cause* appeared in 1965. Rolle's book, subtitled *The Confederate Exodus to Mexico*, was an excellent study. In 1966, as his last task as editor of the *Alabama Historical Quarterly*, Peter Brannon published "Our Life, in Brazil," by Julia L. Keyes. Also, the first doctoral dissertation on the subject of emigration after the Civil War, "Confederate Emigration to Brazil: 1865–1870," was completed by Douglas Grier in 1968 at the University of Michigan. Grier's volume was the most complete work up to that time on the subject of Confederates in Brazil.[6]

Important Portuguese-language writings began to appear in the late 1960s. In 1967 the first modern account of the Southern colonization by a living Brazilian descendant of Confederate emigrants, Judith MacKnight Jones, was published. Entitled *Soldado descansa! Uma epopéia norte americana sob os céus do Brasil*, the work was a very good but lightly annotated overview using original sources of the American Southerners in Brazil. By 1972 Frank P. Goldman had completed *Os pioneiros americanos no Brasil: Educadores, sacerdotes, covos, e reis*, a relatively well-researched but inadequately documented survey of American emigration to Brazil. Neither Jones nor Goldman provided complete coverage of all Southern colonial ventures in Brazil. In both studies, details concerning the Lansford W. Hastings colony at Santarém on the Amazon were notably absent. In fact, except for James E. Edmonds's popular piece "They've Gone—Back Home!" and Frank Cunningham's "Lost Colony of the Confederacy," which appeared in the *American Mercury* in 1961, very little had been written about the Hastings colony since Hill published his work in 1936. In 1979, however, the deficiency was at least partially corrected with the publication of Norma de Azevedo Guilhon's *Confederados em Santarém*, an award-winning volume with some of the best information to date on the Amazon colony. Guilhon, a Brazilian, is the wife of the former governor of the state of Pará, where the town of Santarém is located. Guilhon utilized several sources on the subject for the first time. Four years later, in 1983, David Afton Riker, a descendant of the Hastings colonist David Bowman Riker, completed a family recollection entitled *O último confederado na amazônia*.[7]

From 1980 to the present, other research on Confederate emigration came to press. Beginning in 1980, Daniel E. Sutherland published significant studies expanding the context of emigration. These included "Looking for a Home: Louisiana Emigrants during the Civil War and Reconstruction" in *Louisiana History* (1980); "Exiles, Emigrants, and Sojourners: The Post–Civil War Confederate Exodus in Perspective" in *Civil War History* (1985); and *The Confederate Carpetbaggers* (1988). In 1981 Betty Antunes de Oliveira, a descendant of American emigrants living in Rio de Janeiro, compiled and published an excellent reference volume on the movement of former Confederates in and out of the port of Rio de Janeiro entitled *Movimento de passageiros norte-americanos no porto do Rio de Janeiro*. Also related to emigration but principally concerned with the development of the Protestant church and Freemasonry in Brazil was David Gueiros Vieira's 1980 work entitled *O protestantismo, a maçonaria e a questão religiosa no Brasil*. In 1982 Charles Willis Simmons completed the first study to look closely at the racist tendencies of the emigrants, "Racist Americans in a Multi-Racial Society: Confederate Exiles in Brazil," for the *Journal of Negro History*. In 1985, Eugene C. Harter's study *The Lost Colony of the Confederacy* was published. Harter, a former diplomat who served in the United States Consulate in São Paulo, provided the researcher with a view of the colonies from the perspective of a descendant of American emigrants who was raised in Brazil. In 1986 Frank J. Merli edited "Alternative to Appomattox: A Virginian's Vision of an Anglo-Confederate Colony on the Amazon, May, 1865" for the *Virginia Magazine of History and Biography*. In 1987 William Clark Griggs completed the first in-depth scholarly study on a single Confederate settlement. Entitled *The Elusive Eden: Frank McMullan's Confederate Colony in Brazil*, the work drew on previously unused source material from both U.S. and Brazilian archives. It was published by the University of Texas Press. In 1990 Michael B. Montgomery and Cecil Ataide Melo published the first study of the emigrant's language, "The Phonology of the Lost Cause: The English of the Confederados in Brazil," in *English World-Wide*.[8]

The Book's Plan

The scholars whose essays appear in this volume extend the examination of the *confederados* in three ways. First, they continue the historical study of the nineteenth-century emigration to Brazil initiated by Hill, Grier, Guilhon, and Griggs by focusing on the Norris colony near Santa Bárbara. They explore the context of that particular settlement, the people who went there, and the reasons why they did so. Second, following the incipient work of Clark, Goldman, and Oliveira, the book's authors also seek to bring better light to the study of the ways that the Americans influenced Brazilian culture. Here, especially, it is important to separate fact from boast and prejudice. Did the *confederados* change their neighbors and the future course of Brazilian society? If so, what was their influence? Finally, picking up on the studies of Jones and Harter, the contributors to the book examine the community of descendants as it still exists in the twentieth century. Who are the *confederados* today? What is their heritage, and why do many still see themselves as part of a distinct people?

While the first essays in the book primarily concern the event of, and the context of, the migration, the latter essays primarily concern the initial and continuing influence of the Americans on Brazilian society and the preservation of elements of the American, Old South heritage in that society. It is well to remember that this is a collection of essays and thus does not purport to tell the full story of the migrants and their descendants. Where appropriate, the editors have summarized the flow of related events and identified important elements not otherwise mentioned, thus providing the necessary context for the collection. In addition to the essays, the volume includes an annotated biography and the first complete presentation in an academic publication of the often-quoted first-person account by Sarah Bellona Smith.

In brief, here is what follows: In chapter 1, the book's editors provide the historical setting for the emigration from the South to the environs of Santa Bárbara following the American Civil War. Cyrus and James Dawsey offer quick summaries of (1) the postbellum conditions in the Southern states that led to an interest in migration, (2) the formation of colonization associations to help promote emigration to Latin America, (3) the conditions in Brazil that attracted Southerners, and (4) the initial settlement in diverse colonies and eventual consolidation near Santa Bárbara, Brazil. The essays by Griggs and Jarnagin have much to say about the migration itself and its context, so special care is given to fill in, rather than duplicate, information that is provided in chapters 3 and 4. Finally, an important purpose of chapter 1 is to offer a framework that will aid understanding of the important first-person account by Bellona Smith that follows in chapter 2.

Chapter 2 presents the narrative by Sarah Bellona Smith Ferguson, written when she was quite old, about her experiences as a child. Bellona's story begins in November 1865, when the Smiths left their home in Navarro County, Texas, and joined Frank McMullan and others who planned to form a colony in the province of São Paulo, Brazil. The group sailed from Galveston aboard the ship *Derby* in early 1866. There was a scurrilous plot by the ship's captain, mutiny by the Confederate exiles, a storm, and shipwreck off the coast of Cuba.

Bellona Smith recounts how the refugees were befriended in Cuba and how McMullan arranged passage from Cuba to New York, and from there

C. B. Dawsey & J. M. Dawsey

by steamship to Rio de Janeiro. In Rio, they stayed in the foreigner's hotel, and Bellona met the emperor. The emigrants went to Santos, then to Ribeira de Iguape; from there they traveled upriver in dugout canoes to their homestead on the Juquiá.

The Smiths built a house, cleared land, planted a crop, and through hard work tried to carve out a new beginning. They were isolated pioneers who would walk miles on Sundays to worship with other Americans. But perhaps they were too lonely, for after two years, in spite of their efforts and the success of their crops, they decided to move again. Thus, they left the Juquiá and traveled by foot and oxcart into the interior of the province of São Paulo, near where Col. William H. Norris and a number of other Southerners had settled. There, they tried again, and this time were successful. In all, it had taken the Smiths almost two full years to make their pilgrimage from Navarro County to their new home in the environs of Santa Bárbara.

In chapter 3, William Clark Griggs directs our attention to the principal colonies that were established in Brazil. He focuses primarily on reasons why the Southerners chose to leave the United States, the leaders of the colonies, the process by which the colonization agents recruited emigrants, the trips to Brazil, the types of people who actually went to Brazil, how the groups of emigrants were organized, and the successes and failures of the colonies.

Chapter 4, written by Laura Jarnagin, places the migration of the Smith family and other Southerners into the broad context of the relocation of families within the scheme of nineteenth-century capitalism. Distinguishing dominant core-states from subordinate peripheral areas, Jarnagin shows how the emigrant Southerners and the host Brazilians "acted in the [world] system, perpetuated it, [and] caused it to expand and mutate."

In chapter 5, Cyrus and James Dawsey introduce the second important theme of the book: the Southerners' influence on Brazilian society. In particular, they look at three areas of influence. The first part of the chapter addresses the claims made by Sarah Bellona Smith Ferguson, Douglas Grier, and others that the emigrants contributed in a significant way to the advancement of Brazilian technology and agriculture. In the second part of the chapter, the authors examine Blanche Henry Clark Weaver's important thesis that the emigration marked the establishment of Protestantism and North American–styled schools in Brazil. Since chapters 6 and 7 are devoted to the Baptists and the Methodists, the authors limit most of their study in chapter 5 to the Presbyterians.

Chapter 6 recounts the beginning of the Baptist church in Brazil. In the chapter, Wayne Flynt shows how the Southerners took their religion with them to Santa Bárbara and, after having settled, petitioned the corresponding secretary of the foreign mission board to send missionaries to continue the work started by the Baptist emigrant ministers Ratcliff, Thomas, Pyles, and Quillin. In the second half of the chapter, Flynt turns his attention to the missionaries that the Southern Baptists sent to strengthen the work. After duly noting the first arrival, the Reverend W. B. Bagby, who in 1881 took over the work in Santa Bárbara from Quillin, the author focuses more closely on the missionaries Daniel and Puthuff, who arrived from Texas in 1885.

In chapter 7 James Dawsey explores the beginning of Methodism in Brazil, a denomination which, like the Baptist church of Brazil, is closely allied with the post–Civil War migration. The chapter focuses attention on three figures who were keys to the implantation of Methodism in Brazil: the emigrant Reverend Junius E. Newman; the first missionary to Brazil supported by the Methodist Episcopal Church, South, the Reverend John J. Ransom; and the person who was perhaps most responsible for defining the role of Methodist education in Brazil, Annie Ayres Newman Ransom.

In chapter 8 Cyrus Dawsey introduces the third important theme of the book, namely, the immigrants' preservation of their distinct identity as *confederados*. He traces some of the previously mentioned processes such as migration, religious worship, settlement on the land, and consolidation of the community near Santa Bárbara. The focus of the essay, however, is on the site that has become strongly associated with the descendants of the nineteenth-century migrants. Known as *Campo*, the one-hectare parcel of land was originally set aside for burials because cemeteries were off-limits to the American Protestants. The site has been maintained over the years, and its chapel and cemetery are often shown in the popular media accounts of the *confederados*.

Chapter 9 concerns the efforts of the American descendants in Brazil to establish their identity. John Dawsey examines how the descendants, particularly as portrayed by Judith MacKnight Jones and Eugene Harter, have remembered their community's history and how they have used that knowledge to reconstruct a special identity for themselves.

Chapter 10 probes an important distinguishing cultural feature of the *confederados*: their use of the English language. Authors Montgomery and Melo carefully analyze six elements of pronunciation exhibited by eleven individuals whose speech was recorded in a videotape documentary produced during the early 1980s.

C. B. Dawsey & J. M. Dawsey

In the final chapter the editors recapitulate the salient points of the preceding chapters and mention some common themes that might lead to further investigation.

A postscript written by Eugene C. Harter follows this concluding chapter. The author is a *confederado* descendant who has spent a lifetime immersed in the history of his people. His addition, therefore, offers an insider's view as he tells the story, not only as the narrator, but also as one of the actors.

Finally, the book provides a special reference section by James Gravois and Elizabeth Weisbrod, who prepared an extensive annotated bibliography of the significant scholarly material pertinent to the history of the migration and settlement in Brazil. Their compilation should prove invaluable to future researchers as they track elements of the saga of the *confederados.*

One

Leaving
The Context of the Southern Emigration to Brazil

Cyrus B. Dawsey and James M. Dawsey

When the Confederate exiles left the United States during the mid-1860s, they were responding to a combination of interacting "push" and "pull" conditions, some real and some imagined. As we will see in chapter 4, these conditions often involved complex webs of personal and institutional relationships that extended across national boundaries. Disappointment over the outcome of the Civil War was a major reason for the movement. Most of the migrants were people who had been a part of the social and military fabric of the Old South, people who, with great loyalty to the ideals of the Confederacy, could not bear the thought of living subject to the hateful Yankees. Some of these sentiments lingered on in Brazil, as demonstrated by the continued prominence of the Confederate battle flag at the preserved American *Campo* chapel near Santa Bárbara (described in chapter 8) and emphatic gravestone inscriptions at the nearby cemetery (e.g., "Once a rebel, twice a rebel, and forever a rebel"). The victorious Union was cursed for decades, and some expatriates in Brazil were apt to demonstrate little courtesy or hospitality when they encountered fellow Americans who came from a state beyond the Mason-Dixon line.[1]

The Vanquished South

The migrants left behind a region ravaged by war where they had been afraid and their lives had been filled with stress. Many accounts, such as the diary of the Confederate officer Douglas French Forrest, describe the social and economic disintegration occurring in the South at the end of the war. By mid-May 1865, Confederate currency had lost its value. Out of pity, Forrest gave some money to two sick soldiers and purchased $600 of Confederate paper money for $3. Kirby Smith's army had been dispersed, and "the whole country for miles around was filled with predatory bands, utterly irresponsible, recognizing no rights of property, utterly de-moralized." These bands stole anything that was useful and destroyed every-thing else. Forrest and his companions guarded their possessions as best they could. A horse thief was caught and hanged.[2]

Rumors abounded: The disbanded troops of the North were rioting. "Violence and anarchy," Forrest heard, "defies description, surpassing, if it were possible, that of our own land." Andy Johnson's cabinet had resigned. Sherman was about to establish a Western Confederacy. President Davis was safe in Nassau.[3]

At first, Forrest half believed the rumors and refused to accept defeat. He was angry and remained convinced of the justice of the Southern cause. He found it difficult to contemplate reunion. "[The great powers of Europe] little understand the South," he wrote on May 24, "if they suppose us capable of soon forgetting our dead slaughtered by Yankee hirelings, our homes destroyed, our women outraged, our old men murdered! Heaven grant our people virtue and valor in this critical period of our history. I am most anxious to see and converse with the Genl. & earnestly trust he will regard the matter as I do & agree not to quit the country, but to try to arouse the people & to lead them again into the fight in our just quarrel."[4]

As the days passed, however, the reality of defeat set in. By June 3, Forrest vowed "to leave the country without ever being a prisoner paroled or other-wise of our detested foes." On June 4, Forrest wrote that although "no one seems to have any decided plan of action," he was adhering to the project of crossing the Rio Grande into Mexico. "[I] am purposed to quit the South *malgré eux* on my noble horse. I have considered the question from every standpoint, & am sure that my notions are not Quixotic, but according to right reason. There is no reason why I should put myself into the hands of the loathed Yankees." And the next day, Forrest joined General Walker on what he called "the Mexican scheme" and began the migration to the south.[5]

Daniel Sutherland has argued that the word "disarray" best character-izes that period in the Deep South soon after Appomattox.[6] The father of Bellona Smith, whose first-person account is presented in chapter 2, had served as a bugler in the Southern army in Galveston, and once released from duty, he must have taken several weeks to reach his home in Navarro County. For the Confederates, getting home could be a problem. Forrest hid at night and took special precautions against strangers. Smith must have done the same. A soldier trying to return to Tennessee wrote in his diary that "the tories are worse than before the late surrender, robbing, cowhid-

Leaving

ing, hanging, shooting, etc. To reach my family's present whereabouts we must pass through 70 miles of bad country where I may meet many who will recognize me. There be some to meet with whom is to kill or be killed."[7]

Bellona Smith did not report what Alfred Smith encountered in Navarro County when he returned home after the war. Returning soldiers and war refugees expected to find their houses burned, family and friends missing, property stolen or confiscated, and plantations destroyed. One Southerner expressed his reservations about going back in this way: "It will be a sad home-coming, without a home to go to. The family circle is broken by the death of our boys, and many dear old friends will be missing. Then we are uncertain as to whether we shall be able to save enough from the wreck of our fortune to enable us to live even in a very modest way."[8]

Sometimes, what the returnees found was even worse than imagined. The fabric of the South's government, economy, and society was in great disarray. Describing South Carolina, J. S. Pike wrote:

> The banks were ruined. The railroads were destroyed. Their few manu-
> factories were desolated. Their vessels had been swept from the seas and
> rivers. The live-stock was consumed. Notes, bonds, mortgages, all the
> money in circulation, debts, became alike worthless. The community
> were without clothes and without food. Everything had gone into the ra-
> pacious maw of the Confederate Government; vast estates had crumbled
> like paper in a fire. While the shape was not wholly destroyed, the sub-
> stance had turned to ashes. Never was there greater nakedness and deso-
> lation in a civilized community.[9]

Given the situation in the South at the end of the war, it is not surprising that many desired to leave and go elsewhere. In chapter 3, William Griggs describes at length the condition confronting Bellona Smith's father as he made the decision to leave Texas. The largest number of people relocated within the United States, following the trail west or moving to the North in search of employment.[10] But perhaps as many as 10,000 went into exile in foreign lands—most often to Latin America.[11]

There were many reasons why those who migrated to other countries did so. Some, like Forrest, appear to have decided almost on impulse. They despaired of the South's ability to control its own destiny; they feared imprisonment and reprisals; and they hated the Yankees. With indefinite plans and focused on the "push" conditions of the collapsed Confederacy, they followed their instincts and fled.

Restlessness played a part. Alfred Smith had moved to Texas from Georgia, where he had been taken in by the McMullan family; before that, he had spent some time in Alabama. By the war's end, tens of thousands of refugees roamed the South. Many had become homeless at the beginning or near the beginning of the Civil War, and they were accustomed to moving around. Damage to abandoned property had been much more extensive than to that possessed by their civilian neighbors who had stayed behind. In her book on the subject, Mary Elizabeth Massey entitled one of the chapters "Half the World Is Refugeeing."[12] Half the world found little home to which to return.

Although most of the bands of semimilitary outlaws, such as encountered by Forrest, had been brought under control by the end of 1865, lawlessness, violence, fear, hunger, poverty, ruin, and social disorder were to mark the South for many years.[13] Many of those who left the region were belligerent and bitter. Judith MacKnight Jones claimed that one of the Confederate emigrants to Brazil, Clay Norris, so hated the North, that even when he was old, if someone asked him about the war, he responded with a stream of curses directed at the Yankees.[14] Bellona Smith Ferguson wrote that the exiles Bowen and McMullan were "disappointed and sore over the 'lost cause.'" Some of the exiles did not accept the fact that the war had ended; some were disgusted with their own leaders; most blamed the Yankees for what had happened to the South.

Premonitions of reconstruction horrors were common. Northern merchants and speculators moved into the Southern states after the war, taking away economic opportunities from Southerners. Many Southerners who wished to regain their fortunes—or just to feed their families—were pessimistic about their future in the South. The idea of living and working alongside of their freed black labor frightened many Southerners.[15] Some who left wanted to re-create the Old South in a different country. Southern pride and honor motivated much of the exodus.

Adventure was another reason why some wished to leave. Gold, treasure, and images of tropical paradise attracted many of the Southerners who went to Latin America. The tract of land in Brazil selected for colonization by the Reverend Ballard Dunn was supposedly a site where a pirate had buried his treasure. When first arriving on the banks of the Azeite River, Bellona Smith's family camped near two "sailor men . . . gold seekers." Another Texan, a J. M. Keith, actually struck a fortune in São Paulo prospecting for gold, tin, silver, copper, and other minerals.[16] The descriptions of exotic foreign lands were appealing to the war-suffering Southerners, but for those who made the move, the reality of life in the tropics proved to be quite different from what had been promised.

Attracted to Brazil

So many Southerners talked of emigrating that associations with the purpose of gathering information concerning conditions overseas appeared, and agents began to scout out territory that might be suitable for colonization. William Griggs discusses these efforts more fully in chapter 3. One of the best-known associations was the Southern Colonization Society of Edgefield, South Carolina, which selected Dr. Hugh A. Shaw and Maj. Robert Meriwether "to explore the Southern and Western Territories of the United States and especially the great Empire of Brazil."[17] The Shaw and Meriwether report describing the human and physical geography of parts of Brazil was first printed in the *Edgefield Advertiser* in May 1866. Later, it was reprinted in several different places and was included in the very popular book *Brazil, the Home for Southerners*, by the Reverend Ballard S. Dunn.[18]

Another explorer who represented a group of Southerners contemplating migration to Latin America was Gen. William Wallace Wood, who toured Brazil in 1865 on behalf of approximately 600 Mississippi and Louisiana planters. Dr. James McFadden Gaston explored the province of São Paulo on behalf of some South Carolina families at the time of Wood's tour. Brazil, in fact, was the most popular area of exploration, with perhaps as many as twenty agents being sent there on behalf of Southern associations.[19]

The Reverend Ballard S. Dunn, former minister of St. Philip's Episcopal Church in New Orleans, toured Brazil in early 1866. After visiting several coffee plantations in the interior of São Paulo Province, Dunn settled on a tract of land in the Juquiá valley of the Ribeira de Iguape river system near the coast southwest of Santos. He purchased a piece of property of the "most romantic, thoroughly rich, and beautiful country" imaginable for a negotiated price of forty-two cents per acre.[20] The area was described in his book, which became an important recruiting tool.

Besides Dunn, other Southern agents were interested in the Juquiá. James McFadden Gaston would eventually lead a group of South Carolinians to that area; so also would Colonels Frank McMullan and William Bowen, the organizers mentioned by Bellona Smith. McMullan and Bowen spent approximately five months touring Brazil before deciding to acquire property along rivers of the Ribeira de Iguape system near Dunn's site in southern São Paulo. The two agents carefully recorded information that they thought would be of interest to possible migrants: the geography of the area, conditions regarding the weather, agriculture, soils, and so forth. They met with Dunn at Ribeira de Iguape and exchanged information before selecting their tract. Their greater care led to the selection of a site that was less susceptible to flooding than the one chosen by their neighbor, Dunn.

Other organizations besides the colonization associations helped promote the emigration of Southerners to Latin America. Various businesses and entrepreneurs played roles. For example, the Toledo, Young and Company paid a lecturer to travel throughout the South, enticing settlers to British Honduras.[21] Before the war, Matthew Fontaine Maury had argued that the Amazon River had the potential to become as useful as the Mississippi, and he had urged open navigation on the Brazilian river. After the war, his argument for economic development of the Amazon's resources found a ready champion in the Brazilian statesman Tavares Bastos, who promoted the idea along with that of Southern immigration to Brazil. And the Reverend James Cooley Fletcher, who collaborated with Daniel Parrish Kidder on the best-selling *Brazil and the Brazilians*, helped negotiate government subsidies for a steamship line between New York and Rio de Janeiro to be used to help with the migration.[22]

Several foreign governments also promoted Southern emigration. Emperor Maximilian of Mexico was sympathetic to colonization, and he appointed Matthew Fontaine Maury as the commissioner of colonization and Gen. J. B. Magruder as chief of the land office. Maximilian's idea was to induce Southerners to migrate to the Córdova and Tepic regions by promising free passage, 640 acres of land to heads of families and 320 acres to single men, religious tolerance, freedom from taxation for one year, and freedom from any military obligation for five years.

Venezuela also facilitated the migration of Confederate planters by offering vacant or unused lands in the state of Guyana and the territory of Amazonas. Citizenship was also offered to those who stayed for over one year. The colonists were to be exempt from certain import and export duties and from paying taxes for five years. With citizenship would come freedom of religion and speech and also representation in Congress.[23]

But the Latin American government that provided the most support was that of Brazil under Emperor Dom Pedro II. Thus, upon arriving in Brazil, Wood's party was met with music bands, processions, festivities, guides, letters of introduction, and interpreters. The other agents were also received well, and for the migrants who followed, the Brazilians promised and usually provided land for as little as twenty-two cents an acre at easy terms. Help with accommodations and transportation upon first arrival, easy citizenship, and promises of constructing infrastructure to facilitate the movement of crops to market were also offered. Upon arrival, the colonists would stay in Rio de Janeiro in a big hotel which had been assigned by Dom Pedro II to the foreigners. Bellona Smith wrote that the emperor "contributed much toward the expense [of the foreigners], taking personal interest in all who came to his beloved Brazil."

In Brazil, many of the Southerners expected to find a kindred culture. Brazil had been a staunch ally during the Civil War, having accorded the formal status of belligerent to the Confederacy and having harbored and supplied the Southern ships.[24] Although Dom Pedro II had ended the external slave trade in 1850, emancipation did not follow until 1888. Thus, Brazil was the only major nation that retained the institution of slavery after 1865.

But it was economic opportunity more than cultural similarity that enticed Southern planters to emigrate to Brazil.[25] Many saw the beginning of a cotton boom. Brazilian cotton production had increased dramatically during the war years, and exports had doubled. As the Manchester Association had provided Brazilian planters with seeds, Brazil had begun to supply the English textile mills with cotton. English agents in Rio promoted new machinery with the new crop, and railroad interests saw increased cultivation of cotton as a way to expand traffic into the interior of the province of São Paulo. The agents from the emigration societies reported that the Brazilian climate was favorable for cotton farming. The Brazilian cotton bush was said not to have to be planted every year as in North America, but only once every five years. Moreover, two crops of high quality cotton could be harvested each year. The quality of the Brazilian cotton was considered to be better than that of the South, and it brought a better price on the British market.

Accounts of the high fertility of the Brazilian soil filled the letters of the first who arrived, encouraging others to follow. In addition to cotton, Bellona Smith mentioned crops of corn, sugarcane, bananas, potatoes, manioc, rice, black beans, and tobacco while living on the Juquiá.

Not all who migrated to Brazil were planters or farmers. Alfred I. Smith was a music teacher by profession, and among those who made the trip to Brazil were prospectors, machinists, shopkeepers, doctors, dentists, artisans, and laborers. A cobbler who migrated to Santarém in the Amazon region, hoping to make a living by repairing shoes, was disappointed to discover that most Brazilians did not wear shoes.[26] Jennie Keyes's father was a doctor who set up practice in Rio de Janeiro while buying land and settling his family at the Rio Doce colony in Espírito Santo. Jimmy Graham opened up a saloon in Rio.

Letters from the first arrivals and newspaper articles sent back to be published in American newspapers helped fill in details of the Brazilian picture initially sketched by the reports of agents Shaw, Meriwether, Wood, Dunn, Gaston, McMullan, and Bowen. Many of the early letters were optimistic, filled with hope; others sent later, however, betrayed the disappointment of lost dreams.

Most evidence does not confirm that the prospect of owning slaves in Brazil was in fact an important inducement to the migrants. Slavery was still practiced in Brazil in 1865, but importing people in bondage was not allowed. The restriction was to the reported chagrin of some freed American blacks who, even though it meant that they would be returned to slavery, desired to accompany their former masters to their new home.[27] Relatively few American blacks were among the earliest groups, though a freedman named Steve gained notoriety and substantial wealth by operating a lumber business abandoned by his former master.[28] The language barrier and a lack of capital meant that few Americans acquired substantial numbers of Brazilian slaves.

The Portuguese language and the Brazilian culture proved to be greater barriers than anticipated. Able Southern craftsmen found it almost impossible to compete with Brazilians, even with those who were less skilled, simply because of the language. Moreover, the Southerners found it difficult to adapt to the racial mixture of Brazilian society, to the different pace of life, to Brazilian education, and to Brazilian religion.

Settlement in a New Land

Attracted to a promised land under the Southern Cross, families from across the Old South packed or sold their possessions and made the move. Using an unpublished list compiled by the original migrant Henry Steagall, Jones and Goldman identified at least 154 families who arrived in Brazil between 1865 and 1875.[29] Of these, 103 came from Texas, 37 from Alabama, 6 from South Carolina, and 8 from various other states. Between 2,000 and 4,000 people are estimated to have gone to Brazil in the years immediately after 1865, but we have no accurate count of how many were in that country at a given time.[30] Perhaps as many as half of the people returned to the United States within the first decade. Goldman stated that no more than fifty families were present in the largest colony near Santa Bárbara in 1873.[31]

The early settlement pattern in Brazil was highly dispersed. Though colonies were established in the provinces of Amazonas, Rio de Janeiro, and Paraná, the most important sites were in São Paulo. Two spatial trends ap-

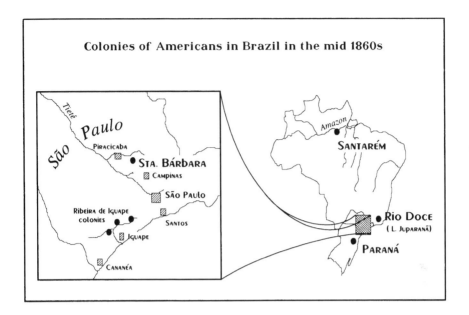

Colonies of Americans in Brazil in the mid 1860s

peared: first, the Americans migrated to scattered locations; second, they moved and consolidated at what was to become the most important site near the town of Santa Bárbara.

The initial dispersion resulted from the process by which the colonies were established. Typically, an individual would go to Brazil, identify an available tract of land, negotiate concessions with the government making himself responsible for parceling the land to the settlers, and return to the United States to recruit colonists. In that manner Frank McMullan, Dr. James Gaston, and Rev. Ballard Dunn took groups to the Ribeira de Iguape river basin in coastal southeastern São Paulo. Charles Gunter founded the colony on Lake Juparanã on the Rio Doce, north of Rio de Janeiro; Dr. John Blue of Missouri led a group to coastal Paraná; and Col. William Norris from Alabama purchased the land near the village of Santa Bárbara, where eventually gathered what was to become the largest group of Americans in Brazil.

Maj. Lansford Hastings, famous for his earlier explorations of the western United States and for the tragedy of the Donner party in California, recruited settlers to go to Santarém in the Amazon region of Pará. As described by Griggs in chapter 3, the Hastings colonists experienced severe hardships on the trip and after they relocated to the tropical forests of Brazil.

C. B. Dawsey & J. M. Dawsey

Conditions for the dispersed immigrants in Brazil were difficult, and within a few years most of the colonies had ceased to exist as distinctly American communities. Often, upon the death or relocation of members of the dominant family, the settlers moved to another colony of Americans in Brazil, returned to the United States, or simply took up the surrounding Brazilian culture. Those who relocated in Brazil most frequently moved to the prospering community near the Norris farm in interior São Paulo. In her diaries, Julia Keyes documented her brief stay at Lake Juparanã, describing the initial excitement of life in a strange land and the later tribulations that ultimately led to the family's return to the United States.[32]

The failures of the scattered sites resulted from many difficulties, some unique, others more general. The climate, soil, and physiography were major problems at most locations. The Ribeira de Iguape region received the bulk of the earliest arrivals in Brazil, but the area near the coast at the base of the Serra do Mar mountains was rugged, damp, and generally not well suited for growing the coffee and cotton planted by the Americans.

Strife within the colonies and competition for leadership weakened some groups. The death of Frank McMullan in 1867 caused severe dissension and accelerated the exodus from the area on the Azeite River settled by Bellona Smith's family.[33] She reports in chapter 2 that her family was the last to leave. They struggled valiantly against the insects, weeds, and mildew but eventually also trekked over the mountains to join others near the Norris farm.

Another reason for the poor success of the sites in coastal São Paulo was the lack of transportation and a bad location relative to markets. Commercial crops produced in the Ribeira de Iguape area could not be moved to market because a good road network and the railroad promised by the government were not built. Financing for the transport links could not be raised because of the high construction costs associated with the rugged terrain and because of the dispersed pattern of the settlement along the Ribeira de Iguape, Juquiá, and Azeite rivers.

Meanwhile, the mid-1860s rail penetration to Jundiaí and the later extension to the vicinity of the colony of Americans near Santa Bárbara provided a substantial boost to that area. Eventually, the railhead became the city of Americana—named after the immigrants. Here, the construction of the railroad was warranted by the more compact settlement pattern, the proximity of a nearby trunk line, and the gently rolling terrain.

The Ribeira de Iguape colonies lasted but a few years, and only slight overt evidence of their presence still exists in the coastal region. Current maps depict a few reminiscent place names such as Presbyterian Chapel

Leaving

and Wright's River, named for the fiery Texan Jesse Wright, who years later
fled Brazil after murdering a neighbor with whom he had a disagreement.[34]
The Rio Doce settlements survived longer than those along the Ribeira de
Iguape, but they too were doomed by the hostile environment and lack of
access.

In the Amazon region, the Hastings group hung on with tenacity, despite many difficulties. Though a cohesive cluster, as present in interior São
Paulo into the twentieth century, ceased to exist, some of the Santarém
colonists prospered, and Anglo familial names are still present in the region.

The only colony truly to persist, for many years keeping its identity as a
settlement of Confederate Southerners, was the Norris colony in the province of São Paulo. In fact, the Norris settlement was not an organized colony. As described in the next chapters, Col. William Norris and his son,
Robert, from Spring Hill, Alabama, traveled to Brazil in December 1865.[35]
They disembarked in Rio de Janeiro and then headed south to the province
of São Paulo to explore the areas described by Gen. William W. Wood. After
examining the Juquiá valley and finding it unsuitable, they traveled inland
to Jundiaí by rail, and then by foot, until they found an area of rolling green
hills and red soil that reminded them of their home in Alabama.

The Norrises bought a homestead approximately ten kilometers from
the village of Santa Bárbara; they purchased a couple of field hands, planted
a crop, built a house, and sent for their families. They also wrote to some
friends, urging them to join the colony.

It was April 1866 before the family and friends arrived. They had voy-
aged on the ship *Talisman*, which had wandered off course to the Cape
Verde Islands, off the coast of Africa, and the trip from New Orleans to Rio
had taken three months. But once in Santa Bárbara, the group quickly
settled down and began to prosper.

Many of the new settlers who arrived in Brazil after 1868 headed to Santa
Bárbara as soon as they heard that the settlement of Americans was growing
and prospering. In 1868, when the colonies at Rio Doce and Juquiá began
to disintegrate, many of those who had first left the South with Gunter,
Dunn, Gaston, McMullan, and Bowen also relocated near the Norrises.

The Norris settlement benefited from site and situational conditions that
were superior to what had existed in the coastal lowlands. The coming of
the railroad has already been mentioned. The geomorphology of interior
São Paulo State is characterized by well-weathered igneous and sedimentary
rocks, and away from the coastal formations, the most prominent features
are basalt-capped cuestas. The igneous basalt and older sedimentaries that

C. B. Dawsey & J. M. Dawsey

Colonel William H. Norris, Prior to Departure for Brazil (*Courtesy of Sarah Norris Crosby*)

are found in the Santa Bárbara area produce soils that are fertile in comparison to those of the failed sites.

The area also presented a landscape that was to some extent similar in climate and topography to the Southern United States. The farms were initially more successful because the favorite crops—cotton and watermelons—were more easily produced. The principal advantage of the Santa Bárbara area, however, was that the terrain was gently rolling and therefore more suitable for the application of the most significant new technology brought by the Americans to Brazil: the moldboard plow. The Americans were able to cut the *cipó* vegetation easily and to turn soil that had stymied Brazilians using hoes.

By the early 1870s, with the exception of the persistent Hastings colony in the interior of the Amazon region, the settlement pattern of the Americans in Brazil had become concentrated in the rural zones south and east of Santa Bárbara. Many of the Southerners who initially went to Brazil did not stay, but those who did, clustered in a community that was able to preserve its culture with remarkable success. During the following decades, the community not only survived but also influenced the larger society in important ways.

Two

The Journey
The Sarah Bellona Smith Ferguson Narrative

Edited by Cyrus B. Dawsey and James M. Dawsey

The first accounts of the emigration to Brazil, for the most part written or compiled by colonization agents, are extremely valuable to the scholar. These include Dr. James McFadden Gaston's *Hunting a Home in Brazil*, Ballard S. Dunn's *Brazil, the Home for Southerners*, and Lansford Warren Hastings's *Emigrant's Guide to Brazil*. Many of the emigrants sent letters to family and friends back in the United States describing their new homes, trials, and triumphs. They also wrote articles and essays for American newspapers, often urging other Southerners to join them. And a few of the emigrants wrote more extensive accounts of their journey to Brazil and their settlement there. Of interest are John Codman's *Ten Months in Brazil* and Hasting Charles Dent's *Year in Brazil*. One of the finest first-person accounts is the diary of Julia L. Keyes, entitled "Our Life, in Brazil." Published in the *Alabama Historical Quarterly* in 1966, it comprises a wonderful overview of life in Brazil and the Gunter colony experience in particular.[1]

Many other primary sources are available. One base of data about Brazil is found in the papers of George Scarborough Barnsley, a Georgian who was one of two non-Texans who sailed to Brazil with Frank McMullan. The Barnsley papers are extensive, but the largest caches are located at the Southern Historical Collection at the University of North Carolina and at the William L. Perkins Library, Duke University. Other important Barnsley papers are found at the Tennessee State Library and Archives and at Emory University. The Blanche Henry Clark Weaver Papers is a valuable research collection containing important primary material. At present, these papers are in the possession of William Clark Griggs.

Any serious student of Confederate emigration to Brazil must also utilize the excellent primary manuscript material available in several Brazilian archives. Of real importance are the National Archives of Brazil, Rio de Janeiro; Archives of the state of São Paulo, São Paulo; the Archives of the

Brazilian Institute of History and Geography, Rio de Janeiro; and the Archives of the Palace of Itamaratí in Rio de Janeiro.

Several articles containing first-person accounts by persons who emigrated to Brazil also are available to the researcher of American emigration. Edwin Ney McMullan, Frank McMullan's younger brother, wrote an account of the troubles of that group in an article entitled "Texans Established Colony in Brazil Just after Civil War," in the semi-weekly *Farm News* of Dallas, Texas, in January 1916. Another article on the same subject, "Sailing Down to Rio in 1866–67," was written by Eugene C. Smith, a McMullan colonist, and published in the *Brazilian American* of Rio in March 1931.[2]

While most of these documents and papers are readily accessible, one of the most interesting and informative accounts written by an emigrant generally has not been available to the scholarly community. This account, written by Eugene Smith's sister, Sarah Bellona Smith Ferguson, focuses on the McMullan colony. The narrative is one of the most extensive first-person accounts written after the end of emigration to Brazil. Although manuscript versions of the narrative have circulated privately among family and friends and have reached the hands of a few scholars, and although Sarah Bellona Smith Ferguson herself published versions of her story, first in 1916–17 in four parts in *Farm and Ranch* and then, twenty years later, in 1936 embellished in the *Times of Brazil,* Bellona Smith's account has not received wide circulation among American scholars.[3]

Bellona's story generated extensive interest among the descendants of the Southern colonists living in Brazil, and as a result, several fuller, unpublished versions of her manuscript are extant. One, a longhand account in the Weaver Papers, is dated May 29, 1935. Unlike the earlier versions, this manuscript includes a listing of McMullan colonists.

Bellona Smith's last and fullest account has never been published in English or Portuguese. It is the account included in this book, and it dates from April 1943, when the author was eighty-six years old. Bellona Smith Ferguson wrote the narrative in longhand for her nephew, Oliver Ferguson, and in the 1970s it was passed down to the Reverend Cyrus B. Dawsey, Jr., a friend of the family, who at the request of the family, translated it into Portuguese and also passed it on for inclusion in this book. For the most part, this 1943 account is based on the version that was written in 1935 and then revised in 1936. Although Bellona described her task as "almost too much for one whose memory is dimmed by the many passing years" and claimed to follow "childhood memories and a few notes previously written," her tale has the earmarks of one often told.

Here, we have given much attention to preserving the original language of Bellona Smith Ferguson's narrative. However, there are places in the account where we have found it necessary to correct the author's punctuation. As is often true of handwritten documents, Bellona Smith Ferguson's account was written with few paragraph divisions. At times, she used commas when she should have used periods, and sometimes she used periods when commas were called for. Oftentimes, she included slashes to identify sentences or parts of sentences. She used capitals irregularly, not always at the beginning of sentences, and not always with proper nouns. Ferguson seldom employed the apostrophe with possessives. She often used dashes in the place of quotation marks or to identify Portuguese words. She used ampersand and abbreviations for the words "brother" and the Portuguese *santa* [saint]. Besides regularizing the punctuation, we have corrected spellings or have added words or parts of words to complete the sense that Bellona intended. These editorial additions to the text are clearly set off by brackets within the text. Where we changed the spellings of words, care was taken to include the original in the endnotes.

"The American Colonies Emigrating[4] *to Brazil— 1865 "*
By Mrs. [Sarah Bellona Smith] Turner Ferguson

Foreword.[5] Strange to say, I have been just lately asked by several persons and acquaintances, both old and new friends, to give an account of the Southern families who emigrated to Brazil soon after the Civil War. It is a pleasing task, but almost too much for one whose memory is dimmed by the many passing years. But having a willing mind and realizing how few of us now remain to tell the story, I shall endeavor to do so by following my childhood memories[6] and a few notes previously written to refresh my failing memory.

Other colonies. There were at least three other colonies besides McMullen's[7] which came from the Southern states soon after Gen. Robert E. Lee surrendered to Grant at Appomattox in 1865. I should say "so-called colonies" for I do not think any of them succeeded in getting rated as genuine, properly organized colonies. One of these was the Gaston-Meriwether[8] Colony. This one landed at Santos and found homes near Santa Barbara, district of Campinas. [The colonists] bought land independently from the *fazendeiros* [planters] and were in no way bound by colony authority. Another was led by Ballard[9] S. Dunn, destined to settle on the Juquiá, but only a few of these people ever reached Lizzieland,[10] as Dunn had named his new projected homeland in honor of his wife, whose death caused the failure of the enterprise. Then there was Tarver's[11] Colony who went to the

Rio Doce,[12] quite a lot of them, but after a few years they broke up. Some returned to the States—others drifted to Santa Barbara, which had gradually become the nucleus of the American people in Brazil and is now known as Vila[13] Americana. There have been many mistaken impressions regarding[14] these Southern emigrants, so I shall confine myself strictly to personal knowledge of the matter.

Frank McMullen–Bowen colony. One writer speaking of these emigrants said "a number of hot-headed secessionists, rather than take the oath of allegiance" etc. Now I do not think them hot headed, but brave-hearted hero[e]s. These high-toned gentlemen—ex-Confederate[15] soldiers—were not influenced by "appointed agents of a social club," as a late writer states, nor were they in any way connected with a society founded for that purpose. On the contrary, [the emigration] was an independent move on the part of the individual.

Neither were our fathers needled into the movement. My dad, for instance, had already sold out to go to Mexico, having a premonition of the reconstruction horrors that followed Yankee rule when Mr. Frank McMullen came along with his proposition to head for Brazil. I was only ten years old, but remember it perfectly.

McMullen and Bowen. Early in 1865, Bowen and McMullen, disappointed and sore over the "lost cause"[16] and fully resolved never to submit to nigger rulers appointed by the Yanks, struck out to find a home for themselves and families. After traveling extensively over South America, especially Brazil, they reached the city of Iguape in the province de São Paulo, as the state was then called. From the government [and] especially favored by Dom Pedro II, they secured a grant of land of size sufficient for a colony on the headwaters of the Juquiá, a tributary of the Ribeira, beyond the section selected by Dunn. This grant of land comprised a part of three small rivers—the Azeite, Rio do Peixe,[17] the Guanhanhã[18]—and a small creek, the Areado.[19]

McMullen immediately returned to Texas, leaving Col. Bowen to make preparations for the Colony. Bowen married a Brazilian lady, *Capitão* [Captain] Martin's[20] daughter, whose home was on the banks of the Juquiá. There, Bowen lived and superintended the construction of a palm-covered ranch, large enough to house the colonists for the time needed to select their own land and build for themselves.

Now, I must take my reader to Texas. But know [that] the full story of our experiences will never be told, for those who knew it best have long since gone to rest. It may be of interest to remark, by way of contrast between the present and olden times, that when we left our home near Spring

Hill, Navarro[21] Co[unty] Texas, we traveled in an old-fashioned[22] covered wagon. This was in 1865, November 9. The nearest railroad station at that time was Milligen. It took two weeks to make the journey. Of course we had a tent and camped out every night on the open prairie. We children thought it great fun, a jolly picnic,[23] an exciting experience remembered with pleasure till this day.

Before we reached Milligen we were joined by Mr. Green, another colonist with his family, traveling[24] as we were in a wagon and surrey,[25] all drawn by horses—his family, himself, three daughter[s], and three sons, whose descendants still live in and around São Paulo. Long may they flourish, for there never was a better man than old man Green. At Milligen, both families—[those of] Mr. Green and A. I. Smith, my father—camped in the suburbs for several days. [Then][26] several other families came up: Mr. Jess Wright, old man Garner and widowed daughter, and the Cooks. For the sake of economy, they all joined in and chartered a freight-car into which they loaded baggage, wives, and children with little room and no comfort for a long, enroute[27] for Houston[28]—our first experience of riding on a rail. We rested about an hour at Houston. Then all aboard again for Galveston—a bitter, cold all-night ride, and most disagreeable, with little sleep, just any old way on the baggage. Just imagine!

Just at daybreak we got the first view of Galveston [C]ity and were delighted at the beautiful bay with its many ships at anchor, the first we had ever seen, looking like a denuded forest, while the old engine bell clanged its noisy way, ding-dong, and whistled into the station. As the sun rose, we disembarked and all bewildered found a little shabby eating place, where we got coffee and bread [for the] children, while the fathers bustled around and soon found the camp where most of the colonists had already congregated. Our tents were soon up, and then [we] began a long wait for others who for one reason or another were delayed. The McKnight brothers arrived about this time—Mr. Calvin McKnight with his new son. His birthday delayed them 2 weeks.

Misfortune dogged us from the first and kept us in Galveston two months or more. The ship on which we finally embarked was an old dilapidated[29] brig, called Brig *Derby*, captained by one [Alexander] Causse.[30] The vessel had to be repaired and provisioned, and then just as all was ready to sail, the Yanks seized the brig to prevent the southern rebels escaping. Nor would they let us go until a heavy fine was paid, which nearly exhausted our resources. There are some who think our people were on a charity basis, but it was not so, for each one paid his quota, and paid heavily.

On looking back now, one wonders why sensible men with such a crowd of helpless women and children should undertake such a hazardous venture as crossing the great ocean in a sailing [ship]. The only excuse I can find is that sailing vessels had made the voyage successfully; and brigs were still used in those days. One thing is sure: our [ship] tacked along in the Gulf of Mexico, and though we sailed on the 22 of January 1866, we did not come in sight of Cuba until the evening of February 25. We were to have put in at Havana for fresh water and fruits. On February 25 the day was calm, weather clear and bright. Most of us had got over seasickness, and whatever the old folks feared, the youngsters were having the time of their lives. The afternoon [was] still clear and beautiful. In the distance were seen two white-sailed[31] ships, and a great whale lay in full view basking on the still waters. [Then,][32] a sudden gale struck from the north about night-fall. The fury of the storm came on after dark, a great flood of water pouring over the deck, and down the hatchway, filling the lower deck ankle deep. And here came Parson Quillin,[33] shaking his head saying, "Oh, we are gone up, gone up!" Scared? There is no name for it!

The Captain was an Americanized Spaniard. We learned afterward that [he] had been bribed by the Yankees to wreck the vessel somewhere on the coast, and that was why he had never sailed out to sea. Soon after the storm began, he tied up the helm and retired to his cabin, leaving that whole crowd to the mercy of the waves and storm. When the trick was discovered, McMullen and Judge Dyer[34] and other resolute men entered the [cabin] and at the point of [a] six shooter forced the captain to loose the helm. He immediately called on the sailors to cut away the mast, which our men, pistols in hand, prevented.

But it was too late then to steer the ship out to sea for safety. Our own men and boys had managed the pumps during the night, for the fury of the waves kept the deck filled with water. Besides, the ship sprung a leak which required more than the sailors could handle. About two hours before daybreak the ship struck the rocks. The wind and waves drove her forward over one ridge after another until after drifting about two hundred[35] yards, she settled into a kind of trough of rocks beyond the depth where the waves could do nothing but batter the vessel back and forth like a cradle, "rocked on the bosom of the deep," whilst we waited in fear until daylight revealed the green shores[36] of the island of Cuba. The storm, though somewhat abated, still heaved the ship to and fro. And the breakers[37] dash[ing] onward to the sandy beach seemed to forbid our ever reaching safety.

The captain, now with smiling face and cheering words, knew a thing or two. He and the sailors somehow arranged the ropes[38] and began to lower the people one by one—secured by ropes around the waist, like descending a well. First went two sailors who loosed [the passengers][39] from the ropes as they reached the rocks. Then, each [person] must look out for [him]-self[40] by jumps from boulder to boulder, onto[41] the shore beyond the foaming water. Sufficient hands were let down first to help the women and children in crossing over, it being a dangerous feat for even a strong man. Advantage was taken while the brig lay on the lee. Captain Causse seemed to want to make up for his previous behaviour by doing all that could be done[42] to save the people. It is to his credit that all were saved. One daring feat deserves mention. In order to save a baby, he took the sleeves[43] of her coat in his teeth and thus with free hands he climbed[44] down the rope and delivered her to her father. This I saw myself.

To describe[45] our feeling or paint the scene is beyond our power. From the shore we looked back at the old brig and saw the great gaping hole in her side, from which the baggage and provisions were gradually washed out to sea—some[46] of which was recovered. We heard afterward that the two other vessels seen the eve before had not been so fortunate.[47] Most of [the] passengers they carried were lost. Our wreck was on the eastern extremity of the island of Cuba—with no dwelling in sight on a desolate shore. However, some natives living further inland soon appeared.[48] Also some of our men went scouting around, and before midday a rich Cuban[49] came to our rescue.

A kind act. This was Don Vermey, a prosperous brick and tile maker. He kindly sent oxcarts driven by coolie slaves to convey the whole crowd to his extensive *fazenda* [estate]. His house [was] a great building, large enough to house our whole people, and in this we took shelter for two days and were fed at his expense until our own supplies, baggage, and tents were brought from the wreck. Many of our goods were lost, but the breakers washed many boxes and barrels back to the shore, though out among the shoals, where with much difficulties and risk our men managed to salvage most of the wreckage. So once more the tents were raised and another anxious wait began. The Don supplied potatoes, mandioca roots, and had an extra bullock killed twice a week.

McMullen had hastened off to Havana but, not finding a ship there, sailed on to New York to get a steamer[50] to take the colony to Brazil. This took some time, and whilst waiting his return, many excursions were made exploring the country and enjoying the strange plants, etc., observing and becoming acquainted with the queer customs of the people. We saw the great sugar mills and vast cane fields worked by negro slaves. It was amusing to see the pickaninnies,[51] stark naked playing[52] in the hot sunshine. Here we learned a new wrinkle about sugar: how it was made, and where loaf sugar came from, and why white sugar (called loaf sugar in those days) had that shape. But [we] were shocked to see the common brown sugar spread out on dry ground to dry, with barefooted negroes walking over [it] and stirring[53] it up with long wooden scrapers—like old-style[54] coffee-drying in Brazil. How different sugar is made these days. But then, [what we saw was] considered up to date and wonderful.

At last came word to set out for Havana in time to catch the steamer for New York. Again it was oxcarts—and only a few could go at a time—so [that] it was some days before all reached the railroad station. [We] traveled all night over the worst roads imaginable,[55] driven by coolies whose queer call to the oxen was so-*triste* [sad].[56] And what with the jolts, even a child could not sleep! But just before we were "kilt entirely," the day dawned and found us at Woanahi, where after a day's wait, all took the train for Havana. On that trip, most all day we saw bananas and more bananas. While at Woanahi somebody offered food to the poor shipwrecked crowd, but in the raw. Who was going to do the cooking? When no one offered, my Dad rolled up his sleeves and went to work. And in great pots, out in the open square, he cooked beans, rice, meat, and potatoes—and only one boy, Luis Green, offered to help. Mother wanted to help, but Dad sent her back. But when eating time came, all were there—you bet. Such is human nature.

We got to Havana before the steamer arrived and were sheltered for a week or more in a large car-shed. Our plight attracted the Sisters of Charity, who brought gifts of shoes, stockings, cloth for dresses, and many other, useful articles. To my mind, there are no finer people than the Cubans[57]— cultured, friendly, given to hospitality, beautiful ladies and handsome gents, especially attentive to children, sometimes teasing us, sometimes treating us to candy, etc. Though not understanding a word, their smiles and kind faces won our confidence, and we would trot along to the store, happy and fearless. One gentleman living near the car-shed invited a party of us and our mothers to a breakfast, which was much enjoyed. Then, as we were leaving, the man followed us, singled me out, and gave me a handsome gold ring, and said "my wife gave that to you," in perfect English.

Many such incidents would fill this page, but now we must hurry on to New York, this time on the ship *Mariposa*, a side-wheeler-steamer, on the 10th of March, 1866. Owing to a storm we were again delayed, [and] the Captain cast anchor near the island where Jeff Davis, ex-president of the Confederacy, was then imprisoned.[58] After starting again, we soon struck the cold zone of the North, and suffered intensely.[59] Some had their toes frostbitten. Then came on an awful[60] fog. The whistle must have had a bad cold, for it made the most doleful sounds all night. Even so, we came near having another catastrophe, barely[61] escaping a collision with another steamer on the high seas. All this made us too late for the regular steamer from New York to Rio.

Consequently, we had to wait a month in New York for the next. We were housed [t]here in a hotel several stories high, where one story could have [housed] all of us and more. One day, from the top of this hotel, a party of us watched the *Great Eastern* as it was towed into harbor by a dozen tugboats—a sight never to be forgotten, [for] at that time [the ship was] the wonder of the world, being the great seven-masted[62] steamer that was built to lay the Atlantic cable. Of course we took the opportunity to see the sights of the great city, of which so much had been said—a never-failing astonishment to those greenhorns of Texas.

But if New York was a sight to us, we were a ten-cent[63] show to the New Yorker, and they certainly enjoyed it. One incident must suffice.[64] Mr. Jess Wright had a crate of half-grown hounds, which had followed all the way and shared[65] the difficulties of the journey from Texas, saved even from the wreck. Soon after landing, the crate and hounds were[66] stolen. When the theft was discovered, Mr. Wright was frantic. He was a very large man with a booming voice, and the figure he cut going down the street dressed in Confederate[67] grey with a heavy grey shawl, asking every one for information, may be imagined. Passing a saloon where the thief had hidden, the dogs heard the master's[68] voice and set up a howl. Sixshooter in hand, Wright sprang through the door and over the bar, seized the dogs, and marched out in triumph. Every one in the saloon had ducked out of sight. The dogs finally got to Juquiá, grew up, and became the wonder of the people. When they "opened up," you should have been there to hear.

Some church people of New York gave the colony two large boxes of books, which proved a great blessing to us while in that isolated backwoods of Brazil [since we][69] lost all our books in the wreck. The McKnight brothers, Calvin[70] and Steret McKnight, paid a visit to their old mother in Pennsylvania, whence they had moved to Texas years before. [They][71] got back in time to sail with the Colony, this time on the *North America*, one of the new line of steam-wheelers plying between New York and Rio, [and] at that time considered the last notch in steamship navigation.

We sailed on the 14th of April, 1866, and landed in Rio after a pleasant[72] voyage of 32 days. Not a storm or gale disturbed the voyage. But just as we entered the bay at Rio, a slight collision with a large ship took place. A great hole in our bow threatened to fill the ship, but before the passengers became alarmed, the sailors managed to stop the hole by letting down a heavy sail cloth, [and] so we sailed on to safety. In Rio we were housed in a big hotel to which we had to climb a long flight of steps. By previous arrangement, this hotel had been assigned to the colonies by the good Dom[73] Pedro II, who not only encouraged [the] immigration[74] of foreigners but [who] contributed much toward the expense—also taking personal interest[75] in all who came to his beloved Brazil. There were already many Americans in the hotel when we got there, besides the many who were on the *North America* with us. [These were] independent Southern people from Georgia and South Carolina. Of these,[76] I remember[77] Dr. Gaston and family, old Parson Pyles and family, the Seawrites,[78] and Messers Burton, Minchin, Buford, and Rowe. These all settled near Santa Barbara. Mr. Dunn and some of his Colony were at this hotel; also, others who had preceded[79] us.

Then, here came the emperor himself to visit the people. [He] came in state, followed[80] by great crowds of people filling the streets. We could see, from the hotel yard, shooting up sky rockets, etc. The Americans rent the inn with "three cheers," threw hats in the air, and all that kind of stuff to beat the band. Then the old emperor inspected the hotel from top to bottom. [He] entered the dining room, even tasted the food to satisfy himself [that] all was right. How few today give the old Dom credit for his foresight[81] in bringing foreigners in to develop[82] Brazil, realizing as he did that the riches here lying dormant would never be developed by the natives. The outcome has proved his wisdom. It was Dom Pedro II who set the wheels rolling that [are][83] making Brazil—now fast becoming—the richest and most powerful[84] nation of the world.

We had about five days in Rio, plenty of time to see the principal[85] sights, the gardens and avenues famed the world over. Almost too soon we put out again on board the *Marion*[86] for Santos.

Here, many other Americans disembarked, while our Colony proceeded down the coast to the city of Iguape, the long looked for end of our journey. But not so to be, for it took several weeks before we could ascend[87] the rivers to the government ranch on the Juquiá, as herein before[88] mentioned. There had been some dissatisfaction among the people for some time. Mr. Nettles had left us at Norfolk,[89] Virginia. The McKnight brothers remained in Rio because the eldest daughter was sick. She died there. Afterward they came on, and finally came to Santa Barbara. It was Calvin[90] McKnight who taught the Americans how to make *pinga* direct[ly] from cane juice[91]—up to then Brazilians made pinga from molasses,[92] dripping[93] from sugar making—thus making it a paying business. And until the price went down, much money was made by the cane planters of Vila Americana. Parson Ratcliff[94] and wife never reached that government ranch on the

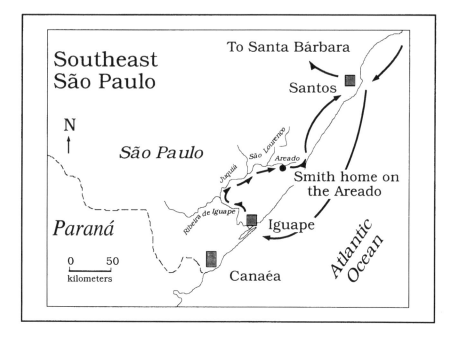

Juquiá, nor Mr. Weingeutter.[95] Both somehow went on to Santa Barbara before any of the others got there.

Most[96] of us stuck together [un]til[97] Frank McMullen's death led to the breaking up of the Colony. Frank was a fine character, highly esteemed by all, and by his death we lost not only our leader but a personal friend. His uncle, old Judge Dyer,[98] a very hard, overbearing man was the cause of the dissatisfaction, first, last, and always. And we felt desolate indeed when [McMullen] was gone from us forever. They took his remains down the river to bury him in the city of Iguape. One of Frank's[99] sisters, Mrs. Odell, soon followed him to the grave. His mother and young brother Ney returned to Santos, [then] settled in Campinas, [and] finally went back to the States. Dr. Moore[100] and wife, Frank's[101] sister and brother-in-law, also lived for awhile in Campinas, and afterward in Santa Barbara, where he practiced dentistry and taught his profession to others who also made a commendable[102] success of it.

It is just as well to say [that] we stayed at that shack on the Juquiá quite 2 months.[103] And while there, [we] were fed by the government—had a commissary[104] and drew rations every Saturday like soldiers in camp. After McMullen's[105] death it was every man for himself. Some returned to the

States at once. But about a dozen families went on up the rivers and founded homes, some on the Rio do Peixe, others on the Guanhanhã, while Smith, Tarver, and Bowen settled on the Areado. Our trip up the river from Iguape, and subsequent life of three years in the wild woods there, make another story.

The colon[ists']¹⁰⁶ trip up the rivers. Perhaps I should mention that our ship the *Marion* got into the waters at the mouth of the Ribeira¹⁰⁷ at low tide and rammed her nose into the mud on [a] sandbar out a ways from the city. So we had to wait for high tide, but at last we landed safely. After so many accidents our people were a tired out set, and long together made us almost hate each other. But no serious quarrel happened among us.

The heads of our colony¹⁰⁸ hurried up the river to Col. Bowen's,¹⁰⁹ and the rest of us took shelter as best we could in a large empty house. Some camped in the street. The first day, while¹¹⁰ my mother was cooking out in the street, a nice Brazilian came along, and his heart expanded to the point of asking us to go to his house. We could not understand except by signs and a few words understood by my brother Eugene¹¹¹ who had studied Portuguese¹¹² on our route.¹¹³ [But] we caught on, and were only too glad to accept his offer and were soon domiciled quite comfortably. This man had a *venda* [store] in front and a large house where we lived several weeks.

In the meantime¹¹⁴ we had some fine times rambling around the old Jesuit city of Iguape. On one side, not far from a great garden [that] we supposed had been abandoned by the Jesuits, who had just recently been banished from Brazil, we came across the foundation of a monastery. It was to have been one of the largest ever built and planned¹¹⁵ by those indomitable fanatics. Though abandoned, the foundation stones still bore witness to the courage and skill of those old Jesuit¹¹⁶ fathers. Their trail may be seen all over Brazil, indeed all over South America—and in the most inaccessible places imaginable, just to capture the wild indians for the Holy Church. However small the hamlet may¹¹⁷ be, there is always a large handsome church steeple and bell tower, with a spacious front enclosure for *festa* [festival] purposes. The Iguape¹¹⁸ church is not behind the best seen in larger cities.

It was the month of June when we were there, and for the first time¹¹⁹ we witnessed an old time *São João festa*, the 24 June, and I have never seen any thing since to half equal it. The square was filled with all kinds of grotesque figures of animals, effigies¹²⁰ of men and women mounted on poles, two alligators, and last of all two battleships¹²¹ set opposite each other. And when the fireworks¹²² were set off, [there was] such a bombardment as set the echoes ringing, till the two were demolished. The alligators also went for each other, to the finish of both. After the display was over, a nice man and wife invited our party to his house for coffee, cakes and other *doces* [sweets], all new to us. The cakes were made of *mandioca* [manioc] starch, served by black slaves, handed round on[123] waiters. We were seated on a kind of low divan, some on rush mats on the floor. The most honored guests took the hammocks. There were never less than two or three in every house in those days. The substitute was a small bench made of planks, box-like,[124] not at all unlike a small trough.

Brazilians are the kindest people in the world and treat strangers with the greatest consideration. We made friends with many nice families. Though unable to speak our language, they would come around and by signs take us to their homes and entertain us by showing all their nice fancy-work, of which they are very fond and great experts. But our young ladies and young men blushed when they brought out their underclothes, all so beautifully embroidered,[125] never dreaming it was improper, not knowing American ideas about such things.

Memories! Precious memories make me loth to leave that queer little city. But word came at last that the river boat had returned after taking the 1st passengers up river. The *porto* [port] was some distance from the city. How we got there, I can't remember. But we camped there a day. During the day a sailor-man came up to our camp with a large bunch of bananas. [He] said he wanted them cooked three ways: boiled, fried and baked. [He] said he did not intend to die in debt to his stomach for a bite[126] of bananas. We had a big laugh, and my mother did as he directed, and that one bunch was enough for a whole troop of people. The sailor was a stranger to us. This story is told to extol the bananas of Iguape. None such can be found anywhere else in Brazil. Take me back to the land where I first saw bananas, has been my song ever since I left there.

The boat that took us up the river was a kind of makeshift[127] steamboat, accommodating[128] only a few passengers. Consequently we had to go in bunches. Our party was the last. [It was composed of] only three families. When going at full speed, the boat stopped in mid stream. Just as the sun went down, there we were unceremoniously[129] dumped into two great dug-out canoes, the men in one, women and children in the other. One old lady exclaimed, "I will not go alone with no man with us." So a young man got over into our dugout. Of course we were crowded in with bag and baggage. These canoes were manned[130] by two natives, one at each end with poles and oars. The old ladies took it fine, and the girls were gay and flirted with the young man—but me! I was scared, for darkness soon came on and it began to rain. Imagine us out in an open dugout in the middle of a great river, ignorant of when or where we would land. It was no fun—dark as Egypt, except when flashes of lightning showed nothing but water. The rain became heavy and threatening,[131] and thunder added to the situation.

At last, about midnight, we landed at [the] port of a big *fazenda*. Glad to once more be on land, we dragged[132] our dripping selves up a long slippery steep path to the house where some of our people were housed.[133] Among others who met us at the door was a young English man. His good sense helped the mothers. He told us to cover our heads and crawl in among the rough[134] rice that partly filled the great hall. This was done and we soon fell asleep, and awoke next morning dry as powder to a bright sunny morning, ready for eats and the next adventure.

In the meantime,[135] the men folks in the other canoe had gone ahead. In the dark, [they] had missed the landing place and poled on up to a small hut where the *camaradas*[136] [companions] landed them. There, they passed[137] the rest of the night round a fire kindled by one lone match my brother Penny happened to have in his pocket. Next morning they came back and were glad to find their wives and children all safe and sound.

On continuing the journey next day, nothing of interest transpired—except one little incident which came near being serious. A bad boy that had annoyed[138] the colony all the way, got to cutting up as usual and fell overboard into the great swift-overflowing river. He was only 5 years old—Eddy Cook. His dad stood up and yelled: "Save my child! Save my child!!" Though the native men did not understand a word, one of them put the boy's[139] dad to shame by jumping out, and after a short swim [he] caught the child and brought him safely back. None but his own family would have cared had he died, but he lived to be a very nice looking young lad. I saw him years after in Santos and hope his manners improved as much as his looks.

We saw very few homes enroute[140] up river, only now and then a small hut built on the steep banks of the river. These were covered with palm leaves and looked more like a corn crib, than a house. We passed one of these where Mr. or rather Parson Ratcliff had taken shelter with his wife and old Mrs. Weingartner[141] and daughter for company. And there alone was born little Nand Ratcliff, who lived to be almost a young lady when her dad went back to the States from Vila Americana. After holding the Baptist church together at the *Campo* for years, he was left a widower with 4 children, one a boy, when he took them back to Texas. We next passed a place, a small town called Xiririca[142] built on the left bank of the [Ribeira], just at the point where the river takes a bend to the right. I can't remember how many days we spent on this trip, but know we camped on the banks in the wild forest. One night's[143] experience is enough. The rain came down, a steady gentle downpour, but by this time we had learned not to mind very much. There was not room to set up the tent, so each took such covering as he had, spread a kind of shelter from one small sapling to another crawled under, and slept with rain dripping all around, too tired and sleepy to fear the *onças*[144] [jaguars].

At last we reached the government house, if such could be called "house," covered with palm leaves, with walls of palm slats set up picket fashion,[145] three inches apart. [The house had] no windows, no inside divisions, only a door at each end. When our party arrived on the scene, there were several families ensconced[146] in the building, filling it to its utmost capacity. Besides [there were] several tents pitched in the open square cleared for that purpose. Our tent was soon set up—and then began the weary wait, for Frank lay sick at Col. Bowen's,[147] and no one cared to move till we knew the outcome.

It was a trying time for all, especially Dad and Ma, for they were devoted to him. Frank, when a boy, was one of dad's pupils, and it was Frank who, when grown up, led my dad to Texas. His father, old Hugh McMullen, had been a father to my dad when he first started in life, and finally gave him a homestead in Texas. So the joke on pa was that he'd follow Frank to the end of the world and die for him if need be. And Frank was truly worthy of their devotion.

We must have remained at this house a month or more. The good church people of New York [had given us a] gift[148] of two boxes of books, principally[149] religious, of course[150]—also many Sunday school books. And with Parson Quillin[151] on hand, we had Sunday school with plenty of singing led by Dad. We woke the echos with songs never heard in those valleys[152] before.

McMullen's[153] death broke the cords that bound the Colony. Dad and a few others went up the rivers to spy out the country. When they returned, several families [set] out together, each in his own dugout. But soon [we] separated and went on alone. We camped every[154] night (just as we did before, on route[155] to the shack Bowen built). Sometimes [we camped] in a hut called *o porto*, a stopping place for travelers. Such was an open shed, in one of which was stored the largest dugout we had ever seen. We made our beds down in it, believe it or not! Here it rained, so we were there two days and nights.

The most interesting part of this last trip was passing the three great falls. These falls consisted of a gradual descent over rocks and boulders for a hundred yard[s] or more, waters foaming along between, leaving the rocks bare. But the main stream flowed through a channel at the right, at

The Journey

the end of which the waters fell almost perpendicularly with terrific force. Passenger and baggage had to be [lifted] over the rock at one side, while the empty boat had to be pushed up the roaring current by the two men, who by main force, with poles in hand, literally[156] lifted the boat perpendicular[ly] forcing it upward, the weight depending on the two poles. One [wrong][157] move would have been fatal. The channel was about 10 or 12 feet wide and fell at least 20 feet. Such must be seen to be appreciated. [It] reminds one of Stanley's[158] travels in Africa.

After this, we went poling on through dense forests on each side, finally passing the mouth of the Rio do Peixe, then the Guanhanhã, then to the mouth of the Areado, our final destination. These three creeks emptied[159] into the Azeite, which at this point took [a][160] right-angle[161] bend. On the property[162] formed by this abrupt bend was found a typical house of those days, mud daubed, surrounded with orange[163] trees, *mandioca* plants and other plants. We landed and found two sailor men living there—pro-tem gold seekers. One was named Bob Smith, the other Mr. Crawley.[164] [Both were] strangers to us. They had quarreled and Crawley[165] had moved over to the opposite[166] bank, built a little hut where he slept rather than share the shelter of his enemy. But [he] had to cross over every day to eat. One could wade at this place on the Azeite. In the open[ing] Mr. Crawley[167] had made, we pitched our tent.

Mr. Tarver had gone before us and [had] befriended an old Brazilian by the name [of] Camargo.[168] [He] became our good friend for the whole 3 years we lived [there]. He had a wheel for gritting *mandioca* roots, a press for extracting the white juice which when settled made the starch called *tapioca*, and an oven for drying out the *farinha* [flour]. So he allowed[169] our boys to use his outfit to make our own *farinha*. They would clean a lot of roots at home, shoulder the load and spend the day, and bring home a bushel of *farinha*, the bread of Brazil at that time. Mrs. Tarver let her featherbed[170] go to this man Camargo. They did not want the feathers, but the cloth was useful, so they emptied[171] the bed out into the river, which floated white with goose feather[s] for days.

The rain kept us in camp for several days (the Crawley[172] camp). The owner of the house opposite had built a shack on the Areado about two miles up, where his family lived at that time. He had a large *roça*[173] [crop] of corn, sugarcane[174] and bananas, potatoes and the inevitable *mandioca*. This squatter claim was on the extreme end of the colony grant. Dad bought out his improvement for 50$000 [i.e., 50 milreis],[175] and the poor old *caboclo* [man from the country] said it was the 1st time in his life he had so much cash in hand. We soon moved up and took possession of our new home, which was to be for the next three years. [This was] on the 11th of August 1866, nearly a year after we left Texas.

The shack was just one long room, walls of palm slats set three inches apart, and covered with palm leaves, with only one door, and dirt floor. The cooking place was on the ground in a corner, the pots being supported on trivets. And such pots! They were made of mud, burnt like tile and shaped like a flat bowl. Food cooked in these pots is most excellent,[176] especially *canja* [chicken soup] made of new rice and chicken. You should eat *tatu* [armadillo] cooked in its own shell set on a trivet. Dad and the boys soon made two partitions, forming a hall between two rooms. A lean-to[177] was also made for our kitchen. We had brought a small stove from New York. They[178] knocked up some rude slabs for door shutters, drove short posts in the floor for beds. The springs were made of palm slats.

Here we lived for two years on the left bank. The fields lay over on the other side, where they built a nice house and hog pen. And by the end of the 2nd[179] year, a good house was erected—or rather, I should say, begun.[180] In the meantime,[181] more land was opened up for rice, corn, black beans, and sugarcane.[182] The first year, we suffered for fresh meat, but the boys trapped *tatus*[183] and other small animals. [We] also learned to make fish baskets from the natives. So we got along fine. It was tough at first, for the wild birds made such queer noises. We thought it was *onças*[184] or other wild beasts. Our days were too[185] busy to feel lonesome until[186] Sunday came. But we had our books for Sunday, until the afternoon, when we small ones would paddle up and down the creek or cross over to the cane patch and chew cane.

We had our lessons every night around the rude table Dad had made out of a solid slab sawn out of the root of the giant *figueira* tree.[187] This tree had been felled by the *caboclo*, who said it took three days hard chopping by two men to bring it down. The wide spreading roots peculiar to the wild *figueira* made it so that they had to build a scaffold to stand on, at least twelve feet from the ground. I could write a whole page trying to describe this tree, and then miss it. One has to see to understand.

By the time we were getting settled, the Tarvers had chosen their place— land where we landed on the banks of the Azeite. And Col. Bowen's family had moved farther up beyond us on the Areado. A wide public road was being opened from the mouth of the Areado to lead over the mountains to the seacoast,[188] where it would reach a town called Peruíbe.[189] Lou Bowen was superintendent[190] of the work, and they built their new house up a ways on this road. But we never went up or down that road without

The Journey

being scared half to death, for fear of the *onças*,[191] which were plentiful. Often, troops of monkeys[192] passed overhead,[193] for, wide as the road was, the branches of the great trees met above and easily gave the monkeys a chance to cross. So we had two neighbors.[194] Most of the others settled on the Peixe and Guanhanhã. We were able to visit each other quite often. (We three neighbors, I mean.)

About this time, our oldest brother Eugene decided to make a break for himself, though only 20 years of age. He first went over the mountain, opened a clearing near Peruíbe, built a hut, and planted a crop. He then married Miss Sue Bowen. Parson performed the marriage at the home of the bride. The following day we had a big dinner at our house, both families being the only guests. About the middle of the day, Mr. Crawley[195] passed by on his way to Peruíbe,[196] this being the only way to get salt and other needs, and Mr. Quillin, not being satisfied without some outside[197] witness, called the couple in and married them over in Crawley's presence—who signed the paper. Crawley had married the widow Flint and had moved to Peruíbe and became Eugene's neighbor. But [he] soon left there and went on to Santos, and finally on to Santa Barbara.

The first year was tough, as we had to get used to so many strange sounds, queer birds and animals. The food also was so different. Our clean rice gave out. Then we had to clean the rough rice by means of a hand mortar[198] with a pestle. This task fell to us 3 little-ones, me [and] my two younger brothers, Virgil and Tully. In the afternoon we would beat out enough for breakfast and next morning sufficient for dinner and supper.

For sugar, we made molasses of the cane planted by the man who sold us the place. He had left the mill, which consisted of two palm logs about 5 feet long placed horizontally[199] on posts. [The mill] was turned by hand. Each[200] roller at opposite ends had two cross sticks. It took a boy or man at each end [to turn the rollers]. The cane knots had to [be] mashed first by an ax or club. One held the cane while the others turned the rollers. It was my task to boil down the juice to molasses—one *bacia*[201] [kettle] in the morning, one in the afternoon. The juice fell from the rollers into a wide wooden tray.

From the beginning, we had plenty of bananas—*bananas da*[202] *terra* [plantains]—which we baked and called "our sweetcakes."[203] For meal, we had a steel hand mill. It was so hard to grind sufficient for bread [that] we soon dropped off to bread once a day and substituted[204] *farinha.* After the 1st[205] six months we had chicken and made our own bacon. Of flour we had none,[206] and when hungry for chickenfrie, we made *canja.* We had sweet potatoes,[207] *cara* [roots of Dioscorea vines], vegetables and onions, also *mandioca-mansa* [cultivated manioc], and learned to make *porvilho*[208] [manioc flour] cakes—and on the whole lived fine.

I am loath to leave the 1st years of our life on the Iguape rivers and our simple amusements. Fond memories picture[209] us wandering through the woods, making swings of the hanging vines, following the trail to the boys' traps, or poling up and down the creeks in a dugout watching the king-fisher, hearing his call, and the sapsucker tap-tap. Then [we would hear] the great *tucano's*[210] [toucan's] queer honk-honk away up in the trees rob-bing the little bird nests; then, the lone sad notes of the *perdiz* [partridge], while the white anvil[211] birds' clanging bell rang out now and then. The cooing wood doves plaintive note and, at twilight, the whipporwill[212] sent thrills along the spine. Our first acquaintance[213] with the black army ants was a surprise. These ants march in droves, a black mass covering the ground ten or 15 feet wide. And everything alive that falls in their path, must hurry[214] itself,[215] or fall a victim to their hungry jaws. In the case of young birds in nest, tiny bones is soon all that's left to tell the story. A cricket, grasshopper, or *barata* [cockroach] has no chance with them. If they strike the house at night, there is no more sleep. We would get up, make a fire in the yard and wait patiently till they passed on. Afterwards, we learned that if we lay still they would not bite, and they certainly were a blessing to clean the house of bugs.[216]

My dearest recollections[217] of these times is of father, then, with only a sprinkle of grey. He was a very well-read man, and in the lonely forest life, [he] tried to make up to us all we missed by our isolated circumstances. We had quite a good assortment of books of our own, besides many from the boxes belonging to the colony, and we were stimulated by a natural bent [that we had] inherited, [and by][218] dad's influence. So we had our daily lessons and at night studied till bed time. And never was the singing omitted.[219] As [we] gathered round the table by candle light with song book in hand, even the monkey must have stopped to listen. Dad was an old-fash-ioned[220] vocal singing school teacher, so he taught us the music notes as well as songs.[221] Every few days a new hymn was learned from the new books—besides glees and comic songs.

Our mother's part must not be forgotten. She kept house and kept us youngsters well clothed as far as she was able. She was a good cook, a very neat housekeeper, and, strange to say, she never complained of all our hard-ships. Her motto was "The Lord will provide." [T]here she gave me my first lesson in sewing, by hand of course, and taught me to make embroidery and draw thread work. Sitting with her candle at her end of the table, with work in hand, [she] would join us in songs as she felt like it. She taught every child to read by the time we were 6 years old. (My oldest brother read at 4 years.) And [she] told us Bible stories till we knew them by heart, and made us toe the mark or we caught the switch we needed.

It must have been in the latter part of the first year [that] we found out Parson Quillin was preaching to those on the Guanhanhã. Our first visit over there was by water or by an old trail over three mountains. But now we learned [a new way to go] by cutting a new trail with only one mountain. Even this trail was a tough proposition, for unless we started early, we could not get there in time. But it was play for us. As we climbed, we had special spots named from *Pilgrim's Progress*.[222] One was "hill difficulty," then beyond, "the valley of humiliation," and so was born in our early minds the inspiration[223] to follow Christian to the celestial city of God. Of course we were afraid of meeting *onças*.[224] And [one] day, brother Penny ran ahead and hid until[225] we came by. Then he began to growl. Sakes[226] alive! Were we frightened? You should have seen us run, down the mountainside[227] until[228] we found [out] it was a joke.

Quillin was much above the average preacher. [He was] a very learned man and brought his very superior collection of books. Such a library was unusual in those days. And we sat spellbound[229] under his preaching. Our "meetinghouse" was in the shade of a tree, with rude seats and [arranged] just any old way. But lessons were just as interesting and hymns just as sweet [as they are today], and we made the wood ring with "There Is a Happy Land" and all the rest of those old Sunday school songs, which have never been beaten by modern hymns. It was while Quillin was preaching on Ezekiel's valley of dry bones, that I made up my mind to join the Church [at] the first opportunity.[230] [This][231] came years afterward, at the *Campo*, while Parson Newman was preaching in an old abandoned *venda* [little store] on the road from the *Campo* to Santa Barbara.

Enough of this.

Now I turn to our work, the work we did in those never-to-be-forgotten three years in the *sertão* [hinterland] of Iguape. One of the first things after felling the big trees and planting a hill of coffee [was] building a rice house and then a rice mill to prepare the rice for market. Dad and the boys first made a dam on a small stream about half a mile above us.[232] [This was] on that same big road mentioned before. [They] bought an old six mortar[233] mill with large water wheel. This was set up with timbers sawn by hand and covered with palm leaves. When this mill got to work, we children did not have to beat rice anymore. On an old abandoned[234] *roça*[235] [cleared land] on our side of the creek, they planted grass for pasture.[236] And my!

House Constructed by Alfred I. Smith Near the Juncture of the Areado and Itarirí Rivers. Sarah Bellona Smith lived in this house during the family's stay on the McMullan grant in 1868–69. (*Photograph by William C. Griggs, 1983*)

how that bermuda grass did grow. In six months it was knee deep and ready for the two horses bought from Bowen. His horses had all died from *fava*[237] [lima beans] except these two.

Now was when Dad determined to build a real American house, weather boarded, and covered with shingles. To find timber to split was no easy job, but at last he found a tree. And while he and Penny and Marsene[238] rived the boards, Eugene and Preston, with one *camarada*,[239] sawed the lumber for posts, doors joists, rafter, and planks for floors. To get these boards hauled to the home was the next question. This was done on the backs of those two horses, and Marsene[240] and I were the drivers. We would ride bareback to the place, tie a dozen boards together—a dozen for each side, pack mule fashion. Then [we would] scramble on top of the boards and ride away down the narrow trail singing as loud as you please, happy as kings!

Another thing, we had to have shoes. But how to get them? Brazilians did not use shoes in those days. Dad was called "jack-of-all-trades and good at none." He made cobbled shoes. But where [to] get the leather? All he had was deer skins, but these were no good unless tanned. Knowing something of oak tan bark, he set out in the *mato*[241] [woods] testing the bark, and happened on the very famous tan bark of Brazil, simply by taste. Soon, he dug a trough, and the tanning was so good, the leather was ready in a week. He made our lasts or forms, for each of us. Then the shoes, the wooden *pisadas*[242] [footwear]. Thus we were shod. Natives with bare[243] feet and shirt tails out, we could not get used to.

Again, Pa and [the] boys raised their own tobacco. [They] actually made a wooden screwpin and press, and one brother made tan rope tobacco to sell—we called it "tan rope." One can hardly realize the hardships of our people.

The time was fast coming [for] us to leave and seek a more civilized country. Both Bowen and Tarver had left, [as had] all those on the Guanhanhã and Peixe, except Quillin, who had moved down to the big river. Brother Eugene had moved over near us and built a nice house, not far from Tarver's. Here was where the first grandchild was born, Mrs. Eugenia Smith Becker, known now as a retired missionary. We children were surprised one morning to hear Dad say, "Sarah (as he always called Ma), this won't do. We got to get out of here somehow."[244] To go back down the river was out of the question, owing to [the] lack of cash to pay ship passage to Santos. To foot it over the mountains[245] was the only way for [us to leave].[246] Next morning, he and brother Penny set out and traveled on foot, first to Peruíbe,[247] then on to the coast, to Santos. There, by train to Jundiaí,[248] the terminus at that time. They walked on and on to Campinas, and finally reached the Americans.

The first house [of the Americans] was not far from the present station of *Rebouças*.[249] On inquiry—"who lives here?"—the man said, "Smith." Dad took off his hat and said, "I've a great mind to shoot you. I have traveled thousands of miles to get rid of the Smiths, and the 1st man I meet is Smith." Smith laughed and took the stranger in and helped him find the other Americans. And [he] also put him on track of a *fazenda*, which Dad rented. And [Dad] left Penny with old man Perkins, while he went back to get the rest of us.

At this time we had a nice, well-built[250] house, not quite finished. Our coffee was white with flowers. [There was] a great field of rice, ready to harvest, and plenty of every thing—but neighbors, and a close market. His description[251] of the wonderful *serracima* [mountain view] set our hearts on fire to be off, and immediate preparation began. Our movables[252] were to be packed[253] over the mountains on the shoulders of our boys and two *camaradas.* It took three days to make one trip there and back. After some days, we all picked up a small load and started out. Mine was part of our lunch and Dad's carpenter-square. Brother soon relieved me of that. I even soon dropped my package of onions. The smallest boy, Tully, had a bag of peanuts, but left them in our mill house as we passed by. We left Eugene and family to gather the rice and sell what he could for cash. [He was to come][254] away next year, which he did—first settling[255] on a coffee place near Campinas where his eldest son Ira William Smith was born. This was Willie Smith, known as cousin Buddie, the father of Henry and Archie[256] Smith and their 5 sisters.

I shall never forget that trip over the mountains,[257] crossing the many streams, sometimes waist[258] deep. The boys would pick Ma up and carry her over the worst places, but I waded with the boys, and soon lost one shoe in the mud. Then, [I] kicked off both stockings and the other shoe. Tired and completely worn out, just at nightfall, we came to the river and crossed over to Peruíbe,[259] where we rested a day. Then [we traveled] in boats down the river and through a long *canal* [channel] where we could almost touch the mossy banks with our hands. It was amusing to watch the crawfish—lots of them on the black mud, between low bushes—for miles. Next came the town of *Conceição.*[260] Here we passed one night. Next day, having arranged two bullockcarts, we loaded up and traveled 40 miles along the coast to the bayou which we had to cross over to get to Santos.

When we got to Santos, we were glad to run upon the Cook[261] and Hanney[262] families. This was in February 1871, and happened to be carnaval time—the 1st time we ever saw that *festa.* On the way over the mountains,[263] we passed an open place where the Cooks had buried[264] their baby boy, [and] left him alone in a vast forest. Ma soon bought me shoes and a hat, and I had a good time visiting Brooks Hanney. [I][265] watched her make wax-lemons, filled with water, to pelt the young men on the street. Then we saw the grotesque figures[266] that rolled along, followed by the happy crowds wild with excitement. Such things were new to us. And serpentines and *lança-perfume*[267] [carnival spray] had not been invented then. But the effigies in those days were funny: devils with horns, and four-footed[268] beast, and what not.

While we were on the beach we saw some queer looking object, which on investigation proved to be some huge sea monster. Some one had set the back bone joints on end,[269] and they were each at least two feet high [and] more than a foot wide. [I] don't know if they were whale or not, and whatever flesh[270] covered those back bones could have swallowed several Jonahs.

After a few days in Santos to make some purchas[es] the journey was continued on the train, which first climbed[271] the great mountain—or rather, was pulled up by cables hitched to engines stationary at the top, a bit of English railroading still considered a wonderful feat. It was a thrilling ride, beautiful view all the way. An old barefooted[272] slave remarked to my brother, thinking to enlighten an ignorant[273] foreigner,[274] "Não precisa viazar. Já estamos ahi." [Don't worry. We are almost there.] Brother smiled and let the old man think we had never ridden[275] on a car before.

Passing São Paulo, the town was seen from the window, a small town with low scattered houses on a hill quite a distance from [the] station of [the] same name. How little we knew that [that] little insignificant looking town would grow to be the second greatest city in Brazil and the most prosperous city in all South America as it is today, 1936.

At that time the railroad had only got to Jundiaí,[276] beyond which lay our destination near Campinas. In those days too, all country traffic and merchandise was carried over rough roads on pack mules and ox carts. We were several days delayed at Jundiaí[277] before we found a way to reach our destined stopping place. We happened upon an old cart man who had two empty carts returning to Camp[inas], in one of which he agreed to take us not only to Campinas, but on to the "Fazenda do Bocudo"[278] that now belongs to Charlie Vaught. [I] can't remember how long we were on this trip—two weeks maybe. It was enjoyable at first, seeing open country [and] after three years in the woods, to watch cattle grazing in pastures, as we passed the coffee *fazendas* with neat houses all in a row. But it became tiresome,[279] with so much red dust and the squeaking carts and pack mules,[280] camping each night at the mule shelters on the road['s] side. The cart man had his wife along to do the cooking, but we cooked for ourselves and afterward sat round the camp fire trying to talk to each other and learning new words of Portuguese.[281]

These cart men and muleteers[282] deserve a better pen than mine. They should be told by songs and story, having now passed forever from the old days[283] of seventy years ago. Now, trains pass along the same route[284] and unseen whistles make the echoes. The horn of the whizzing[285] automobiles sounds along the road, while airships[286] drone above. And not an echo is left to commemorate the existence of those hot, dusty toiling[287] workers whose footsteps are heard no more. And who cares? Or gives them a thought? Now they are gone from the scenes of life where they toiled, lived, laughed, danced, and suffered, as their fathers had done for ages before them with the same heart beats and longing for better things, no doubt!! Who knows?

One thing is sure: those things—conditions—would have been the same yet if England and other nations had not come and built railroads and developed the country. A glimpse of the people, and customs of the people of those times would be almost unbelievable. The cartman,[288] for instance, went barefooted, shirt tails out; and the wife [dressed] in a chemise—bare arms, a wide skirt tied round the waist, barefooted as well,[289] bareheaded except sometimes she wore a shawl or handkerchief tied on her head.

Now behold our cartman with his old battered straw hat as he footed the dusty road, his long pole to guide and drive the slow-going oxen. [There were] two men for each cart, drawn by ten or 12 yoke. These great heavy carts, clumsy, with wheels made of solid slabs of *cabriúva*[290] [hardwood] fastened to the axle, which turned with the wheel. The floor extended[291] to a sharp point out on the tongue, like the bow of a ship. The only light thing about it was the body made of plaited *taquara*[292] [bamboo strips], about 5 feet wide, and long enough to reach round the front and back to the hind end, leaving an opening for entering or loading up. The heavier the load, the louder the squeak. And the louder the squeak, the prouder the driver, as he urged the oxen, calling each by name, while his companion slowly walked on in front with his pole touching them up or turning them as needed around, over the rough places, and up and down hill[s]. The two wheel-oxen always held the whole weight back going downhill,[293] and pulled the most going up. One has to hear the driver's strange words to appreciate them. [They had] different call[s] to go, stop or turn, or back up. The first word to go was "vamos" [let's go], in a long sing-song way. In a crisis it was "puxa diabo" [pull devil]. To stop, it was "o-é-ou!" To pull back was "fasta-fasta [back up, back up] laranja"[294] or "alegria," as the name might be.

In those days the natives rode horseback,[295] and it was a sight to see a rich *fazendeiro* mounted with his two toes in a small stirrup,[296] with his *pozem* [gang] trotting along behind. If in a gang with ladies along, they all strung out in a row, Indian file. The first trollies in Brazil were[297] made by a Yankee, Mr. Sampson. [The trolley][298] was a kind of buckboard,[299] wheels wide apart, with no floor, only two, wide steel springs connecting the hind wheel with the front. And you may be sure, it was not safe traveling.[300] One had to hold tight[ly] to the seat, or fall through over the rough places.

There were no brick houses when we came to Brazil. Even the great churches were either stone, or dirt and sticks. The better houses were plastered and whitewashed.[301] The plaster was made of cattle dropping mixed with water and sand. Most houses were dirt floored,[302] but some had the bedrooms[303] floored with large, wide, heavy, hand-sawed planks. The 1st grapes in São Paulo were planted by an American, Dr. Reinhart, who had a *fazenda* near Camp[inas]. We camped there one night—near his house. He was a fine old gentleman, and my bro[ther] Penny worked for him after he grew up—worked with the plough. And while he was there, the old man died, and Penny helped to bury him. The old gentleman's sons are known to this day, both in São Paulo and Campinas.

Ploughs were not in use until the Americans introduced them. Coffee was cultivated with hoes, some of them a foot wide. [They][304] were used by negro slaves. Coffee grains were cleaned of trash and pebbles by hand, coffee spread on long tables, and extended rows of negroes[305] on each side, busy picking trash, etc. The pulpador was invented by an Englishman[306] name[d] Beven in 1889 or 90. Parched coffee was beaten by hand in a wooden mortar[307] and pestle, while now even the country people buy their coffee in *pó* [powder], or have their own parcher and grinder. The kitchen utensils in those days were neither pans or buckets, but wooden trays and earthen jars. The stoves were *fogões*[308] [stoves] with a cast iron top, with from three to six holes, such as are still seen in country places. As for sleeping, most of them slept on a rush mat [with][309] a few thin blankets and a smoothed off block of wood for [a] pillow. Or else, the pillows were stuffed with *macela*,[310] a wild flower of the *campo*. One could smell them in passing. Now, even the poor have nice beds, white counterpanes and large pillows. No one wore shoes or socks when we came here. Now, every[311] *caipira* [hick] goes shod. Ther[e] are other differences, but these will show what foreigners[312] have done for Brazil. So here ends my story. S. B. Ferguson. Copied for Oliver Ferguson by Aunt Bel[l]ona, Spr[ing] 1943.

Three

Settling

Migration of the McMullan Colonists and Evolution of the Colonies in Brazil

William C. Griggs

Alfred Iverson Smith, Bellona's father and the patriarch of the large family that emigrated to Brazil after the Civil War with the McMullan colony, was born near Macon, Georgia. His grandparents were Huguenots who escaped to the United States after persecution of the religious sect began in their native France. The family first settled in South Carolina but moved after the American Revolution to the area around Macon, Georgia, where over the years they became relatively wealthy as farmers. Although raised on the farm, young Alfred decided that his future was to be something other than an agriculturalist, and in the early 1840s he left for Alabama to search for his star. Less than fourteen years old at the time, Smith's efforts in making a living were not as successful as he might have liked, and it was not long before he decided to return home and to wait for a more fortuitous time to pursue a new career. His return route to Macon took him through Walker County in northwest Georgia where he worked for food and lodging at the few farms and settlements through which he passed.[1]

One Walker County farmstead at which Alfred Smith stopped was near the small community of Chestnut Hill. It belonged to a man named Hugh McMullan, whose father came from Ireland before the War of 1812 to support the American cause. McMullan immediately took a liking to the young man, who was, by then, almost exhausted from his travels. McMullan asked Smith to stay as long as he liked while he recuperated. After learning that Alfred had a better than average education, he suggested that the young man try his luck as a teacher and that he remain in the area. There was not, at that time, a school at which McMullan's children Frank (age seven), Martha Ann (five), Milton (two), and Eugene (one) would be able to attend. Having no agenda other than returning home to Macon, Alfred accepted the suggestion and boarded with the McMullan family until he could begin his school. During that period, Hugh McMullan became almost like a father to the young man.[2]

Smith's classes, which offered a general curriculum with a specialty in music, grew quickly, and the young man prospered. Young Frank McMullan, Alfred Smith's first student, was only a few years younger than the budding educator, and the two became fast friends as well as teacher and student. When Hugh McMullan decided in 1844 that it was time to move to Mississippi and a new frontier, the parting of Frank and Alfred was painful. They were determined not to let distance end their friendship, however, and they continued to correspond over the years. By 1853 the McMullans settled on new land in Hill County, Texas, but the bonds between the families were as strong as ever, although they were hundreds of miles apart.[3]

The letters to Smith from the McMullan family in Texas were full of praise for the new frontier, and the teacher was encouraged to come to the new state. When, in 1856, Hugh McMullan offered him a homestead in Hill County, Smith could resist the temptation no longer. He moved to the community of Spring Hill, Navarro County, with his wife, Sarah, five sons, and one daughter.[4]

When the clouds of war began to gather in 1860, Smith, like the McMullans, supported the side of the South. According to Bellona Smith Ferguson, in her 1935 account, Alfred Smith was "a staunch secessionist and of southern principles to the back bone. Never owned a negro in his life, but believed in *States Rights*; therefore he could not make up his mind to submit to Yankee rule." Smith soon joined the Confederate army, and he was stationed at Galveston, where he served as a bugler for his company. He never fought in a major battle but was involved in a "few skirmishes," before the conflict ended and the threat of Reconstruction loomed on the horizon.[5]

Like many other Southerners, Smith was extremely displeased with the state of affairs after the Civil War. According to Bellona's account, her father had "a premonition of the reconstruction horrors that followed Yankee rule," and he decided to take his family to Mexico.[6] However, when Frank McMullan outlined plans to emigrate to Brazil, Smith changed his mind and decided to accompany his old friend to South America. According to one account, McMullan is said to have made the following appeal to Smith: "Don't run away . . . [to Mexico] until I tell you about the real South—this new land under the Southern Cross where a gentleman is treated like a gentleman and there are thousands of rich acres waiting for us progressive farmers. I tell you we're going to empty the Old South for the Yankees, let them have it if they think they know how to run it better than we did. I'm taking my family to Brazil, the empire of freedom and plenty."[7] Sarah Bellona wrote that the decision of her father to follow Frank was instantaneous and that "he'd follow Frank to the end of the world and die for him if need be. And Frank was truly worthy of their devotion."[8] The rest is history. The Smiths did go with Frank McMullan to Brazil and had an adventure that few persons ever have the opportunity to experience.

Sarah Bellona Smith accompanied her family to Brazil, where she later married another emigrant, Turner Ferguson, and lived in South America for the rest of her life. She had a flair for history, however, and as she became older she recognized the importance of the drama that she had known in Texas and in Brazil. Bellona, as she was known, began to write of the trying times that she had known, and her accounts were published both in Texas and in Brazil. Manuscript versions by Bellona were carefully saved by other former Confederate families in Brazil. Frank Goldman and Judith Jones incorporated substantial portions of the Bellona account in their Portuguese-language volume, and William Griggs included her story in his description of the McMullan colony. As already noted, her last and fullest account appears for the first time in a scholarly publication in the previous chapter of this volume.

In addition to the McMullan colonists, there also were many others who determined to leave their homes in the South and settle in a new country among a foreign people. As Bellona Smith suggested, the weeks and months following the defeat of the Confederacy were, to many Southerners, times of fear and foreboding. United States laws left no doubt that the rebellion fell under the definition of treason, and statutes provided that such actions could be punishable by death. However, the huge numbers of persons who participated in the war on the Southern side made such stern action impractical, and thus unlikely.

Yet, Southerners had no way to measure Northern sentiment, and actions such as the arrest of Pres. Jefferson Davis on May 10, 1865, led to increased worry and apprehension. The subsequent indictment of Davis for treason and Union refusal to allow a trial—a right guaranteed by the Constitution—led to additional doubts and fears.[9] The execution of Champ Ferguson, a former member of Morgan's Raiders, for alleged murder while participating in guerrilla activities against Northerners in Tennessee and Kentucky was carried out on October 20, 1865. Less than one month later, Capt. Henry Wirz, the former commander of the Confederacy's Andersonville Prison, was hanged for mistreatment of prisoners.[10] Other high officials of the former Confederate States of America were convinced that their capture would lead to terrible retribution, and most quickly made plans for exile. Former Confederate Secretary of State Judah P. Benjamin determined that he would rather "risk death in attempting to escape than endure the 'savage cruelty' which he was convinced the Federals would inflict on any Confederate leader who might fall into their hands."[11]

Yet, many of those Confederates whose rank was not such that they might suffer retribution also were chagrined and outraged at the defeat and worried about their fate under an occupation army. Shortly after Gen. Robert E. Lee's surrender at Appomattox, Georgia writer Eliza Andrews wrote that there was "complete revulsion in public feeling. No more talk about help from France and England, but all about emigration to Mexico and Brazil. We are irretrievably ruined." Georgia physician George Barnsley noted soon after the end of the war that "political prosecutions have not [yet] commenced. The crash and thunder of contending factions at the north are almost heard."[12]

Many individuals who were higher-ups in the Southern government left for safer climes in Mexico, Cuba, Canada, and other countries as soon as the South's loss in the war was finally recognized. However, it was not until July 4, 1865, when Gen. Joseph O. Shelby's "Iron Brigade" of Missourians symbolically buried the Stars and Bars of the South in the waters of the Rio Grande on their way to Mexico, that any organized group of former Confederates left their defeated nation for a new life in a new land. Bound for possible service with the emperor Maximilian and the off-chance to fight once more some day against Union forces, Shelby and his men carried an arsenal of weapons, ammunition, and supplies with them. Accompanying the band of 132 soldiers was a broad contingent of former Confederates, including such notables as Gen. William P. Hardeman, Gen. John B. Magruder, Gov. Henry P. Allen of Louisiana, and Gen. Hamilton P. Bee.[13] The departure of Shelby's men and accompanying high officials of the former Confederacy was the beginning of a significant exodus of Southerners for sites in Mexico with exotic sounding names such as Carlota (named for Emperor Maximilian's wife), Cordova, Tumbadero, Tuxpán, and Zapotel.[14]

Even before the former Confederates made new lives in Mexico, Canada, Cuba, and even Europe, however, another genre of former Confederates was making plans to go even farther away from the reunited Union. Indeed, only one week after Appomattox, on April 16, 1865, Missourians Dr. John H. Blue and his son sailed from Baltimore on the *Warwick* for Rio de Janeiro. Blue, along with Col. M. S. Swain and Horace Manley Lane of Louisiana, eventually became one of the principal promoters of a Confederate colony in Paraná in the southern part of Brazil. With his wife and two sons, Lane sailed from Baltimore on May 16, one month after the departure of Dr. Blue, on the *Gray Eagle* bound for Rio de Janeiro. Other Southerners padded the ranks of the Paraná colony when Judge John Guillet and twenty members of his family sailed from New York on July 1, 1865. After others joined the Blue, Lane, and Guillet families, American numbers in Paraná eventually totaled as many as 200 persons.[15]

By September 12, 1865, another former Southerner, Dr. James McFaddin Gaston of South Carolina, arrived in Rio de Janeiro on the *Wavelet* from New York.[16] Within days, Gaston made contact with a Brazilian agent of emigration, Dom J. C. Galvão, and outlined his ideas for a colony, inquiring where he and his friends might settle in Brazil. To support Gaston's initiative, Galvão provided in-depth information including detailed maps and data on land costs, transportation, and lodging. Gaston also asked about the possibility of support for transportation for Southern emigrants, stating that "there were many people of good standing in the southern portion of the United States, who were able to provide land and the means of subsistence for themselves, and yet would find great inconvenience in affecting the transportation across the ocean unless some systematic means of assistance could be devised by the Brazilian government." Galvão promised to relay Gaston's request to the Brazilian minister of agriculture and to provide an answer as soon as possible. Meanwhile, Gaston canceled a proposed trip to the Bay of Paranaguá after hearing about the merits of government lands in São Paulo Province. He then asked Galvão for permission to go there to search for a suitable site for his proposed colony. This was arranged after Gaston was summoned for a visit with Antonio Paulo e Souza, the secretary of agriculture, and the South Carolinian was provided with a ticket and the endorsements necessary to travel easily about the country.[17]

In one place in her account, Bellona Ferguson referred somewhat incorrectly to the Gaston-Meriwether colony. Eventually Gaston, whose colonists traveled with those of Frank McMullan from New York to Brazil on the steamship *North America*, settled on lands near the town of Xiririca, São Paulo Province. Families in this group included the Pyles, the Fenleys, the Seawrights, and several others. All of these colonists cleared plots of land for farming but found the profession, for various reasons, to be unprofitable. Also, faulty land titles contributed to unrest among Gaston's colonists, most of whom, as Bellona remembers, moved to the Santa Bárbara area, where many other emigrants eventually congregated. Gaston himself went into the shipping business after the colony breakup, "carrying canoe loads of toucinho [i.e., side hog meat, cured bacon] and lard from Apiahy, head of canoe navigation, to Iguape, situated on the bay extending from the seaport of Cananea to that city."[18]

In the defeated South, the enthusiasm for Brazil was beginning to bloom in late 1865, and a reporter for the *New York Herald* suggested in September of that year that as many as 50,000 persons might leave Dixie for Brazil. He noted that perhaps twenty agents already were at work there securing sites for former Confederates eager to leave for South America. Although it is unlikely that there were this many persons acting as agents at that time, interest and activity were in progress.

What appeared to be one of the most important colonization efforts was launched with the arrival in Rio on October 3, 1865, of Gen. William Wallace Wood of Mississippi. With Wood was a contingent of other Southerners, including Dr. James H. Warne, Dr. J. P. Wesson, R. L. Brown, and W. C. Kernan. The group was met at the dock by a Brazilian band playing "Dixie," and they were treated to three days' entertainment by the Brazilian government before leaving for a prospecting tour accompanied by Maj. Ernest Street, a surveyor and civil engineer from São Paulo, and Henry Snell, an interpreter. They left the port city of Santos by rail for São Paulo Province, where, accompanied by Dr. James M. Gaston, they examined a huge tract of land on the Jaú and Tietê rivers. Seemingly delighted with the prospects after nearly a month of exploration, Wood canceled trips to other areas and returned to Rio de Janeiro to discuss land acquisition. Ostensibly to make his reports to emigration agents in the South who had entrusted their business to him, Wood and his entourage left for New York on the steamship *North America* on January 2, 1866. To the embarrassment of Brazilian authorities, Wood was not seen again, having lost his interest in Brazilian emigration after his return to the South.[19]

Before Wood and his group returned to the United States, several more men arrived in Brazil to investigate the country's prospects for Southern emigration. On October 28 the Reverend Ballard Smith Dunn arrived in Rio de Janeiro aboard the *Adelaide Pendergast* from New York to search for lands for a southern colony.[20] Dunn, rector of St. Phillips Church in New Orleans from 1859 to 1861, served as a chaplain and ordnance officer in the Confederate army during the Civil War. He determined to emigrate to Brazil after a long and painful argument with church leaders about church protocol, provoked by a disagreement concerning the ownership and placement of a baptismal font. After a series of written exchanges between Dunn and the Reverend Alexander Gregg, bishop of Texas, Dunn found his character somewhat impeached, even in his native Louisiana.[21]

On November 11, 1865, Dunn boarded the coastal packet steamer *Diligente* and spent a month examining lands in the provinces of Espírito Santo and Rio de Janeiro. Although Dunn spoke highly of what he saw and the persons that he met during the expedition, he nevertheless was not convinced that the areas where he looked were of the quality that he desired. As a result he determined, on January 9, 1866, to resume his survey in São Paulo Province. The first ten days were spent principally in areas along the coast at the settlement of Cananéa and the Colony of Cananéa and along the Itapetininga, Garahu, and Pindavina rivers, then to the town of Botujuru. From there, Dunn went down the Jacupiranga River to the Ribeira de Iguape, a broad river which flows into the ocean at the small village of Iguape. On January 20, Dunn was set to proceed with his explorations when, in Iguape, he unexpectedly met Dr. James M. Gaston, at that time still prospecting for lands for his own colony. The two determined to join forces in their search, and they left on the twenty-fourth to ascend the Pariquera River. The lands there, once again, were not what Dunn wanted, and the quest continued. Upon reaching the Juquiá River, however, Dunn's aspect changed entirely. "At every turn of the beautiful stream," wrote the rector, "I felt like exclaiming 'Eureka! Eureka!'" Dunn proclaimed the land fit for virtually any crops, including coffee, tobacco, cotton, or sugarcane. He resolved to secure a government tract of 614,000 acres as a colony site and to name it Lizzieland after his wife, Elizabeth.[22]

On June 30, 1866, Dunn concluded a favorable agreement with the director of public lands, Bernardo Augusto Nacente Azambuja, which provided for land at forty-three and one-half cents per acre. Emigrants were to be able to purchase as much property as they wanted; however, Dunn was to be responsible for all payments to the government, with full title being granted after the debt was paid. Colonists were to be allowed to bring in all "implements of agriculture, manufactures, machines, and utensils . . . for their own use," with no import duties, and the government was to provide provisional housing to emigrants upon arrival. The Brazilian government also agreed to furnish the transportation costs, paying for one ship for every two provided by Dunn. Finally, the agreement allowed Dunn's colonists to disembark directly at Iguape—at the head of the Ribeira de Iguape—instead of going through Rio de Janeiro.[23]

Parson Dunn returned to Louisiana and recruited colonists for Lizzieland, and on April 1, 1867, the steamship *Marmion* sailed from New Orleans with 260 emigrants. They reached the harbor of Rio de Janeiro on May 16 and docked one day later. All were taken to a magnificent building called Government House, or Casa de Saúde, a structure formerly belonging to a Brazilian nobleman and located on the Morro de Saúde—one of the many hills that dot the landscape in Rio. At this mansion, called by the colonists the Emigrant Hotel, they were provided with food and housing while waiting for transportation to their new homes on the Juquiá. According to one account, the group from the *Marmion* broke up in Rio, with some going to gold and diamond mines at Minas Geraes Province and others joining the colonial venture of Charles Grandison Gunter on the Rio Doce. Many remained in Rio rather than join established colonies.[24]

If some emigrants who came to Brazil as a part of Dunn's party left it in Rio, there may have been others who joined it for the trip to Iguape on May 24, as the newspaper *Correo Mercantil* in Rio reported that 257 North American emigrants were on board the *Marmion* for this leg of the journey. As soon as possible, the entire group traveled by steamship up the Ribeira de Iguape as far as it was navigable, then boarded long thirty-foot canoes for their final journey up the Rio Juquiá. Although land was secured and crops were planted, a disastrous flood destroyed the first year's work of the Dunn colonists, causing a wholesale desertion of the site to other parts of Brazil or a return to the United States. Dunn himself left for the United States before the tragedy, supposedly to recruit more colonists. However, the New Orleans minister never returned to Brazil, much to the chagrin of those who had followed him to that country.[25]

On November 26, 1865, while Ballard Dunn was still examining lands in the Espírito Santo and Rio de Janeiro provinces, two more Southerners, Dr. Hugh A. Shaw and Maj. Robert Meriwether, arrived in Rio on the *North America* as agents of the Southern Emigration Society of Edgefield, South Carolina. The men were mandated by the society to look at all of the lands that the Brazilian government had made available for settlement. After their arrival in Brazil, however, the two men realized the enormity of the project and determined to visit only those properties which were in the province of São Paulo, an area which one historian noted were supposed to be "best adapted to the wants and necessities of the southern people." Like General Wood and Ballard Dunn, Meriwether and Shaw joined forces with Dr. James M. Gaston in making their search, accompanied by a guide and an interpreter which were furnished by Brazilian Minister of Agriculture Paulo e Souza. After first examining the area around the city of Santos, a port city out south of Rio de Janeiro, the Meriwether and Shaw party proceeded by rail to São Paulo where they secured the necessary accoutrements and pack mules to go into the interior areas. Their journeys extended as far as 200 miles from the city of São Paulo to Araraquara, but these distant properties did not prove to be the sites for which the men were searching. Instead, they became convinced of the merits of lands near Botucatú, Lençóis, and the valley of the Tietê. This property was, unfortunately, over 100 miles from a railhead, and Meriwether and Shaw were rightfully concerned about the problems that they would face in transporting crops after harvest. As a result, they recommended to the Edgefield District Southern Colonization Society properties around Campinas, on the highlands north of the city of São Paulo and relatively near the railroad. Two Southerners, wrote Meriwether and Shaw in their report to the Southern Colonization Society in South Carolina, already had located on lands in that region. Despite the work of Robert Meriwether and Dr. H. A. Shaw, the society did not sponsor a colonization effort to Brazil. Yet, both Meriwether and Shaw determined to make the country their new home.[26]

On December 9, 1865, about two weeks after the arrival in Brazil of Robert Meriwether and H. A. Shaw, the ship *Ann & Lizzie* arrived in Rio de Janeiro from New York. On board were several men who were also to have significant impact on the colonization of Brazil by Southerners. From Texas were Maj. Frank McMullan, Col. William Bowen, and McMullan's close friend and neighbor, Civil War hero Capt. S. S. Totten. All were from Hill and Navarro counties in the north-central part of Texas. From Alabama, but also on the *Ann & Lizzie*, came Charles Grandison Gunter and his four sons. McMullan, Bowen, and Gunter all were to play an important part in emigration from the Southern states to the land of the Southern Cross.[27]

Upon their arrival in Brazil, McMullan, Bowen, and Totten spent over two months exploring the government lands north of the coastal town of Cananéa. Their search was thorough, and although they saw several river valleys that they believed might support a colony from Texas very well, they were reluctant to make a decision until additional surveys were made. After ascending the Ribeira de Iguape from the seaport town of Iguape, McMullan and Bowen determined to go up the Juquiá River, where Ballard Dunn already had selected properties for the establishment of Lizzieland. They went beyond Dunn's selection, however, believing that area to be too low and subject to high water during some seasons. McMullan and Bowen ascended a tributary of the Juquiá, the São Lourenço, where they found lands more to their liking on the Peixe, Itararí, Guanhanhã, and Areado rivers. "Here," McMullan wrote, "the homeless may find a home, and the outcast a 'resting place, with none to molest and make him afraid.'" Leaving William Bowen in Brazil to prepare for the arrival of a colony, McMullan left Rio de Janeiro on the *North America* for New York on June 3, 1866, as the first leg of his return home to Texas to assemble a group of like-minded Southerners who wished to settle in a new land under a different government.[28]

The efforts of Frank McMullan to establish a colony in Brazil show his great dedication to Confederate emigration. He returned to Texas, then assembled a group of 154 men and women and their families, including the Smiths, who desired to settle on the lands that he had located on the São Lourenço River in São Paulo Province. Although guarantees were promised by the Brazilian government for the lease of a ship, shipowners were reluctant to honor the guarantees because they lacked knowledge concerning Brazilian debt payment. Therefore, McMullan, his uncle, Judge James H. Dyer, and others scraped together enough money to lease an English brig, the *Derby*, in New Orleans.

Legal chicanery caused delays and heavy fines before the ship could sail for Galveston where the would-be colonists were camped on the beach, waiting for a ship and their leader. Even after the *Derby* arrived, however, the delays continued as Union officials in Galveston at first refused to grant permission to sail for Brazil. Finally, the ship was released on January 25, 1867, and after the payment to the collector of the port of "a big sum that impoverished our people very much," the *Derby* was on its way.[29]

Troubles were not to end, however. While he was still in New Orleans, Frank McMullan learned that the captain of the *Derby*, Alexander Causse, was implicated in the seizures and delays of the brig. After the *Derby* was at sea, McMullan called a meeting of the colonists to make a decision as to their future course of action. Assembling in the saloon of the little ship, many of the passengers called for stern action against Causse, possibly even hanging the man they considered to be a traitor to their cause. Cooler heads prevailed, however, and the captain was given a stern warning that no other problems should occur or consequences would be harsh.

When a strong tropical storm appeared, however, Causse was back to his old tricks. Probably because the *Derby* was heavily insured by the ship's owner, Causse added sail when other ships in the area were taking it down, and the brig barreled toward the rocky shores of Cuba. To make bad matters worse, Causse even tied the ship's wheel, then went below to his quarters, leaving the ship to its fate. Only the discovery of the treachery by one of the colonists allowed McMullan and Judge Dyer to roust the captain and force him back to the bridge to steer the careening vessel. Despite best efforts, however, the *Derby* hit the rocks near Bahia Honda, Cuba, and was irreparably wrecked. Fortunately, none of the colonists were killed, although one suffered a painful injury.[30]

Almost without money but still full of hope, Frank McMullan journeyed to New York to confer with the Brazilian consul about assistance in continuing to Brazil. Efforts eventually were successful, and after about a month in Cuba, the colonists boarded the steamer *Mariposa*, bound for New York, where the McMullan group was to board the steamship *Merrimack* and continue its journey. A terrible winter storm delayed the *Mariposa* off the coast of Virginia, and the colonists spent several days in port at Newport News before the ship could continue, arriving in New York on March 26. The layover in Virginia caused them to miss the sailing of the *Merrimack*, and as a result, they were stranded in New York for a month before another vessel, the *North America*, sailed on April 22. The McMullan colonists were accompanied by other Southerners, including 100 additional would-be emigrants. Dr. James M. Gaston and his group headed for the colony at Xiririca. Charles Meriwether and H. A. Shaw also sailed on the *North America* on their return voyage to Brazil.[31]

The McMullan colonists arrived in Rio de Janeiro within days after those of Charles Grandison Gunter and Ballard S. Dunn, and as Bellona Ferguson indicates, all were lodged at the Emigrant Hotel at the same time. The McMullan group left within days for Iguape and, following a routine similar to that of the Americans who headed for Dunn's colony on the Juquiá, sailed up the Ribeira de Iguape on a steamer before boarding dugout canoes for the final leg of their trip to colony lands.

Although the McMullan contingent was spared the catastrophe of flooding that faced Dunn colonists at Lizzieland, they nevertheless had their share of problems. After the untimely death of McMullan of tuberculosis within weeks after their arrival, the emigrants were left without a leader. They also struggled because they lacked available markets for their agricultural produce. The colony began to break up, with most going to other sites, but some returned to Texas.[32]

While Frank McMullan and William Bowen still were exploring lands on the Juquiá and São Lourenço rivers, Charles Grandison Gunter was examining lands north of Rio de Janeiro near the Rio Doce in Espírito Santo Province. Born in Chatham County, North Carolina, Gunter settled in Montgomery County, Alabama, in 1853. Said to have been "an extensive planter" and a man "of financial means," he was described as an irreconcilable Southerner and one of the first persons in the South to consider emigration to Brazil. Gunter first sailed to England with four of his sons before beginning his search for colony lands in Brazil. He arrived in Rio de Janeiro on the English ship *Hailey* from Liverpool on February 2, 1866. With one of his sons, Gunter made two trips, one on the seventh to Mangaratiba, and another on the thirteenth to Itabapoana. Although no further record has been found of his route, Gunter and his son left Campos on March 17 to return to Rio de Janeiro. He made two trips from Rio to Santos—once on April 14, and again on June 26.

Gunter made another voyage on July 19 from Rio, bound for Vitória on

Settling

the ship *Auré*, a first step toward his investigation of the lands along the Rio Doce and Lake Juparanã in Espírito Santo Province, north of Rio de Janeiro. Gunter had determined to secure these government lands for several colonies of Southerners from the former Confederacy. Gunter claimed to have secured a huge tract of 600 square miles which he planned to develop into twenty separate settlements.[33] Describing the Gunter grant, emigrant Josephine Foster wrote the *New Orleans Times* on December 1, 1867, that the property "embraces Lake Juparanã, a fresh water lake, about 20 miles long and 4 wide; twenty American settlements have been made around this lake within the past five months. The land comes up to the lake in hills and bluffs, small bays and arms of the lake forming capes, points, etc." On the eastern side, said Foster, "the land runs back level for miles; on the western side several small lakes make their way in, and a low range of mountains is visible in the distance. The mountains, hills, etc., on that side forms the most beautiful and ever-changing scenery."[34]

In the first months, the families who cast their lot with Charles Gunter found life to be satisfactory, if not extremely comfortable. Crops were planted, homes were built, and families were raised. It appeared that the settlement would flourish. In 1868, however, all of the potential evils of the region beset the former Southerners. Mosquitoes became epidemic. Rain poured through thatched roofs, spoiling much-needed supplies, followed by a drought that destroyed patiently planted crops. Illness followed, with chills and fever affecting entire families. As food supplies became more and more scarce, talk turned to leaving for more hospitable areas such as Rio de Janeiro. The exodus that soon began was the beginning of the end of the Gunter colony, and following a pattern seen in other North American settlements, many left for other areas of Brazil. Some determined to return to the United States.[35]

Less than three weeks after the initial arrival in Brazil of McMullan, Bowen, and Gunter, the ship *South America* docked in Rio de Janeiro from New York. On board were two men who were to have a major impact on American colonization in Brazil. On December 27, 1865, Col. William Hutchinson Norris and his son, Robert C. Norris, first stepped on Brazilian soil. On January 6, little more than one week later, they left Rio for Santos, where they boarded a train for the provincial capital of São Paulo, the base from which they would search for lands for their families and friends. They purchased an oxcart, loaded their belongings, and began a trek to the north to the area near the present city of Campinas. There they located properties that they felt suitable for colonization, then completed papers for their purchase from the Brazilian government. It is likely that the "two

gentlemen from the States" who have "already purchased and settled there" and were mentioned in the report by Meriwether and Shaw to the minister of agriculture were the Norris father and son. Little did the two Alabamians know that their colony was to be the only one in middle and southern Brazil to survive into the twentieth century.[36]

After the Norrises sent for their wives and children in Alabama, thirty-three persons sailed from New Orleans on January 10, 1867, on the *Talisman* bound for Rio de Janeiro. After several days at sea, the ship was overwhelmed by a ferocious storm. When waters calmed, it was discovered that the ship was far off course. The nearest landfall was the Cape Verde Islands, near the coast of Africa! Three days were spent in repairing the *Talisman* before the journey could be resumed. While there, it was discovered that the metal hoops that women used to support their skirts had been stored directly under the ship's compass and had caused the instrument to deviate wildly. It was not until April 19 that the Norris colonists finally reached Rio. From there they went to Santos, then to São Paulo, before proceeding to Jundiaí by rail. From there, they continued to Campinas by oxcart. The Norris family went on to the village of Santa Bárbara by horseback and cart, then settled on a *fazenda* named Recanto, where they remained for many years.[37]

Another colony site, this one at the town of Santarém on the Amazon River in northern Brazil, also was to be long-lived. It was pioneered by Lansford Warren Hastings, a remarkable man whose exciting career reads more like fiction than truth. Born in Ohio, Hastings was elected leader, in 1842, of one of the first wagon trains to journey to Oregon. He traveled from there to California, where he saw an opportunity for leadership and power. In quest of the presidency of a California republic, Hastings sought to bring emigrants to the west coast of North America and then overthrow Mexican rule and establish a republic. Hastings yearned to emulate Texan Sam Houston and to become the leader of the new nation. In a book entitled *The Emigrants' Guide to Oregon and California*, Hastings extolled the virtues of the region and was successful in attracting hundreds of families, an action he believed to be essential to his design of independence from Mexico. Hastings's star fell, however, when one group of emigrants, the Donner party, was trapped by a winter storm on the way to California after following the Hastings cutoff, a shortcut recommended in *The Emigrants' Guide*. It was said that one survivor had to be physically restrained from killing Hastings after the rescue of the remains of the wagon train. Without question, the tragedy was the end of Hastings's dream for political power in the American West. After serving in the Confederate army until the end of the Civil War,

Hastings vowed to renew his faded dreams of empire in a new colony on the Amazon.[38]

Hastings was not long in assembling a group of forty-two disaffected Alabamians, and they sailed from New Orleans for Brazil on December 27, 1865, onboard the schooner *Neptune*. Bad luck continued to dog the California entrepreneur, however, and on January 4, 1866, the ship went aground during a gale twenty-six miles from Havana on the coast of Cuba. After making their way to Havana, the colonists dispersed with some going to Mexico, some to Florida, and some taking the *Guiding Star* back to New Orleans, hence to Alabama. Hastings, according to a newspaper account in the *Mobile Advertiser*, "although feeling this calamity very sensibly, is still resolute and hopeful in his enterprise, and informs us that the colonists with whom he has conversed, avow their intention to renew the effort, after a visit to their old home and friends."[39]

Unlike other entrepreneurs who spent months planning their trip to Brazil and made every possible arrangement with the government before venturing for South America, Hastings was in no mood to delay further his exodus from the United States. Undaunted by the wreck of the *Neptune*, Hastings assembled a group of thirty-five Alabamians, boarded the steamship *Margaret*, and set sail from Mobile on March 26, 1866, for the Amazon. Within days of departure, however, smallpox appeared on board. Hastings ordered the return of the ship to Mobile where it immediately was placed in quarantine. The sickness took the lives of eleven of the would-be emigrants, and Hastings's second expedition ended before it hardly began.[40]

Not to be deterred, Hastings was soon on his way to Brazil once more, but this time without a following. Traveling by way of New York, where he arrived on April 28, Hastings conferred with the Brazilian consul, who provided the Californian with letters of introduction to persons in the province of Pará. Hastings left New York on the *North America* on April 30 and arrived in Pará on May 16. Provided with an interpreter, an American identified by Hastings only as Mr. Collyer, Hastings left on the steamer *Manaos* that same evening. Four days later, the ship docked at Santarém, a location which showed great promise as the site of a colonial venture. Hastings was not content to look at the countryside only around Santarém, however, and he continued his trip up the Amazon River to Manaus on May 23. From there, he went back down the river to Santarém and eventually to Pará.

From Pará, Hastings sailed for Rio de Janeiro on June 28, arriving at the capital city on July 16. There, he presented letters of introduction from government officials in Pará to the Brazilian secretary of agriculture. His business in Rio complete, Hastings sailed again for Pará, where he was to finalize agreements with the president of the province. Once negotiations were satisfactorily completed, Hastings sailed again for Santarém on the steamer *Tapajós* along with three passengers from the *Margaret* named Barr, Chaffie, and Sparks, along with Felix Demaret, from Louisiana and Texas. The men made a thorough survey of the region around Santarém. Following a dinner in honor of the prospective emigrants, one Brazilian woman "expressed her heartfelt sympathy for the 'Americans who felt themselves constrained to abandon the homes of their fathers,' and who 'trusted in God that they may find a home of peace and quietude in this prosperous and happy country.'" At Belém, the capital of the province of Pará, on November 7, 1866, Hastings signed a contract with the president of Pará, Dr. Pedro Leão Velloso, validating the establishment of a colony on the Amazon. Hastings sailed for the United States on November 12, arriving in New York on November 30 and Mobile on December 15. Hastings claimed to have traveled over 19,000 miles on the trip with over 10,000 being in the empire of Brazil.[41]

Hastings's agents were busy while he was making final provisions for his grant of sixty leagues of land near Santarém, and on July 12, 1867, a total of 109 colonists boarded the steamer *Red Gauntlet* bound for Brazil. However, upon arrival at the first port of call, St. Thomas, Virgin Islands, a hint of Hastings's former problems returned when adequate money was not available to pay the crew. According to one account, the United States consul at St. Thomas refused to allow the *Red Gauntlet* to continue, ordering the vessel sold to pay wages. As a result, the colonists were stranded until Hastings made arrangements with the Brazilian government for transportation to the colony site at Santarém. Although Hastings died during this trip or on a subsequent voyage, the colony remained in place, even though life there was condemned by some as being very harsh. In 1940, however, one writer was able to locate three of the original Hastings emigrants.[42]

The Americans from the South who emigrated to Brazil were no doubt sincere in their belief that it was to their best interests to leave the United States. Some persons adapted to their new surroundings almost immediately and would have been reluctant to return to their old homes for any reason. Others quickly recognized that their decision had been a mistake and began assembling means to return as soon as they were able to do so. Perhaps the most succinct reasons for dissatisfaction were expressed by the physician George Barnsley, the official doctor of the McMullan colonists. Barnsley noted the principal problems were "dissimilarity of language and customs; difficulties of transportation; low price for skilled labour; differences in religion; inability to vote and be sovereign; disgust for the Brazilian idea that a man who sweats from work is not a gentleman; and finally—the most potent of all, that this country [Brazil] offers and gives nothing for the American, which he cannot get in his own country—nothing worth the sacrifices of exile from his native soil and kindred."[43] Yet, Barnsley returned to Georgia and could have remained there, but he elected to return to his adopted country. Ney McMullan, Frank McMullan's youngest brother, went back to Texas in 1872 but returned to Brazil for good with his family in 1895. There was an allure to the South American nation that many former Southerners simply could not ignore.

Four

Fitting In
Relocating Family and Capital within the Nineteenth-Century Atlantic World Economy: The Brazilian Connection

Laura Jarnagin

In chapter 2, we were presented with an eyewitness account of the Smith's family migration to Brazil. This chapter seeks to place the drama of the relocation of Southerners to Brazil in the post–Civil War era in a broader context. In brief, we will observe and assess the relocation of families, like the Smith family, within the greater scheme of the capitalist world system, particularly as it manifested itself in the Atlantic region of the nineteenth century.

Taking into account various "push" and "pull" factors, plus the characteristics of the migrating population itself, along with its supporters and promoters in Brazil, we find an internal logic to the phenomenon that tends to escape us at smaller scales. In fact, we discover a continuum of capitalist behavior contained herein that transcends national borders and leaves us with an enhanced understanding of what is too often seen as historical oddity.

Broadening the Historical Horizon: The Modern World-System Perspective

The modern world system, as elaborated by Immanuel Wallerstein, is a theoretical construct which is particularly well suited for placing the migration of postbellum Southerners in its more proper perspective, away from being an anomalous quirk in U.S. history and into the mainstream of the borderless nineteenth-century capitalism of the Atlantic world economy. It provides a conceptually well-situated vantage point from which to view not just the actions of a small group of people at a given moment in time but the very socioeconomic processes of which they, their forebears, and their descendants were a part. In so doing, the Southern migration becomes not

66

a sideshow freak in the carnival of U.S. history but a leading actor at center stage.

Although the essential features of the world-system theory are widely familiar to scholars in history and the social sciences, an abbreviated summary of it is appropriate here.[1] In essence, the modern world-system approach seeks to describe and explain the dynamics of capitalism, from its earliest stirrings in Western Europe over 500 years ago to its all-encompassing dominance of today's global economy, not simply as an economic system, but as an imbricated system of economy, polity, and society.[2]

Within this system, there are differentiated zones of capitalist activity, which can be broadly divided into core states and peripheral areas. Core states are characterized economically by a higher degree of variety and specialization of goods and services, more highly skilled labor, and higher concentrations of financial resources; and politically by stronger, more centralized states. In short, they are the command center of the capitalist system, largely determining what, where, and how goods and services will be produced. Peripheral areas, by contrast, tend toward monoculturalism and less skilled labor; in essence, they gear their production to meet the demands of core states.[3] As the capitalist system evolved and geographically spread outward from its European epicenter, it incorporated outlying areas, initially only select portions of Asia, Africa, the Middle East, and Latin America, and ultimately these regions in their entirety.

As a dynamic system, capitalism has been and continues to be characterized by ongoing cycles of expansion and contraction. The locus of the core of capitalism itself has shifted over time, with first one then another state dominating for varying intervals. In the mid-nineteenth century, however, Great Britain was the unchallenged prepotent center of the capitalist world system. The Americas, with the exception of the Northern states of the United States, were part of its periphery, engaged primarily in the production of raw materials.[4] In turn, the economies of the periphery were dominated by an agrarian-based capitalism, producing surpluses that were sold elsewhere throughout the system.

While the broad characteristics of the capitalist world system are known to us, we are less familiar with how individuals acted in the system, perpetuated it, caused it to expand and mutate—in short, how individuals simultaneously contributed to its dynamism and were the unwitting agents of forces far beyond their control, or even the control of any given country. We do know that as the system became more refined and specialized, it required—directly or indirectly—the services of a broad spectrum of skilled occupations and professions: landed capitalist proprietors and well-to-do farmers (who in many respects were lay scientists, engineers, and business managers rolled into one); merchants, large and small; lawyers, bankers, engineers, physicians, educators, clergy, diplomats, military officers, statesmen; and a host of other bourgeois/gentry occupations.[5]

If one were to use the analogy of a beehive, these would be the worker bees in the capitalist system. But who were they, as individuals? The phenomenon of postbellum Southern migration to Brazil provides us with a convenient population of worker bees to study, not just in terms of those individuals from the South, but also of their counterparts in Brazil, and a community that straddled both worlds.

We hope to show that the Confederate migration to Brazil is essentially the continuation of a logical historical trajectory within the nineteenth-century Atlantic world economy's periphery. Once one discards nation-state borders as the unit of analysis and adopts the perspective of the wider capitalist system, the logic of that trajectory becomes more apparent. What we are allowed to view, then, is a pattern of socioeconomic behavior and mentality that persisted through multiple generations across dissimilar societies and that may be regarded as a manifestation of the culture of agrarian capitalism. As a culture, it was propelled by networks of personal contacts, whether of family or friends. It flourished best within nonconfining, noninterfering political institutions and was supported by certain cultural and religious values.

Push and Pull Factors

If one argues that this migration proceeded along a logical, historical continuum, then the classic mode of viewing migrating populations in terms of push and pull factors becomes something of an artificial construct. Nevertheless, push and pull categories are useful for sorting out the historical data conceptually and are thus beneficial for understanding the phenomenon at hand.

In chapters 1 and 3 we have examined some of the more immediate push and pull factors involved in the migration of Southerners to Brazil. On the push side, one has only to point to the economic ruin and psychological trauma resulting from defeat in war. However, as historians of the event have been careful to observe, devastation did not translate into hasty abandonment of home and country. Emigration societies were organized and advance agents were sent to Brazil. Individuals like William Norris even financed their own trips for scouting purposes. In short, careful plans were laid by many of the migrants prior to committing to the move. Not all were economically ruined, either. One source gives the average financial assets brought by migrants to Brazil to be between $500 and $1,000, although some brought considerably more. The Gunters of Alabama, for example, took £3,000 and $2,000 to Brazil with them, and their first harvest there was valued at almost $20,000.[6] One migrant, J. D. Porter, gave no-nonsense advice to prospective migrants concerning what to expect in Brazil, depending on what financial assets they would or would not be able to bring with them: "Brazil offers . . . good land and cheap, good climate and assistance to come and enjoy these blessings. But these will only be blessings to such [as] have the will to labor and endure the privations and hardships of pioneer life or such as have a little money, say $5,000 to live without laboring with their hands."[7]

On the pull side, as we have seen, Brazil's attractions as understood by many migrants lay in such features as a perceived benevolent monarchy, a degree of tolerance of religions other than Roman Catholicism, contractual arrangements between advance agents and the imperial government that included easing the bureaucratic regulations for these particular immigrants, making public lands available for purchase (often with government-backed loans), and promises of improved infrastructure such as new roads and railroads into communities established by Southerners.[8]

The continuation of the institution of slavery in Brazil also held appeal for at least some prospective migrants, although as already noted in chapter 1 the subsequent history of the migrating population reveals that few ever acquired slaves, and those that did apparently did not retain them for long.[9] This aspect of the Confederate experience in Brazil has posed a certain dilemma for historians: was slavery an important pull factor in the decision to migrate or not? Once again, comments by J. D. Porter are instructive: "The rumors you have heard to the contrary, not withstanding, slavery will not be abolished soon in this country, and when done, as most probably it will be, this government is not going to make paupers of Africans. In proof—Negroes are advancing in price, and Southerners are all wanting to buy."[10]

When this observation is taken together with Porter's comment quoted earlier, however, one gets the impression that acquisition of slaves would very much be a function of a migrant's financial resources; migrants were advised to plan to work with their own hands if they had less than $5,000 to bring to the effort. Thus, it would appear that it is too simplistic to state the issue in terms of whether potential migrants were attracted to Brazil because slavery was still being practiced.

While it cannot be denied that these push and pull factors go a long way toward explaining the migration, they do so at a somewhat superficial level. The historian cannot help but suspect that there were less visible, behind-the-scenes forces at work as well. Advance agents, such as Lansford Warren Hastings, W. W. Wood, James McFadden Gaston, Frank McMullan and William Bowen, Robert Meriwether and Hugh A. Shaw, and Ballard S. Dunn, no matter how impeccable their credentials, simply could not have sailed into Rio one day, had an audience with the minister of agriculture the next, and with the emperor himself shortly thereafter—not in a hierarchically structured, protocol-conscious society like that of nineteenth-century Brazil.[11] The appropriate groundwork had to be laid, and that groundwork would have had to hinge definitively on personal connections and favors.

To a large extent, we know the essence of that groundwork and those contacts. The Brazilian protagonists of this drama were liberal reformers, who were in political ascendancy in the mid-1860s. Their presence, dominance, and direct role in bringing the Southern migration to fruition are often noted by historians and will be discussed at greater length.[12] At this point, however, a brief outline of their main objectives is necessary. Among the reforms they advocated and promoted were organized immigration to offset the growing shortage of agricultural labor, the formation of free colonies, simplified naturalization laws, religious toleration, opening the Amazon to world trade and commerce, and the gradual abolition of slavery. All of these objectives, taken as a whole, were calculated to improve the commercial performance of Brazil in the world economy.

And yet, the fact that Brazilian liberals just happened to be casting about for credible immigrants at the same time that Southerners just happened to be looking for a new home cannot be dismissed as felicitous coincidence. Granted, many educated Southerners were familiar with Brazil in passing as a result of a number of things which occurred in the 1850s. These range from the U.S. naval expedition that explored the Amazon from headwaters to mouth, to the effort of Southern states to develop an economic sphere of influence that would have included Central America and the circum-Caribbean southward through the Amazon valley, as well as the works of Protestant missionaries Kidder and Fletcher, including *Brazil and the Brazilians*.[13]

Familiarity with Brazil, however, is still not a completely satisfying explanation of why Confederates set their sights on the land of the Southern Cross without the addition of personal networks and contacts operating in the background. Although here we do not claim exhaustive research into the individual links in this presumed chain of contacts, we will follow some promising leads which provide a glimpse into the more complex scenario that must have existed at the time. The significance of what is known, however, goes a long way toward demonstrating how the inner workings of the world economy made for a logical set of contacts that ultimately brought many historical threads into the weave of the Southern migration to Brazil. In order to understand that convergence, however, it is first necessary to describe some of those many threads, beginning with the more salient features of the migrants themselves, then moving on to their promoters and supporters in Brazil.

Characteristics of the Migrating Population

Identifying who the Smiths and the other Southern migrants were in the greater scheme of things will be accomplished by examining their motives for migrating, their socioeconomic backgrounds, the kinship networks among them, and some of their historical antecedents as an identifiable group within U.S. history. To begin with, a distinction must be made that narrows the community upon which we are to focus. As is noted in the existing literature of the migration, there were basically two types of émigrés. One was a set of individuals who had few, or at best dismal, prospects in life to begin with, irrespective of the war. In New York, where the Brazilian government established an agency to handle what was initially anticipated to be a large number of North American migrants, they were usually recent Irish and German immigrants who took advantage of free-passage offers. From locales such as Galveston, Mobile, and New Orleans, it was the occasional "wharf rat."[14] Their decisions to migrate appear to have been far more spontaneous, their forethought simplistic, their actions aleatoric.

The second general type of migrant can be characterized as a "purposeful" migrant.[15] These are the emigrants with whom we are concerned in this study. Such were the A. I. Smiths. Among other common characteristics, these migrants had an appreciable degree of choice in the matter of resolving to migrate; indeed, there were many Southerners who evidently considered the idea seriously but ultimately rejected it. Those who did choose to move—or "remove," in classic nineteenth-century parlance—did so largely with a strong sense of finding not merely equal but in fact greater opportunity at their new destination than was to be had in their present, immediately foreseeable, and even past (prewar) circumstances. For instance, Robert Lewis Dabney, an eminent Virginia Presbyterian clergyman, wrote the following to his brother in early 1866 about what he expected to gain from migrating: "Could these hopes be realized, we should have nothing to regret, after the local ties were once surrendered, and the actual labours of removal gotten through: but might find ourselves in a better situation than we ever were before, even during our good days. Our chinquepin [*sic*] region [of Virginia] was a hard country at best: and nothing but a set of social circumstances acceptable to our feelings & habits made it a tolerable home."[16]

Most of the purposeful migrants had studied their options with care over many months or even years, relying on reports made by the several advance agents and/or becoming members of the emigration societies mentioned in chapters 1 and 3. They weighed relative costs and benefits, insofar as they were able, prior to migrating. Not surprisingly, therefore, we also find that they came from relatively privileged, though not especially wealthy bourgeois/gentry backgrounds; in short, they were neither Frank Owsley's "plain folk of the Old South" nor its most affluent inhabitants. One advance agent, Robert Meriwether, wrote a retrospective summary of his farming experiences in Brazil from late 1866, when he purchased lands, to mid-1872 and was able to confirm the wisdom of his scouting expedition undertaken with Dr. Hugh A. Shaw in 1865. Among his observations are the following remarks comparing the productivity of the land in São Paulo with areas in the U.S. South: "Products, compared with So. Carolina and Georgia (Edgefield) District, and Baker Co. S.W. Ga: where my experience in planting was considerable previous to 1865 are as 4 to 1. Four acres of land to one bale of cotton, and from 10 to 15 bushels of corn to the acre in those States: Here a bale per acre of cotton, and in some instances more than two; with 40 bushels of corn, and sometimes 60 per acre."[17] Not surprisingly, we find Meriwether concluding his testimony by saying "I . . . have no reason to regret my choice."[18] Those migrants who had been less vigilant in their preparations to migrate, or who may have had less in the way of financial assets, however, appear to have been those who were more likely to return to North America within a relatively short time.[19]

The bourgeois mentality of the nineteenth century not only allowed for but depended upon a willingness to be open to opportunity and to act when it presented itself. In the Americas, maximizing opportunity often meant by definition being mobile as well, leaving one locale for another. New ventures of this nature were seldom undertaken by individuals alone but rather in conjunction with family and friends. Thus, it was the family unit, in concert with an extended social and kinship network of clans from a like social strata, that was the strategic organizing principle for structuring economic activities. Over time and space, other families would be incorporated into these networks with an eye toward strengthening and diversifying the

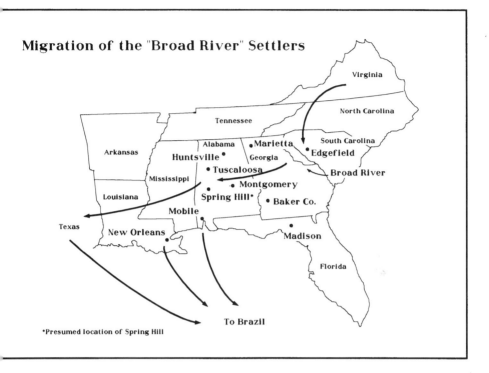

Migration of the "Broad River" Settlers

*Presumed location of Spring Hill

group's horizontal linkages as agrarian capitalism expanded in the periphery. If anything, these individuals were the purveyors of that capitalism.[20]

When one looks at the group of migrants from Alabama identified for this study, one readily finds these same principles at work, both in terms of the generation that migrated and in terms of their forebears. More specifically, an examination of the surnames occurring in the target group of Alabamians reveals that many of these families were descendants of what has come to be known as the Broad River group of the Georgia–South Carolina border region. Leaving a nucleus of intermarried, prominent merchant-planter families of Virginia and North Carolina in the post–Revolutionary War years of the 1780s, the offshoot group sought new opportunities in commercial agriculture along the Broad River of northern Georgia and the neighboring valley of the upper Savannah River.[21] This does not mean that the occupations of the numerous members of this network limited themselves to planting or commercial activities. Rather, we find these individuals engaged in a diversified spectrum of the bourgeois/gentry professions outlined previously.

The most ardent advocates of opening the Alabama territory—and other lands farther west—to American settlers came from this nucleus. Once land grants in Alabama were made available from the federal government, many of the Broad River group were among the first to make their way to one of two localities—Huntsville in the north and Montgomery in the center. In the case of Montgomery, companies were formed expressly for the purpose of facilitating the movement of Broad River families into the area, a similar approach to what would be used again a few decades later when Southerners moved to Brazil. Although the Broad River group would play a pivotal role in the early economic development of Alabama, as a group they were often held in contempt because of their relative success. As one historian has expressed it, "Broad River capital came chiefly from agriculture, of course. . . . But their investments were a great deal more diversified than those of most Alabama planters."[22]

Ties to the older Broad River communities were not severed with the move to Alabama, however. One of the emigration societies formed to facilitate migration to Brazil was located in Edgefield, South Carolina, a major Broad River community. Its advance agent, James McFadden Gaston, was the author of the widely consulted book *Hunting a Home in Brazil.* His brother, Dr. J. B. Gaston of Montgomery, Alabama, migrated to Brazil along with Charles Grandison Gunter and his family, also from Montgomery. Dr. Gaston's brother-in-law, S. D. McConnell, was a member of the Florida Emigration Society of Madison. From that emigration society also came A. J. Dozier, who was also one of Charles G. Gunter's sons-in-law. Furthermore, James McFadden Gaston's father-in-law, the noted scientist Richard Trapier Brumby of Marietta, Georgia, served as an agent for prospective emigrants from that state.[23]

Brumby, who at one time lived in Alabama, was also an ardent supporter of John C. Calhoun's nullification movement of the 1820s, having been described as one of the "most talented and effective of all Nullifier editors" when he ran the *Tuscaloosa State Rights Expositor.* One of Calhoun's law partners in South Carolina was William Lowndes Yancey, who later became a famous Alabama "fire-eater" in the 1850s and 1860s, advocating a radical Southern rights position. Two of Yancey's sons, Benjamin and Dalton, were later among the Alabama emigrants to Brazil. Furthermore, John C. Calhoun's brother-in-law James Edward Calhoun of Edgefield had spent time in Brazil while in the U.S. Navy serving on the *U.S.S. Boston,* probably in the late 1840s or early 1850s. He is said to have made "a number of friends in Brazil" while there.[24]

At all events, the South Carolina migrants to Brazil included members of at least three of the "first families of Edgefield"—the Brookses, the Butlers and the Pickens—all of whom were intermarried with the Calhouns. Another scion of the Calhoun family, James M. Calhoun, was a state representative from Dallas County, Alabama, in 1839 and again in 1842, when one William Hutchinson Norris also served in the state legislature. The Norris family of Spring Hill, Alabama, and of Broad River descent, as we already know, later moved to Brazil.[25]

Other connections within the migrating community with linkages to the Gunter family are also to be had. Charles G. Gunter's son William Gunter was married to the former Ellen Poellnitz. Although William and Ellen did not migrate to Brazil, Ellen's two sisters and their husbands did. One of these gentlemen was Robert A. Hardie, who was probably related on his mother's side to the U.S. diplomatic representative to Brazil between 1857 and 1861, Richard Kidder Meade. Meade may also have been distantly related to the Keyes family, a branch of which was located in Spring Hill, Alabama, and migrated to Brazil along with the Norrises of the same town.[26]

This abbreviated sampling of the linkages that ran through the community of purposeful migrants is but the tip of a proverbial iceberg, both at the time of the migration and for several generations prior. From this kinship matrix spanning several generations precipitates out a notable set of individuals who gave definition to the expansion of capitalism in the periphery of the world system. Among them, for example, are many of the leading seventeenth- and eighteenth-century planter-merchant families of Virginia, such as the Burwells, Cabells, Carters, Randolphs, and Taliaferros, among others; explorers Meriwether Lewis and Willard Clarke; the notorious filibuster William Walker, who brought havoc to California and imposed himself as president of Nicaragua temporarily; Matthew Fontaine Maury, the naval officer who advocated incorporating the Amazon into the Southern commercial orbit; his cousin, William Lewis Herndon, who actually mounted the late 1850s expedition of the Amazon valley as per Maury's instructions; and a host of other "agents of Manifest Destiny."[27]

This exercise in uncovering other connections both through time and across the geographic expanse of the South (and beyond) could be continued indefinitely. Suffice it to state here that the gamut defined by this network ranges widely across those who advanced the capitalist frontier in the Atlantic periphery. As will be seen in the next section, individuals from this same socioeconomic milieu would be responsible for bringing about the migration of Southerners to Brazil and would be the dominant elite in those Brazilian communities where the more successful purposeful migrants established themselves.

The Brazilian Connections

A logical point of departure in attempting to understand the Brazilian setting of the migration is with an individual who constituted one of the stronger links in this chain of events—Aurélio Cândido Tavares Bastos. Tavares Bastos was the quintessential liberal reformer of his time and one of the movement's most eloquent and exigent figures. An adviser to Emperor Dom Pedro II and an unabashed admirer of the United States who wanted to duplicate the American republican model in Brazil, Tavares Bastos was intimately linked to the Protestant movement in Brazil and with Freemasonry.[28] Protestantism and Freemasonry in mid-nineteenth-century Brazil had close ties with the Anglo-American commercial community and the attendant diplomatic corps of Great Britain and the United States, both of which were intrinsically engaged in advancing the commercial interests of their compatriots and respective nations.[29] Tavares Bastos was convinced that Protestantism was the route to what was termed progress. His ideology in turn led him to advocate liberal economic principles, including opening the Amazon to international commerce, establishing navigation lines between Brazil and North America, free coastal navigation of Brazil, civil marriage, constitutional rights for Protestants, and, above all, the separation of church and state.[30]

Among Tavares Bastos's multitudinous activities and interests during his relatively short life was his work as founder and president of the Sociedade Internacional de Imigração (International Immigration Society), which came into being primarily to further the cause of Southern immigration to Brazil.[31] The members of its board of directors were equally fervent and prominent liberal reformers. By promoting Southern immigration to Brazil, Tavares Bastos and his colleagues simultaneously promoted their ambitious political agenda.

Tavares Bastos and the Reverend James Cooley Fletcher, coauthor of *Brazil and the Brazilians*, were personal friends. In addition to his role as a Presbyterian missionary in Brazil, Fletcher also served in the early 1850s as first secretary of the U.S. legation in Brazil. In addition, he was the son of a banker and enjoyed traveling in similar, monied circles in Brazil.[32] Fletcher's closest Brazilian acquaintances included a childhood friend and close adviser of Emperor Dom Pedro II, intellectuals and educators who admired Anglo-Saxon culture, and notable politicians and statesmen.[33]

In short, Fletcher was "the linking agent between the companies, impresarios, Protestants, and [Brazilian] liberals."[34] The specific interactions between Fletcher and the international commercial community in Brazil have yet to be established. Certainly, ferreting them out would provide us a fuller understanding of the Confederate migration. What we can claim is that within the world of Protestant clergymen and international merchants, we find a fluid community of individuals who were accustomed to commuting between the United States and Brazil with some regularity.[35]

From the linkage between Tavares Bastos and Fletcher, a complex network of relations in both Brazil and the United States is opened up. Although the reaches of this network are beyond the scope of what we can pursue here, a few examples of how these relations may have abetted the migration of Southerners to Brazil can be demonstrated.

One of the more promising lines of inquiry in this regard concerns the role of Freemasonry in the migration effort. An oblique hint that Freemasonry may have been one of the routes by which prospective migrants were recruited comes from a letter written by Robert E. Lee in 1866 to one Robert W. Lewis of Virginia. Evidently, Lewis had written to Lee seeking his opinion as to whether Southerners should undertake to migrate, and most of Lee's reply addresses that point. (Lee was not particularly in favor of it, by the way, stating that "the South required the presence of her sons . . . to sustain and restore her.") At the very end of Lee's letter, however, there is the following: "In answer to your question as to what portion I hold in the order of Masons; I have to reply that I am not a mason and have never belonged to the society."[36]

Why had Lewis inquired about Lee's possible Masonic connections in a letter that had obviously dealt largely with the question of emigration to Mexico and Brazil? We know that several of the Southerners who migrated to Brazil were active Masons once there, including such leaders among the migrant communities as William H. Norris, Dalton Yancey, and Charles G. Gunter. It is also known that Freemasonry in Brazil went hand-in-glove with the Protestant community, especially the Presbyterians.[37]

Furthermore, one of the members of the Sociedade Internacional de Imigração who helped arrange passage for Southerners migrating from New Orleans, Charles Nathan, was also a Mason.[38] Nathan, a British merchant in Rio, had formerly resided in New Orleans. As a member of the immigration society, he was instrumental in arranging passage for a number of the Southern migrants who left from New Orleans.[39] One can conjecture that the Reverend Ballard S. Dunn, the Episcopalian who, as we have seen, led migrants from New Orleans to the ill-fated colony of Lizzieland in southeastern São Paulo, may have been a Mason himself and could have known Nathan in that context in New Orleans.

But were there ever any direct connections between Southern migrants who were Masons and Brazilian Masons? In at least one known case, the answer is yes, and from that case, the multifaceted role of the liberal reformers in the migration is reinforced. That one known instance involves an Alabama migrant, Dr. Russell McCord, who evidently settled in the northern portion of Rio province in the vicinity of the town of Macaé. His surviving Masonic certificates for the years 1872, 1874, 1875, and 1879 include the signature of one Joaquim Maria Saldanha Marinho, a friend and colleague of Tavares Bastos's and at one time a coeditor of the influential liberal newspaper *Diário do Rio de Janeiro*, along with Quintino Antônio Ferreira de Sousa Bocaiúva. Bocaiúva, in turn, was one of the more active directors of the Sociedade Internacional de Imigração and spent time in New York heading up the society's agency in an effort to promote Southern immigration to Brazil.[40]

In addition to being a lawyer and an imperial politician, Saldanha Marinho held the title of grand master of the Grande Oriente do Brasil ao Vale dos Beneditinos, one of two branches of Brazilian Masonry, and the one to which Dom Pedro II himself belonged.[41] Saldanha Marinho is described as having worked with enthusiastic ardor and dedication in the cause of Freemasonry and was particularly active politically in the mid-1860s in the cause of forging a separation of church and state.[42]

In late 1865, just as the various expeditions by advance agents and other Southerners to Brazil were getting underway, Saldanha Marinho was appointed provincial president of Minas Gerais, one of the sites considered for the settlement of Confederate émigrés. In fact, one migrant wrote home to his cousin in 1867 that he considered Minas Gerais to be preferable to São Paulo, since there was a greater abundance of lands to be had there than in the Campinas region of São Paulo, but with the same climatic advantages.[43] By October 1867, when the movement of Southerners to Brazil was in full bloom, Saldanha Marinho was the new president of São Paulo, the province in which the most enduring Confederate settlement, Vila Americana/Santa Bárbara, was located. His predecessor in that same office had been none other than Tavares Bastos's father, José Tavares Bastos.[44]

Another signatory of McCord's Masonic certificates was an even more prominent Brazilian—José Maria da Silva Paranhos, better known as the Visconde do Rio Branco, one of the most imposing and distinguished political figures within the Brazilian empire. Rio Branco also held the title of grand master of the Grande Oriente do Brasil.[45] Within Brazilian history, however, Rio Branco is best known as the author of the first piece of emancipation legislation, the Lei do Ventre Livre (law of the free womb), which was passed in 1871 and marked the beginning of Brazil's seventeen-year circuitous trek toward a final abolition of slavery.

In the early 1850s, however, Rio Branco was one of the directors of a company formed in London to construct railroad lines for the government of Brazil that were to run from the city of Rio to the provinces of Minas Gerais and São Paulo. Among the other Brazilian directors of the company was Dr. Caetano Furquim de Almeida, a wealthy planter, commission merchant, and member of a major modernizing clan of Rio province, the Teixeira Leites of Vassouras, who were advocates of railroad construction as early as the 1840s.[46] Furquim de Almeida was also a close friend of Tavares Bastos and of the Reverend James C. Fletcher—one of Fletcher's "money men" acquaintances.[47] Furquim de Almeida promoted Tavares Bastos's immigration schemes with the Rio financial community, although he and Fletcher later disagreed about the future direction of the Sociedade Internacional de Imigração: Furquim de Almeida did not want to limit the society to promoting just Confederate immigration, while Fletcher wanted it to be devoted exclusively to that end.[48]

In the personages of Furquim de Almeida and Quintino Bocaiúva, we have a window that opens onto a distinctive set of Brazilian elites whose socioeconomic behavior and values bear a remarkable resemblance to the purposeful migrants from the U.S. South. From the ranks of these Brazilians came the strongest supporters and advocates of the migration, and it would be in the communities where they were hegemonic that the most successful migrants would also be found. Like their Southern counterparts, extended families or clans constituted the main organizing principle for economic advancement. Also like their Southern counterparts, horizontal linkages through marriage with other clans provided social mobility and economic diversification into a broad spectrum of activities integral to the agrarian capitalism of the periphery, such as landholding, international commerce, finance, railroad building, and politics.[49] A very small sampling of this community will suffice to illustrate the point.

As noted previously, Furquim de Almeida was a member of one such clan, the Teixeira Leites of Rio province, whose interests and control extended into coffee production, international commerce, and railroad building. In addition to coffee, Furquim de Almeida's commercial firm—Furquim, Joppert and Company—had business connections with the sugar producers of the Macaé-Campos region of northern Rio province, where Alabamian Russell McCord had settled.[50] Among the McCords' social friends during their time in Brazil were the Carneiro da Silvas of the Macaé-Campos region. The Carneiro da Silvas, not incidentally, were one of the most prominent sugar-producing clans in all of nineteenth-century Brazil, due in large part to their unparalleled leadership in modernizing sugar production, but also to their major commercial role in the international sugar market as well.[51]

Through Quintino Bocaiúva, we can establish connections with prominent clans of São Paulo Province, including individuals who were members of an association of *paulistas* (residents of the state of São Paulo) formed to assist the Confederate immigrants.[52] Among these were the Barão de Iguape (Antônio da Silva Prado) and Luís Antônio de Sousa Barros, whose families were interrelated. The Silva Prados were a nouveau riche clan as of the nineteenth century, having been among those most responsible for opening up new commercial agricultural lands in São Paulo Province earlier in the century, much like their Southern counterparts.[53]

Although the Silva Prados did not reach their social and economic pinnacle until the 1890s, the mid-nineteenth century found them actively engaged in building the kinds of horizontal linkages with other clans that broadened and diversified their interests. Described as being gentry to the core, the Silva Prados had family members who were engaged in the cultivation of coffee, sugar, and cotton, as well as members who were commission merchants, bankers, and railroad builders. A member of one of the clans with which the Silva Prados were linked, the Sousa Aranhas, later became active in the founding of the first school established by the Confederates in Campinas in 1871.[54]

The Silva Prados and the Sousa Barroses were also interrelated with the prominent Monteiro de Barros clan, which had branches in São Paulo, Rio de Janeiro, Minas Gerais, and Espírito Santo. The profile of this clan closely parallels that of the Silva Prados in its diversified socioeconomic activities, which included many linkages with foreign commercial families. It is mentioned here not to repeat the pattern that has already been delineated but rather to provide an instructive postscript. In the early twentieth century, a scion of one branch of the Monteiro de Barros clan, Eduardo de Oliveira Adams, married Julia Norris Jones, daughter of Leonard Jones and Julia Norris, members of two of the more prominent Alabama migrant families. Eduardo's sister, Helena da Silveira Adams, married José Benaton Prado, a probable relation of the Brazilian nephew of Charles Nathan, Newton Benaton.[55] In another branch of the clan at about the same time, another Monteiro de Barros descendant married Alberto Rudge, Jr., the great-

Fitting In

grandson of one of the partners of the Anglo-American commission house of Rio and Baltimore, Maxwell, Wright & Company.[56]

While the similarities in family and clan behavior between the purposeful Southern migrants and their Brazilian promoters are fascinating enough in and of themselves, there remains yet another similarity between the two communities that is equally instructive and engaging. It has to do with politics. The Southern migrants had come from defeat in a contest in which they had championed a strong states' rights stance. The connections with the political movements of Calhoun and later the Alabama Yanceyites among some of the migrants are especially worth noting in this context. Meanwhile, as of the 1860s, the migrants' Brazilian counterparts were just entering a political struggle that would be couched in similar terms. Proponents of the Brazilian liberal movement, which later grew into the successful republican movement of the 1870s and beyond, championed what might be termed a provinces' rights position, as decentralized in its objectives as the states' rights movement had been in the South of the United States. Political systems structured along these lines inherently aided and abetted the core states within the world economy by virtue of keeping peripheral states relatively weak, thus allowing the economic elite in the periphery a relatively free hand in maintaining and advancing their role as producers of primary export products. In the case of Brazil, however, supporters of decentralization ultimately won their struggle, whereas the same cause had been defeated in North America.

By 1869, Tavares Bastos and his clique had founded the Clube Reforma, also known as the Clube Radical, which eventually became the Partido Republicano. São Paulo figured prominently in the republican movement, with members from most of the bourgeois/gentry clans previously mentioned at its forefront. This included, for example, Joaquim Egydio de Sousa Aranha, the member of the Sousa Aranha clan who had participated in founding the school in Campinas and who later became the president of the Partido Republicano.[57] As of 1889, the republican movement successfully displaced the Brazilian monarchy.

Contrary to popular belief, the economic elite of Brazil's nineteenth-century commercial export agriculture—and particularly the more progressive-oriented, bourgeois/gentry set described heretofore—were increasingly at odds with the Brazilian monarchy, a fact that became more salient from the early 1870s onward. The discordant relations between the two cannot be distilled into a simplistic dichotomy of planters being pro-slavery and the monarchy anti-slavery. In fact, most planters looked forward to the day when a slave-based economy would be a thing of the past. Just how to abolish that institution, however, became an exceedingly complex matter, due to the fact that from mid-century onward, the exigencies of export agriculture became increasingly intricate and turned on the key variables of capital, labor, and technology. Unlike any previous century in modern times, the nineteenth century presented export agriculture with a wide array of new and rapidly changing options in these key areas. In many respects, there were too many options, too many choices, too many unknowns, too many possible combinations in much the same sense that the late twentieth century is being overwhelmed by the information revolution. The challenge to nineteenth-century commercial planters was twofold: to find the right combinations of capital, labor, and technology that would assure success, not ruination; and to stay afloat through periods of experimentation. Furthermore, no planter could look at any one of these factors in isolation—such as slave versus free labor—and hope to make an informed, successful business decision. Nor could an individual planter act in isolation; there were not only the ups and downs of the international market to consider but the often pivotal impact of government structures and policies as well.

As of mid-century, a host of events and trends either had taken place or were taking place concurrently that warrant labeling that time a turning point that set the stage for the deterioration of relations between export agriculture of the Brazilian center-south and the monarchy in the succeeding decades. In terms of the dynamics of the capitalist world system, one can argue that mid-century represents a turning point from a process of capital widening to one of capital deepening in Brazil. The two concepts are distinguished as follows: capital widening is a stage in which, for example, markets are extended or new and latent natural resources are explored; capital deepening is a process in which more capital-intensive techniques of production are adopted.[58] Most notable among this confluence of occurrences were the cessation of the slave trade to Brazil in 1850, the proliferation of railroads into the coffee-growing regions, and the rapid expansion of the international market for coffee.

Whereas planters had always anticipated that a host of problems would arise from and be compounded by the cessation of the slave trade, it was not until the early 1860s that the initial impact of this confluence of factors was felt, that a sense of impending crisis drew nearer, and that demands on the imperial government for change first began to find organized voice. It was the search for solutions to export agriculture's mounting problems—a search that would perpetuate and benefit the capitalist world economy as it was then structured—that set up many of the pull factors that would ultimately translate into the migration of Southerners to Brazil in the post–

Civil War years. More specifically, even though the Brazilian monarchy never veered from acknowledging that export agriculture was the preeminent, unchallenged source of Brazil's wealth, it would be the very structure and functioning of that monarchy that ultimately was identified as inhibiting export agriculture from realizing its full potential.

Both Tavares Bastos and Saldanha Marinho concerned themselves with issues confronting Brazil's export agriculture and were among the critics who first began to articulate a coherent and comprehensive overview of the problems facing Brazil's export agriculture that ultimately translated into a divisive political debate in the last two decades of the empire. Tavares Bastos's seminal work *Os males do presente e as esperanças do futuro* remains a benchmark of the problems facing export agriculture in Brazil at mid-century.

As editor of the prominent liberal newspaper the *Diário do Rio de Janeiro*, Saldanha Marinho had championed the cause of a planters' association founded in 1860 in the Rio coffee-producing community of São José da Cacaria. This organization was one of the very few of its kind in Brazil to have been founded as of that date. Saldanha Marinho applauded the fact that this association represented local, private initiative in light of the indifference shown toward agriculture on the part of the then conservative-dominated imperial government. Among the key members of that organization were members of Rio Province clans linked by marriage to the progressive *paulista* clans who supported the Confederate migration to Brazil.[59]

To make a long story short, the Brazilian movement helped bring to an end the centralizing Brazilian monarchy and helped introduce the decentralized republican system in which export agriculture was to enter its golden era. In other words, whereas agrarian capitalism ultimately failed to achieve political dominance in the United States, where a countervailing industrial capitalism had already been implanted, it succeeded in Brazil by the late nineteenth century. Thus, in conclusion, in many respects, the migration of Southerners to Brazil in the post–Civil War era should be regarded as just one more iteration of a common pattern of behavior that was characteristic of generations of a bourgeois/gentry network that was integral to the process of capitalist expansion in the Atlantic periphery. By migrating to Brazil, these purposeful migrants were not fish out of water, although they were certainly navigating in currents that took them farther than the distance from, say, Edgefield to Montgomery. Rather, they were making the next logical move to yet another new opportunity within the agrarian capitalism of the Atlantic world system.

Five

The Heritage
The *Confederados'* Contributions to Brazilian Agriculture, Religion, and Education

James M. Dawsey and Cyrus B. Dawsey

In his study "Confederate Emigration to Brazil, 1865–1870," Douglas A. Grier raised a question that he called "perhaps the most important question that the historian must ask about the emigration movement" to Brazil: "What contributions, if any, did the Americans make to Brazil's economic and cultural progress?"[1] This topic was of interest to Sarah Bellona Smith Ferguson also, for, as we have seen, she ended her account by interspersing examples of changes that had occurred in Brazil since the days of her childhood with examples of contributions to the development of Brazilian society made by Americans and Englishmen, concluding that "these will show what foreigners have done for Brazil." To her mind, Brazil would have remained as it had been in the days of the cart men and muleteers "if England and other nations had not come and built railroads and developed the country." She claimed that Americans introduced the first trollies, grapes, and plows into Brazil, and she implied that foreigners were responsible for such developments as brick houses, modern stoves, kitchen utensils, beds, soft pillows, shoes and socks, and the *pulpador* (coffee pounder).[2] Here, Bellona repeated a view that was common among the early *confederados*. As expressed by another émigré in 1872, foreigners "flocked into Brazil . . . [and] established railroads, telegraphs, steam power, machinery, agriculture with the plow, masonry, and Protestantism. All these new ideas from abroad (for this race has invented nothing) are admired and adopted."[3]

Grier too expressed the opinion that American emigration had a substantial influence on the economic and technological development of Brazil. As evidence of "an impact far out of proportion to its meager numbers," he listed the new technology, especially agricultural technology that the Americans took with them to South America. He enumerated the metal-tipped plow, the kerosene lamp, the sewing machine, the buckboard, a

process for distilling sugarcane into rum, a simplified procedure for sur-
veying land, and the introduction of four new crops—upland cotton, rattlesnake watermelons, grapes, and pecans.

Although some scholars have attributed these advances to the emigrants,
we should not overstate the importance of the Southern colonists to the
economic and technological development of Brazil. As we have seen in
chapter 4, the emigration of the *confederado* farmers fits within the broader
framework of economic development where the periphery planters supplied raw materials to the industrialized center. Not just instruments for
economic development, the Southern emigrants were themselves being
moved by greater forces at work in the world's economy. The high price of
cotton on the international market in the 1860s had led to the expansion
of cotton plantations in the province of São Paulo, and the Brazilian planters themselves were seeking better agricultural technology. In a report to
the *Auxiliador da Indústria Nacional* three Americans noted as early as 1867
that the Brazilians spoke of cotton as a money crop. The Brazilians, they
said, were seeking the best seeds to plant and the best tools with which to
cultivate the cotton's growth. They had experimented with several different
types of plows but had found none that were satisfactory. In conclusion,
the Americans noted that they expected the Brazilians, who were very
smart, soon to find the tools corresponding to their needs.[4]

The Southern émigrés provided some of the know-how being sought by
the Brazilians. Col. William Norris's activities when first arriving in Brazil
illustrate the larger economic forces at work. He arrived as a cotton planter,
but during that first year he actually made more money demonstrating the
use of the American plow than producing his own cotton crop. Norris was
hired by José Vergueiro, owner of the Fazenda Ibicala in Limeira, to teach
Southern agricultural methods to his employees. Eventually, José Vergueiro
became the largest cotton producer in Brazil.[5]

The kind of cotton technology that the Southerners took with them from
the South of the United States to Brazil followed the development of the
periphery and probably would have been introduced even without the emigration of that particular group. A different type of example is to be found
with the textile mill Carioba, founded in 1875 in the vicinity of American
settlement. The founders were not North Americans but the Brazilians
Antonio and Augusto de Souza Queiroz, who hired the Southern engineer
William P. Ralston to help set up the factory. A few years later it was sold
to the brothers Jorge and Clement Wilmot, Americans who developed it
into one of the province's most productive textile mills. One of the inno-

vations used by the Wilmots at the Carioba was the hiring of recently arrived Italian immigrants from the textile regions in Italy, who brought their European expertise with them.[6]

The immigration of 4,000 *confederados* after the Civil War was soon dwarfed by the large influx of Italians, Germans, and Japanese that followed. Proper perspective is given by the colporteur Hugh C. Tucker, who arrived in Brazil in 1886 and right away noticed the great number of Italian immigrants in São Paulo and observed the economic forces driving them there.

> When I first went to São Paulo, my attention was attracted to the large numbers of Italian immigrants to be seen on every hand. They were already coming in considerable numbers to the State even before the emancipation of the slaves: but after the emancipation act, the coffee planters contracted for them in much larger numbers. They had been arriving in Brazil at the rate of 10,000 or 12,000 annually, and the year of the emancipation 104,000 came: in the year 1891 more than 132,000 were admitted. Within the last twenty years about 1,000,000 Italian immigrants have entered Brazil, and the great majority of them have located in the State of São Paulo, proving valuable substitutes for the slaves who when freed began at once to leave the plantations and drift to the towns and villages.[7]

The Southerners' influence upon Brazilian agricultural technology does not so much reflect brilliant ability on the part of the individuals who emigrated to Brazil (though some demonstrated considerable ingenuity) as it demonstrates the process of diffusion from one culture to another. The Brazilian planters were seeking the knowledge and ideas possessed by the Americans. These were novel and stimulating to the Brazilians, and some of the American tools were more efficient than those commonly used in the region.

Of the tools carried to Brazil, the moldboard plow apparently drew the most attention. Soon after arriving from Texas, Thomas McKnight and John Domm began producing steel-tipped plows, and demonstrating the use of the implement became a major activity. Increased use of efficient plows affected the local agriculture and made it possible to farm areas that had not been suitable for cultivation by the Brazilians using the more traditional simple hoe. The skill of plowing was as important an introduction as the tool itself, and the Brazilian government eventually recruited members of the American colony to demonstrate plowing techniques. Especially remarkable was the immigrants' ability to control their horses, often merely by the use of voice commands.[8]

Though not as large as normal Brazilian *fazendas*, the farms of the Americans near Santa Bárbara were visibly productive. Some of the Americans became administrators of Brazilian-owned plantations, and from those positions they promoted the spread of North American agricultural technology. Lee Ferguson, son of one of the original colonists, was the manager of a *fazenda* belonging to the prominent Piracicaba resident Luiz de Queiroz. He was an enlightened owner, and the well-managed tract was converted into a demonstration farm. When it was later donated to the state of São Paulo, it became the Luiz de Queiroz Agricultural College of the University of São Paulo.[9] Today it is one of Latin America's most prominent technical schools.

An important technological introduction in the local region was the buckboard wagon with steel-rimmed wheels. The dominant mode of rural transport in interior São Paulo at the time was the oxcart, a heavy, slow, and cumbersome vehicle that rode on two solid wooden wheels affixed to a rotating axle. The lighter and faster wagons of the Americans quickly proved superior, and they soon replaced the oxcarts throughout much of the area. Diffusion of the wagons was accelerated when a Swiss immigrant named Krähenbühl established a company whose major activity was their manufacture.

Most of the Americans first to settle in the area of Santa Bárbara planted cotton. The heavy rains and caterpillars (armyworms) destroyed much of the crop in 1871, but an unusually dry summer brought a bounteous crop in 1872.[10] In June of that year, an observer from Campinas reported that "the Americans have been very prosperous this year. They have just finished or rather are just finishing their cotton crops. Nearly all of them have made over a bale to the acre, and some of them, from 700 to 750 lbs of lint cotton to the acre. Their corn crops too are very good, yielding with little cultivation from 40 to 50 bushels per acre."[11]

But the caterpillars returned, and many Southerners soon switched to the two crops already dominant in the area—coffee and sugarcane. Thomas McKnight, in addition to producing plows, is given credit for perfecting a process for distilling *pinga*, Brazil's potent rum.[12] The achievement and the associated profits did not please many of the strict Methodist and Baptist settlers.

In the region surrounding Americana, Santa Bárbara, and Piracicaba, floral evidence, such as an occasional pecan tree, still marks the presence of the Americans. Their most successful introduction was the large striped Georgia rattlesnake watermelon from seeds that Joe Whitaker took to Brazil in his coat pocket. By the turn of the century the harvest was so large that 100 boxcars were needed to transport the crop to market. When the railroad could not provide them, the American farmers threatened to deposit the rotting fruit at company headquarters. A temporary setback to the watermelon enterprise occurred a few years later when the fruit was blamed for causing an epidemic of yellow fever.[13]

Time has placed the agricultural and technological contributions of the Southerners in historical scale. The very large American plantations like those of John Christopher Judkins, Duncan McIntyre, and Sam and James Johnston, for the most part situated near Rio de Janeiro, had no real impact on the development of the country. Basically, these were transplanted antebellum plantations which prospered for a few years but were soon abandoned—at least partly in response to the first steps taken by Dom Pedro II in 1871 to emancipate Brazil's slaves.[14]

The more modest family farms near Santa Bárbara persisted well into the twentieth century, and there the Southerners left visible marks. They did not create many new industries but contributed to existing Brazilian enterprises in the late 1800s by making them more productive. For example, they demonstrated that one person could handle one animal and a plow to more efficiently perform farm operations of plowing, harrowing, and planting. It is difficult to determine whether the innovations of the Americans in the region near Santa Bárbara actually represented new technological introductions in Brazil. The local novelties—the plow factory in Santa Bárbara, the cotton gins, the wagons transporting watermelons to the railway station, the cornbread, houses with glass windows and brick chimneys, and so forth—did become part of the regional patrimony, and like the heritage of immigrants from other nations, some elements have been incorporated into the Brazilian culture.[15]

Religion and Education

In 1992 the Brazilian agriculturalist Zilmar Marcos expressed his view that the Southerners' major contributions to the development of Brazil were not in agriculture but in their beliefs and values, their progressive minds, their capacity for action, and their technical competence that they brought with them to their new homeland.[16] In this regard also, the historian Blanche Henry Clark Weaver claimed in a 1952 article "Confederate Immigrants and Evangelical Churches in Brazil" that the Southern colonists made significant contributions to Brazil in two fields, religion and education, and that otherwise they did not affect the general course of history there.[17]

The Heritage

Weaver's study has been a foundation for much subsequent research. Thus, Grier's 1968 dissertation listed the introduction of Southern Protestantism and of American schools, specifically the Escola Americana and the Colégio Piracicabano, as long-range contributions of Southern colonization;[18] and Jones's *Soldado descansa* utilized several long passages from Weaver's article to show the extent of the *confederado* contributions to Brazilian Protestantism and education.[19] Likewise, in this volume, Wayne Flynt and James Dawsey in chapters 6 and 7 have drawn deeply from Clark Weaver's well. Weaver's thesis is that:

> the permanent establishment of missionary work of the [Presbyterian Church in the United States, the Methodist Episcopal Church, South, and the Southern Baptist Convention] can be attributed to the activities of these colonial groups. This not only marked the beginning of the steady growth of the evangelical churches, but also led to the establishment of schools under North American sponsorship. Consequently, the contributions of southern immigrants to the religion and educational life of the country were far greater than might be expected from such a limited number of people.[20]

Concerning the implantation of Protestantism in Brazil, Weaver argued that the Southern émigrés took their religious faiths with them to Brazil. There, they "established Protestant churches for their own worship . . . [and] their settlements served as centers from which evangelical missions to the Brazilians could be successfully launched."[21] In broad outline, she claimed that mainline Protestantism, though begun in Brazil before 1865, was strongly boosted by the arrival of the Americans. Ministers such as Alabamian Junius Newman, one of the founders of the Methodist Church in Brazil, and Elijah Quillin, a fire-and-brimstone Baptist, were among the early settlers. Letters to relatives in the United States expressed the need for spiritual leadership in the colony and for evangelization of the native population. Southern Presbyterians, Methodists, and Baptists responded to the call. The calls from the American colony near Santa Bárbara gave impetus to the Protestant denominations that had, until that time, experienced only sputtering growth. Though a congregational church had been started in Rio de Janeiro in 1855 and the Northern Presbyterians U.S.A. had been active in Rio and São Paulo since 1859, little growth had taken place prior to the arrival of the Southerners.[22] In fact, "the significance of their [i.e., the *confederados*'] presence in the country is more readily apparent," Weaver wrote, "when earlier failures of American Protestant efforts in Brazil are reviewed."[23]

The missionaries had in mind the spiritual welfare of the *confederados*—and also, the Brazilians. Although "it was due to the urgency of [the immigrants'] pleas that the southern churches established their first missionary projects in Brazil,"[24] the concerns of the missionaries stretched beyond the American community. "Many came to feel that this group [i.e., the Southern emigrants] might fulfill a great destiny if they were instruments through which the 'true gospel' could be spread in Brazil. Consequently, as soon as the language was mastered, the missionaries beigun [*sic*] a ministry to the natives."[25]

Presbyterianism in Brazil

There is much to commend Weaver's view that the Southern immigration played a significant role in the founding of Protestantism in Brazil. This is especially the case with regard to the Baptists and Methodists in Brazil. In the next two chapters, the authors will explore the role that the *confederados* played in establishing those two denominations in that country. The late nineteenth-century missionary movement to Brazil was largely based in the United States South, and many who went to Brazil preached their first South American sermon not in Portuguese but in English to a freckled, fair-skinned congregation at the *Campo* chapel.

Weaver's article, however, does not adequately describe the beginning of the Presbyterian Church in Brazil, which was much less influenced by the immigration of Southerners than were the Methodists and the Baptists. Presbyterianism in Brazil finds its nineteenth-century roots with the Reverend Ashbel G. Simonton from the Northern branch of the denomination, the Presbyterian Church U.S.A., who arrived in Rio de Janeiro in August 1859.[26] There, Simonton found a thriving congregation led by Dr. Robert R. Kalley, a Scottish physician who "was a Presbyterian in doctrine, but . . . [who] gave to the church that grew up as the result of his labors, a congregational form of government."[27] Dr. and Mrs. Kalley were accomplished linguists, and soon Simonton also was preaching in Portuguese to the Brazilians.

Simonton was joined by the Reverends Alexander L. Blackford, and George W. Chamberlain, from the North. By the time that the Southern branch of the Presbyterian church first sent a representative to work in Brazil in 1869, these Northerners had founded numerous Presbyterian congregations in the provinces of Rio de Janeiro and São Paulo. They also had started a semimonthly journal, the *Imprensa Evangelica*, in 1865 and a seminary for training ministers in May 1867.[28]

The Heritage

More important, Simonton and his colleagues had ordained the first Brazilian Presbyterian minister, the Reverend José Manoel da Conceição, in 1865, at the same time that they had officially organized the Presbytery of Rio de Janeiro. Conceição, a former Roman Catholic priest, was an eloquent speaker who before conversion had served appointments as a priest in Água Choca, Piracicaba, Santa Bárbara, Taubaté, Sorocaba, Limeira, Ubatuba, and Brotas; much of the early Presbyterian success in that region of the province of São Paulo should be credited to his eight-year ministry, from 1865 until 1873, when he died. Giving credit where credit is due, the historian Duncan A. Reily claimed that Conceição was a principal reason for the growth of the Presbyterian church.[29]

With regard to another common misconception: it is not exactly true that the Southern branch of the Presbyterians decided to set up their permanent mission in Brazil, as later did the Methodists and especially the Baptists, in response to appeals from the *confederados*. In fact, the General Assembly of the Southern Presbyterians, meeting in 1866, explicitly refused a request from the Synod of South Carolina to send a missionary for the Southerners. In spite of the support voiced for the motion by the powerful Robert Dabney, and for emigration in general from the Reverend A. A. Porter, who was the wartime editor of the *Southern Presbyterian*, the assembly decided that "all action on our part in that direction would be at this time premature."[30]

This is not to imply that Americans, at home and in Brazil, did not continue to appeal to the Presbyterian Church in the United States to send spiritual helpers for the emigrants. They did. In fact, one of the most influential expressions of concerns did not come from a Southerner, but from a Northern Presbyterian minister, Alexander L. Blackford. In a long letter to the Reverend H. B. Pratt dated July 22, 1868, and subsequently printed in the October issue of the missions journal of the Southern Presbyterians, *The Missionary*, Blackford wrote:

> I beg you will call the attention of the leading men in your section of the Church to the necessity of helping to sustain ministers of the gospel among our countrymen who are coming to settle here. The Rev. Mr. Emerson, formerly of Mississippi, is here. The Rev. Mr. Baird, of South Carolina, arrived on the 20th. The Rev. Mr. Harvey is in the Amazon region. Their services are needed, and they could do good, but need help. There is not a single settlement of Americans, so far as I know, where the gospel is statedly preached. Their future welfare and influence on the native population depend on something being done for them. We have many times the work already for which our force is adequate.[31]

But concern for the emigrants clearly was not the main impetus leading Southern Presbyterian missionaries to go to Brazil. The publication of Blackford's letter in 1868 coincided with a scouting trip to Brazil by the Reverend George Nash Morton, whose purpose was to search out the best locale in that country to establish a mission for the Southern Presbyterians. Morton's instructions were "to visit the four principal cities on the coast at which the American steamships touch," as he cited them—Pará, Pernambuco, Bahia, and Rio de Janeiro. When in Brazil, Morton "received very kind attentions from Mr. Blackford," who urged him in the direction of the province of São Paulo. Taking upon himself the expense of a trip to the south, Morton then visited Santos, São Paulo, and Campinas.[32]

In his report to the Executive Committee of Missions, presented at a meeting held on the first Tuesday in January 1869, Morton offered arguments favoring locating the mission in Campinas. Important considerations included the comparatively milder climate and cheaper cost of living in that section of Brazil, the openness to the Brazilians in that area to the Protestant message, the strategic location of Campinas at the end of the railroad leading to the port of Santos, and the prospect of working closely with the Northern Presbyterians, whose "mission has been remarkedly successful."[33]

Morton also pointed out that Southern immigrants, like Dr. James McFadden Gaston from South Carolina, were already in the area and were actively "distributing tracts and sowing the seeds of truth,"[34] and he reminded the committee of what had first interested him and his colleague, the Reverend Edward E. Lane, in going to Brazil: "The first thing which attracted Mr. Lane and myself to the South American field was the fact that after the reverse of the war a number of our countrymen had founded new homes among the Brazilian people. It was thought by ourselves and others that the social and commercial relations of these settlers with the natives of the country would greatly facilitate our communication with the latter and afford a rare opportunity of teaching the adherents of an apostate Church the evangelical truths of our own."[35] The focus of Morton and Lane from the beginning was not on the *confederados* but on the doorway into Brazil and the Brazilians that was being opened by the emigration.

Morton's arguments must have sounded convincing to the Executive Committee of Missions, for both Morton and Lane were appointed to Campinas. They sailed, accompanied by Mrs. Morton, aboard the *Winifred* from Baltimore on June 22, 1869, and arrived in Rio de Janeiro on August 14, after fifty-six days at sea. They were warmly received by the Americans and English in Rio, and "Messrs, Blackford and Chamberlain, of the Northern Presbyterian Church, were as kind as they could be."[36] Finally, in the middle of September 1869, the missionaries reached Campinas and began Southern Presbyterian work in Brazil.

In a sense, the Southern Presbyterians were already active in that area before the arrival of Morton and Lane. In their report, the missionaries had mentioned the evangelical work of Dr. Gaston. And as Blackford had mentioned in his letter to Pratt in July 1868, two Southern Presbyterian ministers were already present in the province of São Paulo: the Reverend William C. Emerson from Meridian, Mississippi, who had arrived in Brazil in 1867, and the Reverend James H. Baird, from South Carolina, who had arrived in July 1868. Both men were among the Southern settlers near Santa Bárbara, situated a day's journey from Campinas. There, joined by the Methodist Junius E. Newman and the Baptists R. Thomas and Richard Ratcliff, they preached regularly to the Americans, some of whom were Presbyterians.

The two new missionaries were anxious to get to know the Presbyterians in the area, and soon after arriving in Campinas, they visited the American settlers. As recounted in an October 1869 letter by Lane,

> We have now been in Campinas some two or three weeks, but have not been able, until within a few days past, to procure a teacher to teach us the pronunciation and give us a start in the language. . . .
> I preached at one of the American settlements the Sunday before last, at the house of the Rev. Mr. Emerson. His residence is situated about thirty miles from here; and Mr. Baird, also a minister of our Church, lives near him. They are both engaged in farming, and one of them, I believe, preaches every Sabbath. There were about forty persons in attendance the day I was there. Most of the settlers are from Texas, Alabama, and Georgia, and represent almost all the shades of religious opinions to be found in those States. Brother Emerson told me that there were some fifteen or twenty Presbyterians in his neighbor-hood.[37]

Again, in spite of the missionaries' quick visit to the American community and their ready fellowship with Emerson and Baird, their mission was not directed to the *confederados*. Rather, as Lane reemphasized in that same October letter, he hoped the immigrants would be "instrumental in spreading the gospel . . . [for] I feel that our great business is with the natives; and that which claims our undivided attention now, is to master the language so that we can preach." Lane, however, wanted to help the Americans also, for he was quick to add that he was glad "that there is plenty of missionary work for us to do, even now while pursuing our studies."[38]

The First Southern Presbyterian Presbytery

The missionaries began preaching in Portuguese in February 1870, and by June they reported that they were conducting services regularly in that language to a small group meeting in their parlor in Campinas, and that "two persons [i.e., Brazilians] have made a public profession of their faith and were baptized; and it is expected that, at our next communion, one or two others will do likewise." After three months, about fifty people were attending services, and Morton and Lane began to plan to obtain "a suitable hall, separate from our dwelling-house," where attendance would be even greater. A Sabbath school had been organized, and by October the missionaries counted an attendance of 25 children.[39]

The small congregation in Campinas continued to prosper in 1871, and before long, Morton was "preaching three sermons a week in Portuguese— one on Wednesday night and two on the Sabbath." There had been other Brazilian converts, and after a year, the missionaries' parlor had become "uncomfortably small for the congregation." Morton and Lane rented a larger room, and by January 1872 they reported twenty members to their church. By May, the congregation was taking steps toward self-sufficiency, and Morton reported having "established Sunday collection, the amount of which varies from four to five millreis per week, and which is devoted to paying the expenses of the room in which we worship."[40]

Although Morton and Lane were headquartered in Campinas, they actually traveled a large circuit, preaching three or four times a year at important towns, "to wit: Santa Bárbara, 28 miles northwest of Campinas; Itu, 36 miles southwest; Limeira, 36 miles northwest; Mogy-morim [sic], 40 miles north." On their circuit, they worked closely with the ministers from the Northern branch of the Presbyterian church. Writing on May 16, 1870, Lane expressed his appreciation for the Northern brethren's help: "With the view of improving myself in the language and becoming better acquainted with the wants of our field of labor, I started on the 29th of March on a missionary tour, accompanied by the Rev. Mr. Mckee, of the Sao Paulo [sic] Mission, who kindly volunteered to be my companion during a part of the journey. I found it of great advantage to travel with one who had made similar expeditions before."[41]

Over the years, Morton, Lane, and the Northerners became close friends. They met each other at port when arriving from the United States, and they continued to support each other's work, often going on preaching tours together. And the Northerners too expressed their appreciation for Morton and Lane, even to the point of writing letters requesting that the

South send more missionaries to Brazil—"many more such men as you have already in the field."[42]

Others, besides the Northerners, aided Morton and Lane in their work. We have already mentioned Emerson and Baird and Dr. Gaston's distribution of evangelical tracts and Bibles. In an 1870 letter, Morton mentioned that there were "nine Christian ministers, united by personal friendship and cordial sympathy for the spread of the gospel among all classes of inhabitants," active in the area. These nine had joined together to hire a Methodist who spoke Portuguese, German, and English to sell religious books in the province.[43] In a later letter, Morton described the working relationship he had with these men. Mr. Wingerter, the colporteur, went to an area first. Then he was followed by the preachers.

On the particular trip that Morton described, he, Chamberlain, and a German pastor by the name of Zimke evangelized together. They traveled by horseback and stopped at a number of locales, preaching and visiting. Morton and Chamberlain left Campinas at seven on a Monday morning and reached Limeira, thirty-eight miles away, at four in the afternoon—in time to preach at a theater that night. They stayed three days with the Zimkes, who lived in the area, spending "most of the morning visiting the people from house to house" and preaching at night. "The services were all in Portuguese, and took place in a Brazilian school-house."[44] The next stop was Patrocinio, a village sixteen miles from Limeira. They stayed with the Gastons and preached at a German's house. "Dr. Gaston sent out special notices to his friends, saying that they had often invited him to their mass, and now he wished to return the compliment by inviting them to hear one of his preachers." After visiting the Roman Catholic vicar, who was sick, the ministers went to Moji-mirim, thirty-two miles away. There they preached several times "in the large reception-room of the hotel." They were well received by the vicar, who informed them that he subscribed to the Northern Presbyterian's *Imprensa Evangelica*. Later they were confronted by a government official who, "instigated by two priests," wished to see Morton and Chamberlain's passports. On Sunday, they preached twice before heading home.

> The hall, doors, windows, and all were full of people, who listened most seriously and solemnly to the word of life. When preaching was over, many remained and talked with us until 10 or 11 o'clock at night. I was really sorry to leave, but both Mr. Chamberlain and myself felt obliged to return home. The people took leave of us affectionately; and, after a short rest, we started off, at 2 o'clock in the morning, for Campinas, thirty-six miles distant. We reached Campinas at 11 o'clock A.M., having

been absent a week, and having travelled one hundred and twenty-two miles. May the Lord establish the work of our hands![45]

The Americans in the vicinity of Santa Bárbara were on Morton and Lane's circuit, and the missionaries tried "to preach as much as possible among" them.[46] In truth, however, the immigrants mostly saw after themselves, being tended by Emerson and Baird. Toward the middle of 1870, these two and eleven other Presbyterian immigrants gathered together at the house of William P. McFadden and founded the Hopewell Church.[47] The immigrants were even more ecumenical than were the missionaries, and in August 1870 Lane noted that "the settlers [had] decided to build a church for the use of all evangelical denominations." By December of that year, the small congregation had organized two Sabbath schools. The missionaries "were able to assist them in the matter of books, catechisms, etc."[48]

It was January 13, 1872. More than two years had passed since Morton and Lane had arrived in the area. Two churches had been founded, and many preaching points had been established in the area. Complying with directions from the General Assembly of the Presbyterian Church in the United States, Morton and Lane convened a meeting in Campinas of the Southern Presbyterian ministers in the area—Morton, Lane, Emerson, and Baird—and the ruling elders of the Campinas and Hopewell churches, Gaston and McFadden. These representatives of the Presbyterian Church in the United States then organized themselves into the Presbytery of São Paulo. By order of the General Assembly, the Presbyterian church of Campinas was the constituent member of the presbytery. Hopewell was received into the care of the presbytery.

Presbyterian Education

Morton and Lane were very interested in education—and we have seen how they quickly established a Sabbath school for children in Campinas. Just as quickly, they also established a night school. Morton explained why: "By opening this school at night, we reach many, both men and children, who belong to the laboring classes, and who could not attend during the day. We hope to make it a very important auxiliary to our work of preaching the gospel. It is opened by prayer and reading the Scriptures, and each scholar, as soon as he learns to read, begins the study of the Scripture text. The number reaches to twenty-eight—the maximum which the room will accommodate."[49] The school was a means of reaching many more people than otherwise possible, of introducing these people to the Bible, and of preparing them to read Scripture for themselves.

Other advantages accrued from the missionaries' interest in education. In 1871 Morton started teaching Greek five nights a week to professors at a local college. His goals were twofold: First, after getting the professors to read the Greek New Testament, he hoped to get Greek introduced into the college's curriculum, with the Greek Testament as a textbook. Second, Morton wanted to improve his own Portuguese. As he recounted, "The Principal is one of the best educated men in the province; and as he does not speak English well, I am forced to do all my teaching and hear all the recitations in Portuguese." In this, Morton set a pattern to be followed by other missionaries. Thus, after Nannie Henderson arrived at the beginning of 1872, "appointed to teach a female school in connexion with the mission," she too learned Portuguese by teaching in a local school.[50]

Many of the strong bonds that the missionaries formed with the leaders of the Brazilian community were fostered through their efforts in education. The principal, mentioned above, became a fast friend and an avid Bible reader. Mrs. Caldina, who hired Ms. Henderson, was another supporter. And there were others, some of whom were among the most influential citizens in Campinas.[51]

The idea of opening a secondary school in Campinas offering more than reading, writing, and ciphering came jointly from the missionaries and these influential citizens. Morton seems to have been most interested in finding a means of spreading the gospel and preparing young men to be ministers; the Brazilians, most interested in a school like "the perfected institutions" of North America. The hopes of both missionaries and citizens coalesced. Such "an institution for the education of the rising generation . . . would not only be the means of promoting the interests of true religion, but would be a blessing to the country at large."[52]

The idea caught hold, and by the middle of 1871, Lane had gone to the United States to raise support for the school. Meanwhile, Morton argued for the importance of a school through letters sent home.

If we could only make a start here in the way of establishing a good school, I am sure that we would be well sustained. Some of the most influential citizens in the place have come to see me to talk to me on the subject. . . . [I]f the school be once *begun* they will assist us with both money and students. . . . We have now an opportunity to get a foothold here which we shall probably never have again. We have an opportunity to establish, under the most favorable patronage, an institution which may educate teachers, legislators, etc., for all parts of the Empire. I believe that if one-half of the money could be raised in the United States, the other half could be found here without any difficulty. The most influential citizen in this place says that we may count on at least three hundred students to begin with. Such an opening does not exist anywhere else in Brazil, and I suppose that such does not exist in any other mission field in the world.[53]

By the end of 1871, Lane had garnered significant support for the school from the Presbyterian Church in the United States, including the appointment of a teacher to Brazil, and Morton had reported that "the various journals of the Province . . . were then discussing, in very favorable terms, our project of a college." The time seemed ripe for action, and on December 8, 1871, the missionaries and Brazilians joined together "to establish in Campinas a school of high grade, which is designed to grow according to our means and according to the necessities of the country, into a college of the first order."[54]

The plan was to begin with a preparatory school that later would develop into "higher branches of academic study," namely "Latin, Greek, Modern Languages, Moral Philosophy, History, Literature, Logic and Rhetoric, Political Economy, Mathematics, Natural Philosophy, Chemistry, Applied Mathematics, Civil Engineering, Analytical, Industrial, and Agricultural Chemistry." While morality and religion were considered "the foundation and indispensable concomitants of education," the school was to recognize "entire religious liberty" and to allow the students "to cultivate in their rooms without molestation and frequent on the Sabbath that Church which their parents or guardians may direct." For, the missionaries and Brazilians concluded, "it is on this broad principle of religious liberty, which to-day begins to characterize all the great institutions of learning in the world, that we hope to establish a school which may be open to students of all creeds and nations."[55]

The foundational meeting of the school, held in the missionaries' residence, was presided over by Col. Joaquim Egydio de Sousa Aranha. Morton and Lane presented their plan for the school, read out loud, by the way, by Chamberlain, whose pronunciation was easier for the Brazilians to understand. Several people, including the well-known lawyer Dr. Manoel Ferraz de Campos Salles and the inspector of public instruction Dr. Luiz Silverio Alves Cruz, then spoke in favor of having such a school in Campinas. There was applause and a motion to support the school, which was carried unanimously.

After expressing their gratitude to Morton and Lane, the Brazilians who were at the meeting signed their support. The names read like a Who's

Who of the republican movement in Brazil and include some of São Paulo's most powerful families: Sousa Aranha, Penteado, Campos Salles, Caldeira, Alves Cruz, Amaral, Rangel Pestana, Quirino dos Santos, Camargo, de Moraes, Cerqueira Leite, and others.[56]

The Southern Presbyterians raised most of the money for the school. A matching gift of $5,000 from "a friend of missions, but not a member of our Church," actually a donor from New York, sped the collection, and soon the building program was begun.[57] When Emperor Dom Pedro II visited the city in August 1875 to inaugurate the stretch of railroad reaching Campinas, the first American school in Brazil was holding classes. And when Dom Pedro went to the school, he visited perhaps the most imposing structure in town, a two-story brick building with wooden floors and paneling.[58]

The Confederados

Although the Southern immigrants were keenly concerned with providing school facilities for their children, Grier and others perhaps go too far in crediting the missionary schools to the *confederados*.[59] Actually, the American settlers were not brought into the Colégio Internacional project until June 13, 1872, when at the presbytery meeting held at Hopewell, Dr. Gaston moved that "in view of the proposed measure of establishing an institution for liberal Christian education at Campinas that this Presbytery recommend an expression of opinion on the part of the American population in this section, and that a committee be appointed to confer with the people, and to prepare such a paper as may be a true exponent of the wants and wishes of our brethren and others who have families in this country."[60] The adoption of this motion to survey interest occurred six months after the missionaries and Brazilians, meeting in Campinas, had voted to go ahead with the school.

Also, as we have seen, one should not claim that Presbyterian religion in Brazil began with the *confederado* settlements and radiated out from them. At the time of its founding, Hopewell Church counted thirteen adult and three infant members. And it never grew much larger, probably because important members moved away. By 1872, Emerson had moved to Tatuí and was busy making plans to return to Mississippi,[61] which did not materialize, probably because poor health prevented his trip. He died in 1875 and was buried at the *Campo* cemetery. The Reverend James Baird also did not long remain in the community, returning to the United States in 1878.

In what ways, then, did the Southerners influence the founding of the

J. M. Dawsey & C. B. Dawsey

Presbyterian church in Brazil and the establishment of the Presbyterian school in Campinas? There were many. The migration of the *confederados*, along with the migration of European Protestants, opened the door also to the *confederados'* religion. Brazilians accommodated themselves to the Southerners, and in turn the expectation of being granted a receptive hearing attracted Morton, Lane, and other Presbyterian missionaries to Brazil. Moreover, since kinfolk had moved there, laypeople in the South of the United States took a special interest in Brazil and were more apt to support missions there than in other places. And by no means should we underestimate the testimony of the immigrants' lives to their Brazilian neighbors or the solace afforded to the missionaries by having fellow Americans nearby. As Morton put it after visiting the Gastons: "What a blessing it is, in our missionary journeys, to meet with the warm welcome of a Christian countryman; and what a leaven in the midst of society around them. We cannot tell how much of our success is due to the silent influence of the few pious families scattered here and there through the country."[62]

Undeniably, the greatest influence that the *confederados* exerted on the establishment of Presbyterianism in Brazil occurred at the level of personal linkages. For example, upon arriving in Campinas, the missionaries boarded "with an intelligent and pious American family,"[63] destined to become one of the outstanding Presbyterian families in Brazil.

Susan Porter had been widowed soon after arriving in Rio de Janeiro, when yellow fever had killed her husband. After then losing all of her money to an American confidence man, she moved to Campinas, where, aided by her brother-in-law George Northrup, she opened a boarding house for American and English immigrants.[64] While there, a special friendship developed between the Mortons and the Porters, and later, Susan Porter sent her son to study and live with George Morton. Still later, in 1884, William Porter went to Brazil's Northeast, where he became one of the Presbyterian church's most successful lay evangelists.[65] In a letter written September 18, 1871, Morton described his relationship with the young man.

> The two boys who board with me are Americans. . . . God has not left me without the fruit of my labors in this little school. The oldest boy, about sixteen years of age, a child of the covenant and a Presbyterian, has since his stay in my house been brought under a deep conviction of sin, and been led, as I hope, by the Spirit of all grace to put his trust in Jesus. Last night, after the sermon, he sat with me in my room for more than an hour, talking to me of his sins, of his hope, and of his readiness, by God's help, to bear the cross. He told me of his own accord, "I have always thought of being a doctor (of medicine); but now, since my heart

has been changed, my thoughts have been turned toward being a preacher. I am not worthy; but if God will let me, I wish to preach."

He speaks and writes Portuguese well; commenced the study of Latin and Greek under me, and is making good progress. He is a faithful and diligent student—upright and conscientious in his conduct. I think, therefore, that he is well fitted for the ministry; and I hope that you will join me in prayer to the Lord that he will "count" him "worthy, putting" him "into" it. [66]

Around 1890, we find William Porter in Santos, as the manager of the coffee house of Hard, Rand & Co., and still "a blessing to the missionaries and their work." The Methodist Hugh Tucker sold Bibles in the city and preached in the Porters' house "in Portuguese to a goodly number of Brazilians."[67]

The personal connections between the missionaries and Southern immigrants were many. Besides William Porter, the Mortons also greatly influenced his sister, Carolina. Carolina later studied with and married another Southern Presbyterian missionary, J. Rockwell Smith. Together with her husband and the Reverend and Mrs. John Boyles, Carolina pioneered the Presbyterian mission to the northeastern state of Pernambuco.[68]

Like Carolina, other immigrants married missionaries. Hervey Hall's sister married William Porter, and five of Charles Hall's daughters, Hervey's granddaughters, married Presbyterian missionaries. Interestingly, two of Dr. Gaston's daughters married Northern Presbyterian missionaries.[69]

Nannie Gaston married the Reverend Alexander Latimer Blackford after his first wife died.[70] Blackford and James McFadden Gaston had been friends since the time of Gaston's exploratory trip to Brazil in late 1865, and it had been Blackford who had supplied the information concerning the Protestants that Gaston included in his book *Hunting a Home in Brazil*.[71] Once Gaston moved to Brazil, the two became yet closer as they both worked to propagate the "true gospel." There were many occasions on which the Blackfords and Gastons visited one another, and after Elizabeth W. Simonton Blackford died of "nervous disease" on March 23, 1879, Alexander married Nannie Gaston, and the two started Presbyterian work in Bahia. The other sister, Izzie Gaston, also went to Bahia at the service of the Presbyterian church, and it was there that she married the Reverend J. B. Kolb.[72]

Meanwhile, another child of a Presbyterian immigrant helped establish the church's mission in Ceará, also in the Northeast of Brazil. As mentioned earlier, the Reverend James Baird left Brazil in 1878, but his son Reynalt eventually returned. The younger Baird studied medicine and theology, was ordained a Presbyterian minister, and returned to Brazil also with the ambition of preaching in Brazil's Northeast. On the way, he stopped to see childhood friends in Santa Bárbara, where he fell in love with, and later married, Lucille Bankston. The Bairds opened their work in Ceará in 1896.[73]

Two other Southern descendants went with the Bairds to do Presbyterian mission work in the Northeast: Lucille's sister, Lillian Bankston, and Reynalt's nephew, Charles Thatcher. Lillian Bankston, like her sister, had been trained as a teacher in a missionary school.[74] In fact, a number of the immigrants' children who studied at the missionary schools became teachers in the schools.

The earliest settlers, of course, had been taught at home. Thus, Bellona Smith first studied at home, as did the children of Robert Norris. After a few years, the settlers built a little schoolhouse near Santa Bárbara and began to hire trained teachers to educate their children. A Mr. King, from Canton, Ohio, seems to have been the first teacher hired. He was followed by an Alabamian, Dr. Cicero Jones, who later married into the Norris family. Dr. Jones had arrived in Brazil with only seven dollars in his pocket, and he had taken on various jobs before establishing himself in his own profession. He taught the more advanced courses at the school. Later, Lovie Fielder, Annie Lou Vinson, and Joeld Sanders, all from Alabama, were hired to teach English, arithmetic, and basic science to the immigrants' children.[75]

For their secondary education, many of the immigrants sent their children to the Colégio Internacional in Campinas and the other schools started by the American missionaries. Some of these former students, in turn, became teachers in the American schools. Annie and Mary Newman opened a school in Piracicaba, and as chapter 7 will show, were very important to Methodist education in general. Katie and Mary Hall played an important role in opening the Colégio Americano in Natal. Izzie Gaston had gone to Bahia as a teacher, before marrying the Reverend J. B. Kolb.

The educational links forged by the missionaries, the immigrants and their children, and the Brazilians are so complex that they are difficult to disentangle. For example, Rangel Pestana, one of Brazil's famous educators and one of the original signatories at the founding of Morton's school, took a special interest in Annie Newman, who was a brilliant student and one of the first graduates of the Colégio Internacional. After Annie finished her coursework, Pestana helped her get started in her career by hiring her to teach in his school in São Paulo. One of Pestana's good friends, dating from their days studying law together, was Prudente de Moraes Barros. The

Barros family lived in Piracicaba, which did not have an American-style school.

In the mid-1870s, the citizens of that town approached Annie Newman's father, the Reverend Junius Newman, pleading their need for a school. The elder Newman agreed that a school was needed and urged his daughter to take on the project. She then, with great help from Prudente and Manoel de Moraes Barros, opened a Methodist school in Piracicaba. Later, after 1881, Martha Watts, the Methodist headmistress of the Piracicabano, as the school came to be called, developed a special friendship with the Barros brothers, and when Prudente de Moraes became the president of Brazil, she deeply influenced the government's program of education.

More than in any other way, it was through these difficult-to-trace personal links with missionaries and Brazilians that the *confederados* became so closely identified with the success of the American schools. During the nineteenth and early twentieth centuries the ties between the schools and the Santa Bárbara group remained strong, as many teachers and students were drawn from the community of descendants. To list a few more examples: among the Reverend William Emerson's relatives, Sophie and Suzan Grady became teachers in São Paulo, as did also Mrs. Robert McIntyre and Ms. Mary Alice Clark.[76]

The Colégio Internacional suffered through several outbreaks of yellow fever, and finally, after the death of the Reverend Edward Lane to the same disease in 1892, the Presbyterians moved the school from Campinas to Lavras.[77] The Colégio Americano in São Paulo was opened in 1870 by the Reverend and Mrs. George Chamberlain.[78] By the turn of the century the Presbyterians had started over forty elementary schools, and their Mackenzie College in the city of São Paulo was considered the nation's leading center of engineering education.[79] The Methodists began similar colleges in Ribeirão Preto, Taubaté, Petrópolis, Juiz de Fora, and other cities. Throughout Brazil the American schools were viewed as academically superior institutions.[80] Though administered by churches, they affirmed religious toleration and were marked by progressive attitudes, including the practice of instructing boys and girls in mixed classrooms.[81]

Persistence of Culture

To recapitulate, the innovations in farming that the Americans took to Brazil had an immediate, although small, impact on that country. Items such as the plow and the watermelon were rapidly adopted during the decades after the arrival of the Americans, but the colony at Santa Bárbara was not a continuing source of new technology. Once the knowledge that had been taken from the United States was shared with the Brazilians, the advantageous position of the Americans disappeared. Furthermore, large-scale European immigration into Brazil occurred after the establishment of the Inspetoria de Terras e Colonização colonization agency in 1876, and the Americans quickly became one small group in the flood of many different cultures invading interior São Paulo.[82] The Americans had a definite impact though, in part, because they had arrived earlier than other innovators.

The influence on Brazilian society by the American systems of education and religion was more significant. The schools established by the American missionaries flourished and became models of rigorous practical education. Their administrators and teachers were sought after by the government and other academies, and the techniques that they employed were widely emulated. The American-founded schools remain among Brazil's best, and many are still linked to the churches through which they were begun.

The Presbyterian, Methodist, and Baptist denominations have included small memberships relative to other religious groups, but they themselves have been an important mechanism of diffusion. As elsewhere in the world, the Protestant missionaries helped channel into Brazil elements of Western philosophy and ethics, which influenced Brazilian economic and political structures.

The group of Americans who remained after the original emigration and consolidation in Brazil has maintained itself as a cohesive community and, alongside the missionaries, has exerted an important influence on nineteenth- and twentieth-century education. The impact has been far greater than might have been expected given the original conditions of migration and the number of those who stayed in Brazil.

Six

The Baptists
Southern Religion and
Émigrés to Brazil, 1865–1885

Wayne Flynt

Migration is a familiar theme in Southern history. People leave one place and travel to another for a variety of reasons. In 1860 a young schoolteacher newly arrived in Butler County, Alabama, wrote friends that teaching in her rural locale was "a very unpleasant occupation: I do not know where we wil go to yet but we wil not be apt to stay in butler, I think it is a very good country for farming but ther is no society nor nothing elce her the people is more like hogs an dogs than they are like folks. . . . I will try to stay heare this year without saying much."[1]

Five years later, Southerners had more tangible reasons for leaving. A cycle of drought and bad crops drove the population of many parts of the South to the verge of starvation. The loss of human life and farm animals to the Civil War deepened the natural calamity. A prominent official in Calhoun County, Alabama, wrote Gov. Lewis E. Parsons: "I pledge you my word, I've never heard such a cry for bread in my life. And it is impossible to get relief up here. The provisions are not here and if they were there is no money here to buy with." He closed with the same earnest plea the hungry had directed toward him: "If any thing can be done, for God's sake do it quickly. This is no panic but real great hunger that punishes the people."[2]

Similar cries went up across the state. In November 1865, a Bibb County official reported nearly 600 indigent families containing 2,270 people. Conecuh County listed 728 destitute women and children on January 1, 1866. Tuscaloosa County contained 700 such families with 2,800 people. Louis Wyeth reported from Guntersville in Marshall County that three persons had already starved to death and 3,000 more were destitute. One widow with seven children had not eaten for a week. Benjamin F. Porter wrote from Greenville: "This very moment my wife is dividing our small store with a dozen ragged children who will want again tomorrow."[3]

Cherokee County suffered perhaps more than any other in the state.

Foraging armies containing tens of thousands had spent nearly two weeks there in 1864. Drought destroyed most corn crops that year and again in 1865. Thirty prominent men drafted a petition to Governor Parsons in August 1865 explaining that even once-prosperous farmers were destitute.[4] The following March, citizens held a public meeting at Centre, where they drafted a resolution begging again for help. The audience contained few poor whites, who were then able to receive aid from the Freedmen's Bureau. This was a new class of poor, men who had recently been prosperous citizens. Now "we have no money, we have no cotton, we have no credit." Before, the only destitution known in Cherokee had been among the "old, infirm, decrepit, soldiers' wives, widows, their children and orphans; not so now, nearly all of all classes are in the same category." These were proud people who never before had asked for help; now all was "gloom and wretchedness and woe."[5]

Another public meeting in September 1866 was less specific about the source of assistance. The people who attended requested that federal Maj. Gen. Wager Swayne, Governor Parsons, and the railroads help destitute families to leave Cherokee County. One district contained twenty-three families with 147 members who were utterly destitute, without land or corn; eight of these families desired to emigrate to Texas, eight to Arkansas, five to Tennessee, and two to Mississippi. By late October many of these families had moved west.[6]

Tens of thousands of Alabama poor whites left their lands in the 1860s and 1870s. Between 10 and 15 percent of the entire white population of Alabama migrated out of state, an exodus exceeded only in South Carolina. The total probably exceeded 50,000 with a third of them heading for Texas. Many white farm laborers along the Georgia and Florida boundaries crossed into those states.[7]

For more affluent whites, migration had different sources. Some could not bear to remain in Alabama because residence there carried too many painful memories. A magnificent marble marker in the cemetery at the Hatchett Creek Presbyterian Church in Clay County records the death of a mother on one side and her three sons on the other:

> Sergeant Malcolm Patterson was born July 17, 1839 and was slain in the Battle of Sharpsburg, MD. in defense of his own sunny South. Sept. 17, 1862. Aged 23 years and 2 months. We know not his resting place as we did not recover his body from the battlefield. But have every reason to feel and know that he died as true soldiers die.
>
> Captain Archibald A. Patterson was born July 12, 1832, and was slain in the Battle of Murfreesboro, Tenn. December 31st, 1862 and was bur-

ied near that place not far from the bank of Stone River. Aged 30 years
5 months and 19 days.
Col. Thomas H. Patterson, was born Jan. 13, 1831. He also was slain
in defense of his beloved country near Atlanta, Ga., July 30th, 1864
where his remains are now interred. Aged 33 years 6 months and 17
days. The Sweet Remembrance of the just will flourish while they sleep
in dust.

For affluent families not so deeply affected physically, there were political
reasons to migrate. Having exerted every ounce of their emotional energy
in the defense of slavery and states' rights for a generation, and having
fought the nation's bloodiest war on behalf of those beliefs, they could not
reconcile themselves to defeat. Louisiana's Gen. P. G. T. Beauregard was so
alienated that he negotiated with Brazil, Italy, Romania, Egypt, France, and
Argentina, trying to find some country that would employ his military
skills. Virginia's Gen. Jubal Early once told a friend that if forgiving ene-
mies was essential to salvation, he was afraid that he would be consigned
to perdition. He even refused to donate money to build a monument to
Robert E. Lee because the granite to be used was quarried in Maine. Some
years after the war ended, Georgia's irreconcilable Gen. Robert Toombs
was asked about the latest news of the Chicago fire. "Well," he replied,
"every effort is bein' made to put it out, but the wind is in our favor." Even
Southern advocates of industrialism and cooperation with Northern busi-
nessmen gained no sympathy from Toombs, who described them as "cow-
ardly and venal a lot of place-hunting politicians as ever lived"; "like putrid
bodies in the stream, they rise as they rot."[8]

These streams of economic calamity, emotional trauma, and political resentment converged in a mighty river of migration, most to new territories
in the West, but others to more exotic locations. Brazil, Venezuela, Honduras, and Mexico beckoned, though Brazil's Dom Pedro II and Mexico's Emperor Maximilian offered the greatest inducements. Cheap land, deferred
payment, and continued slavery made Brazil a particularly attractive destination.

Colonization societies sprang up to assist determined migrants, led by
Ballard S. Dunn, rector of St. Philip's Church in New Orleans, and Lansford
Warren Hastings, filibuster and entrepreneur. Estimates of the total num-
ber of Southern immigrants to Brazil vary from 2,000 to 10,000.[9]

Southern evangelicals had earlier thought of Brazil primarily as a dark
and heathen land, a worthy object of the missionary impulse gathering mo-
mentum in their ranks. But now they had another interest—beloved brethren and sisters who left their sacred communities for the Brazilian wilder-

ness. They chronicled this hegira with mounting interest. Perhaps God would use the Confederacy's defeat for the propagation of the gospel in Brazil. This 1860s migration left a lasting impression on the South in many measurable ways. The Southern Baptist Foreign Mission Board had contemplated opening work in Brazil during the 1850s, but to no avail until 1859, when the first missionary family departed for Rio. Health problems ended that initial effort in less than two years. There the matter stood for twelve years until the board received an intriguing letter in January 1873 from the First Baptist Church of Brazil near Santa Bárbara in São Paulo Province:

> *To the Corresponding Secretary Foreign Missions Board:*
> Allow us to state to you that since the year 1865, a number of citizens from the Southern United States have removed to the Empire of Brazil, and are located in this province—viz.: São Paulo and in the District of Santa Bárbara, most of whom are farming, (owning lands, &c.) and permanently settled here. That on the 10th of September, 1871, a number of them, with letters from various Baptist churches of the States . . . did unite and organize a church under the style and name of the First North American Baptist Missionary Church of Brazil, which at this writing contains twenty-three (23) members, with a pastor and such other officers as Baptist churches usually have. That on the 12th of October, 1872, the church in conference did adopt the following resolution—viz.:
> *Resolved*, That Brethren R. Meriwether, R. Brodnax, and D. Davis, be appointed to communicate with the Baptist Board of Foreign Missions at Richmond, Va., in regard to sending missionaries to this country.[10]

Maj. Robert Meriwether, church secretary, was described as "a stirring man" who was married to a "pious wife." The migrants described the prospects for Baptists in their new homeland to be excellent, reported that the American colony was "enjoying some prosperity," and urged the foreign mission board to act expeditiously.[11] They boasted of Brazil's religious toleration (except toward Jesuits, who were banished by law, which doubtless was no source of discomfort to the *confederados*), then added:

> Five or six years experience and intercourse with citizens of this country enables us to state that now is a propitious time to set forth the religion taught in God's word to this people. Generally, they do not like their religion, saying "it begins and ends with money for the priesthood." Really many intelligent Brazilians have a contempt for their practices. "The Baptists," they say, "practice as did the Saviour and his Apostles; they baptized only believers and immersed; who has a right to alter their modes and practices?" The Portuguese translation of the New Testament

is, if possible, more emphatic in describing baptism than the English translation. The presence of our people here has had, and is having, a salutary influence upon the feelings and opinions of this people.[12]

The pastor of the church, the Reverend Richard Ratcliff, had come to Brazil from Louisiana in about 1868. He preached once a month. Another preacher from Arkansas, the Reverend Robert P. Thomas, had also joined the congregation in about 1872 and preached occasionally. A Baptist pastor from Florida named Pyles lived entirely surrounded by Brazilians some miles distant.

In a curious concession to their new homeland, the Southern Baptist émigrés added that "many priests here are men of great ability and learning." This evaluation soon changed for most of them.

When the board hesitated to act, additional correspondence arrived in 1878 urging immediate action. Ratcliff, now a widower with children, had returned to the States after eleven years among the *confederados* as a self-sustaining missionary. He wrote:

Dear Brother—In behalf of Foreign Missions, I would ask the Board to consider Brazil, S.A., as a very important field.

The recent changes in her laws respecting the toleration of Free Masonry, and the civil right of marriage, are some of the fruits of the rapid growth of the "Liberal" party, who wish to separate the Roman Church from the Empire.

The majority of that people would rejoice to be relieved from the dogmas of Rome, that they might exercise their own opinions in matters of religion. They are more than anxious to hear what they call "Protestantism." I speak from an experience of eleven years with them, while a self-sustaining missionary.

The first missionary Baptist Church in St. Bárbara, São Paulo Province, is composed of English-speaking people. And it is the opinion of that church, as they have told you time and again, that if the Board would use them as a nucleus, or an aid, the Board could accomplish more with the same amount of means than in any other field.

They have never asked you for money for themselves, but that you help them preach the gospel to the natives. Their present pastor authorized me to say to the Board, that he would accept an appointment to the Brazilians (he is a teacher of their language), and make quarterly reports to the Board, without charging one cent.[13]

Finally in 1879 the board recommended to the Southern Baptist Convention that it accept the First Baptist Church of Brazil as a self-supporting mission. This the convention agreed to do at its 1879 convention.[14] So the

English-speaking church at Santa Bárbara, led by the Reverend E. H. Quillin, actually began the Southern Baptist mission effort in Brazil.

The first years of all mission efforts are stressful, but few suffer the multiple problems of the Santa Bárbara field. Heading the list of difficulties was E. H. Quillin. He was born in Tennessee in 1829, and his family had moved to Texas, where he was ordained to the Baptist ministry in 1858. He left for Brazil in 1867 and pastored the Santa Bárbara Baptist Church for four years. His wife had attended the University of North Carolina in Chapel Hill and requested joint missionary appointment with her husband. She was a schoolteacher and accomplished linguist, at least according to her husband. The couple had six children.[15]

When the foreign mission board first decided to sponsor the Santa Bárbara mission, critical evaluations of Quillin began to arrive from Texas. B. H. Carroll, one of the most influential figures in Texas Baptist ranks, warned the head of the foreign board that Quillin might well embarrass Baptists. An anonymous source recently returned from Brazil reported that the pastor was a "confirmed *opium eater* and [in] every way indiscreet." He urged the head of the board to warn newly appointed missionary W. B. Bagby, who replaced Quillin as pastor in Santa Bárbara, about him.[16]

A second source of trouble was one of Quillin's converts. The Reverend Antonio Teixeira de Albuquerque emerges from the murky chronicles of the colony either as one of its foremost converts or as its premier confidence man. Teixeira had been a Catholic priest who converted to Methodism before finally joining the Baptists. Teixeira was a fine linguist and reputedly the best pulpit orator in Brazil. At first Quillin raved about his coup and warned that Methodists were circulating malicious rumors about their turncoat. But five months later Quillin conceded that his premier Brazilian convert was an impostor, a drunk, a gambler, and a habitué of houses of prostitution. "He would now make a good Catholic priest—he has every essential element."

Quillin also regretted the apostasy of a Mr. Pyles, a minister from Florida who had settled in the community. Pyles was inclined to "spiritism and speculative theology. I fear he will not be useful."[17]

But clearly not all the problems were external to Quillin. Even if one ignores the rumor of his drug addiction, there was still the problem of his poverty. Theoretically the Santa Bárbara church was a self-supporting mission station as it represented itself to the foreign mission board. But if Quillin is to be believed, there was little support involved. The pastor received no salary, and when the Reverend W. B. Bagby arrived, Quillin resigned to pursue more lucrative opportunities. Although he was crippled

The Baptists

and unable to labor (perhaps the pain from his injury accounts for the charge of drug addiction), he had to support a wife and six children.[18]

Toward this end Quillin proposed an elaborate scheme of missionary education. Arguing that both a practical life and practical preaching were necessary in Brazil, he proposed that the foreign mission board support a mission school for Brazilian children. He and his wife would manage the institution. His elaborate proposal began with the claim that traditional denominational mission efforts in Brazil had failed to convert many people. A free school with an able faculty without a dogmatic or religious course of instruction would be far more successful. For five days a week no religious activities beyond prayers and "moral lectures" would be permitted. Weekends would be devoted entirely to voluntary religious instruction. Such a school, Quillin argued, would unite the community as well as spread the gospel.

The new liberal Brazilian constitution tolerated all religious groups but protected the favored status of Catholicism. Therefore, there was little chance of converting the present generation. But education could reach the young and extend civilization.

He tried to establish a mission school at Piracicaba using $500 or $600 of his own money. But his effort failed, and he lost his investment. So he returned to Santa Bárbara, where he opened a co-ed school with thirty regular students and requested a subsidy of $3,000 annually from the foreign mission board, a request which the impoverished agency rejected.[19]

Upon his return to Santa Bárbara in 1881, Quillin penned a bleak portrait of the American community. The sources of his pessimism were complex: their fear that the Brazilian government was moving toward emancipation of slaves, the continuing Jesuit influence in government, the timidity of the chief executive toward these elements, and the General Congress's indifference toward continuing emigration from the Southern United States. As a result of these tendencies "the hearts of many are failing, and some of our best citizens are busily arranging for an early return to the land of their fathers." To what extent Americans would abandon Santa Bárbara he would not estimate, but he believed that some Southerners would remain and that "North American industry and enterprise will . . . go down to posterity as a living reality, and that the little church that is under the aegis of your Mission Board" will survive and help evangelize Brazil.

The vision the émigrés shared was of dual spiritual citizenship in both the divine and political sense: "We are in Brazil, under Providence we will remain. Yet we are American citizens and in this will also remain. . . . Our chief aim—move forward a little . . . [which] will permeate the circle of

Brazilian life long after our name may have faded [from] the record of time."[20]

After Quillin turned the congregation over to Bagby in 1881, the new missionary momentarily turned the Santa Bárbara congregation into a thriving parish. But Bagby remained only two years, and after 1883 it declined again. In 1885 the Reverend Herbert Soper, formerly of the English Mission in Rio, became pastor. He allegedly introduced the temperance movement to Santa Bárbara but remained only one year. Although Baptists, Methodists, and Presbyterians equally represented the religious preference of the Santa Bárbara colony, even the Baptists conceded that their two rivals were better established and supported. Quillin died in March 1886, and his wife and six children were too poor even to return to Texas. They begged help from Texas Baptists but received little assistance.[21]

When the Southern Baptists began to send missionaries directly from the States, they still managed to tap into the émigré community. Charles D. Daniel and E. A. Puthuff were appointed by the foreign mission board in 1885. Daniel was a native of Monroe County, Alabama, who had lived in Santa Bárbara for several years with his father. The family had returned to America after his father's death, but Daniel spoke Portuguese well and had been infected with a romantic attraction to the country. While attending college at Baylor University in Waco, Texas, Daniel had converted his best friend, E. A. Puthuff, to the cause of missions.

The two were inseparable, participated together as Masons, and finally settled upon a scheme to return to Santa Bárbara together. Daniel would work upon Brazilians, using his Portuguese, and Puthuff, who was already known to the American community in Santa Bárbara, would minister to English-speaking settlers. Puthuff married Emma Fox of Pickens County, Alabama, and the two couples rejected entreaties that they study for a time in the seminary. Daniel maintained that his fluency in Portuguese would allow him to begin preaching immediately, while Puthuff was already an experienced preacher who would not need language training anyway. A lenient mission board, anxious to respond to pleas for help from Brazil, waived its rule and sent the four missionaries on their ways.[22]

Although they traveled to Brazil on the same boat, their destinations differed. The board sent the Puthuffs to Santa Bárbara and had greater need for the Daniels elsewhere. After Daniel brushed up on his Portuguese, he took charge of Baptist work in Pernambuco. He was able to preach extemporaneously in Portuguese and was optimistic about his work in Bahia, even though his wife had preferred to stay in Rio. Almost immediately the Daniels began to request the board to send the Puthuffs to help them, but the agency needed them elsewhere. As a consequence both families slowly became dispirited. Bitter opposition from the Catholic population of Pernambuco turned Daniel into an anti-Catholic fanatic who filled his correspondence with diatribes against "our Catholic soul, mind, and body murderers." Though their purposes were carefully disguised in America, the real Catholic priesthood lived immorally and corruptly elsewhere. Persecuted and ill, the Daniels finally left for Rio.

After a brief period of recuperation they began work in Minas Gerais. Daniel beseeched the board to allow him to organize missions in a new way. He proposed an itinerancy scheme whereby he would hire a native worker to help him, establish a church in São Paulo, then move to Taubaté to begin preaching. Once that work was established, he would leave an unpaid Brazilian overseer in charge and move on to a new station, corresponding with his understudies through sermons and literature.[23]

This plan succeeded no better than his earlier efforts. And he soon began complaining about the lack of support he received from the board compared with that received by Methodists and Presbyterians, who were conducting their mission work with far better resources and skill.

Like the Daniels, the Puthuffs' debts were mounting, their health suffering, and their morale undermined. Conditions in Santa Bárbara were worsening, and the mission board had trouble even paying Puthuff's salary. He wrote from the community in January 1888: "I cannot remain here through another year of doubt and uncertainty."[24] The Puthuffs resigned that year. Two years later the Daniels did likewise in a letter in which Daniel grieved: "If I only had my life to live over again no one could induce me to come to the field until I had first taken a *thorough literary* and *theological* course." He had regretted "ten thousand thousand times" bringing his wife and son to Minas Gerais.[25]

Missionaries, like secular émigrés, found Brazil as tough a frontier for the gospel as it was for Southern crops and culture. But the seed they planted did not die. By 1948 the Pernambuco field, which Daniel had helped to begin, contained 110 Baptist churches, 50 Brazilian pastors, and more than 10,000 members.[26] Brazil remained a center of Alabama Baptist attention. During the eighty years following the appointments of Daniel and Puthuff in 1885, twenty-six Alabama natives served in Brazil under appointment of the Southern Baptist Foreign Mission Board.[27]

The process of immigration often strengthens traditional culture. Although many migrants chose to leave their religion behind as they did families and possessions, others clung to traditional religious values and affiliations in a desperate attempt to preserve as much as they could of their culture. For immigrants to America, the church was "one of the few institutions that crossed the ocean with them, and its influence mounted steadily under the pressure of new circumstances."[28] Perhaps a second or third generation, newly assimilated and seeking identity with the dominant culture, might convert to a new religion. But the very process of immigration seemed to reinforce the importance of traditional religion on the first generation of emigrants. In Southerners, newly arrived in Brazil, we thus see a pattern already familiar to students of immigration to the United States.

A good example of this spiritual function of buffering traditional culture can be seen in the previously cited and increasingly desperate appeals of the little Baptist congregation in Santa Bárbara for foreign mission board support. In a series of twenty-one resolutions adopted by the congregation, two in particular reflect the role of religion in shoring up the faith of pilgrims in a strange land.

> 1. *Resolved,* That in the providence of God we are called to dwell far from the scenes of our childhood, amid a vast moral waste, widely severed from the ineffable pleasures of church associations and the endearing influences of a wide-spread Christian intercourse; and that a consciousness of this loneliness at times hangs heavily upon the heart, and plays rudely with the tender sympathies of the soul, weakening the nerve of moral energy, and fringing the horizon of hope with the mist of a doubtful future.

> 2. *Resolved,* That we believe that some relational recognition on the part of the Foreign Mission Board would dispel our gloom, give confidence to our existence, inspire new life, and establish the unwavering conviction that we do in reality belong to the great Baptist family.[29]

The congregation also pledged to help any American Baptist minister or layperson emigrating to Brazil. Not only did members pledge to support them spiritually, they offered to assist their economic endeavors as well.[30]

Roman Catholicism, Judaism, and the Orthodox Church, which together provided nurture for the majority of immigrants to North America during the late nineteenth century, were not evangelical and thus served the exclusive purpose of buffering immigrants from the multiple shocks of social alienation and nativism. But as correspondence from the First Baptist Church of Brazil makes clear, the *confederados* represented evangelical sects. Their faith required that they aggressively evangelize others, even as it also served the classic role of buffer against heretical indigenous religion and hostile culture. Their religion sought to retain a sense of sacred community, even as it also attempted to enlarge the circle of that community to include native Brazilians.

So, unlike the experience of Old World religionists in America, Southern immigrants to Brazil sought the solace of religion both to strengthen and preserve their own culture and to allow them to serve as the advance agent of an aggressive new religious challenge to traditional Brazilian religion. The Southern evangelical missionary effort in Brazil largely entered the country in the wake of the *confederados* and now flourishes in a circle quite beyond anything that first generation of emigrants could have imagined.

Seven

The Methodists
The Southern Migrants
and the Methodist Mission

James M. Dawsey

The Methodist Church of Brazil celebrated its centenary in 1967. The church dated its "uninterrupted presence in Brazil" from the arrival in the port of Rio de Janeiro on August 5, 1867 of the Reverend Junius Eastham Newman, a minister from the Alabama Conference and part of the migration of Southerners who eventually settled near the property of Col. William Norris in what was then called the province of São Paulo. Newman organized the first Methodist church among the settlers on the third Sunday of August 1871. Two of the nine charter members were Mr. Alfred I. Smith and Mrs. Sarah J. Smith—known to readers already from their daughter's account of the family's migration from Texas to Juquiá, and then to Santa Bárbara. A. I. Smith was the music leader of the congregation.

Given Newman's founding role, and the location and membership of the first congregation, one would expect a close connection between the Southern colonists and the Methodist missionary effort that followed Newman to Brazil. But what was the nature of that connection? What role exactly did the colonists play in starting the mission? And what was the role of the mother church?

It was certainly the case that Southern Methodism, more than Northern Methodism, influenced Brazilian Methodism. As Duncan A. Reily pointed out, the Southern influence was so strongly felt because the large majority of Methodist missionaries came from Southern states.[1] In fact, after an initial effort by the Reverend R. Justin Spaulding and family from New England (1836–41) and the Reverend Daniel P. Kidder and family from New York (1837–40), and except for some isolated activity in Pará,[2] in the Amazon,[3] and in Rio Grande do Sul,[4] all of the Methodist missionary activity in Brazil prior to 1930 was carried forward by Southerners.

Conversely, a very large part of the missionary effort of Methodists in the South of the United States was directed to Brazil. For over forty years,

Brazil was the only South American mission field maintained by the Methodist Episcopal Church, South,[5] and as late as 1907, the mission in Brazil was one of only five foreign missions worldwide supported by the Methodist Episcopal Church, South.[6] In terms of the global effort of the Methodist Episcopal Church, South, from the incipience of the support it directed to Brazil in 1876 to Brazilian church autonomy in 1930, the Brazil mission ranked second only to the China mission in the amount of money expended and missionaries sent to the field. Thus, not only did Southerners labor to implant Methodism in Brazil, but the Methodist Episcopal Church, South, was singularly concerned to do so in South America in Brazil. Naturally, one assumes a connection between the arrival of the Southern colonists and the heightened interest of the Methodist Episcopal Church, South, for missions in Brazil.

The hard labor involved in implanting Methodism in Brazil should not be forgotten. While the literature of the Methodist Episcopal Church, South, sometimes claims that the mission in Brazil was gloriously successful, including it as part of "a growth which under the circumstances is almost without a parallel in ecclesiastical annals,"[7] the establishment of Methodism in Brazil was in fact extremely slow and painful.[8] Daniel Kidder's wife died of yellow fever in 1840, and after he and the Spauldings left Brazil, Methodism was interrupted until Newman's arrival in 1867. But the first missionary to Brazil supported by the Methodist Episcopal Church, South, was not Newman but the Reverend John J. Ransom, who did not arrive in Brazil until 1876. Ransom's first wife also died from yellow fever in Brazil (1880), as did the Reverend James W. Koger, in 1886, the next married missionary to arrive from the South of the United States. The first Brazilian ministers were not received into full connection with the Methodist church until 1890. The so-called Grande Plano, by which Methodism became economically self-sufficient in Brazil, was not instituted until 1924, and complete autonomy from North American Methodism came only in 1930. It took almost 100 years of devoted effort to implant Methodism in Brazil. From 1876 until 1900, the Methodist Episcopal Church, South, sent approximately thirty missionaries to Brazil, and as a result of that effort, in 1900, the Methodist Church in Brazil numbered 2,774 members in a country with a population of 18 million.[9] Seldom has a denomination expended so much effort for so long a time for so few converts.

At the same time, however, it would be unfair to judge the success of the Methodist mission in Brazil in those early years solely by the size of the church's membership. Methodist mission schools helped establish the denomination in the eyes of society. Brazil's third president, Prudente José de Moraes Barros, himself helped bring Methodist education to his home-town as early as 1876, had family members attend a Methodist mission school, and was good friends with several of the early Southern missionar-ies. Although in 1890 the Methodists had only 23 church buildings, they had established 10 colleges and schools.[10] By 1926, Methodist missionaries had helped found 41 schools in Brazil, 16 of them schools of higher edu-cation. At that time, Methodism in Brazil already boasted of 3 conferences, 114 charges, 149 churches, 124 preachers, 234 professors, and 208 proper-ties valued at 19.103:053$700.[11] By 1930, Methodism had clearly estab-lished itself in Brazilian society.

Thus, while it is clear that almost all of the early Methodist missionaries who went to Brazil were from the South of the United States, that the Board of Foreign Missions of the Methodist Episcopal Church, South, was singu-larly interested in Brazil in South America, and that the Reverend Junius E. Newman and the post–Civil War colony provided an important connec-tion between Southern Methodism and Brazilian Methodism, the exact na-ture of that connection is complex. What led the Methodist Episcopal Church, South, to concentrate such extensive efforts on Brazil? What al-lowed Southern Methodism to take root in Brazil? And what explains Methodism's mixed influence in Brazil, in education out of all proportion to the size of its church membership?

The purpose of this essay is to sort through these and other questions that ultimately concern the special connections formed between the colo-nists and the Methodist Episcopal Church, South. In order to focus more closely on the roots of the Brazilian mission, I propose to concentrate at-tention on three figures: the colonist Junius Newman; J. J. Ransom, the first missionary to Brazil supported by the Methodist Episcopal Church, South; and Annie Ayres Newman Ransom, the person who I believe was most re-sponsible for defining the role of Methodist education in Brazil. In brief, my plan is to trace the beginning of the Methodist mission in Brazil to the work of Junius Newman, while looking at the appeal for assistance for Brazil by Ransom and the Methodist Episcopal Church, South, and at how Annie Newman and the colony of Southerners provided a springboard for Meth-odist education in Brazil.

The Colonist Junius Newman and the Implantation of the Methodist Mission in Brazil

Methodist interest in Brazil did not begin with Junius Newman and the arrival of the Southern colonists. It preceded Newman's arrival in Brazil by thirty-five years and can be traced to 1832, when Bishop James Osgood

Andrew commissioned the Reverend Fountain E. Pitts of the Tennessee Conference with the task of investigating the possibilities of opening Methodist work in South America.[12] After raising money to support himself, Pitts arrived in Rio de Janeiro on August 19, 1835, and two weeks later concluded that, sure enough, Brazil offered fertile soil for the "true Christian philosophy."[13] Shortly after Pitts's exploratory trip, as already mentioned, two Methodist ministers and their families went to Brazil: the R. Justin Spaulding's, from New England (1836–41), and Daniel P. Kidder's, from New York (1837–40). After their departure, there was a hiatus of Methodist activity until the arrival of the Reverend Junius E. Newman in 1867.[14]

Junius Newman, born in 1819 in Point Pleasant, Virginia (today, West Virginia), transferred into the Alabama Conference in 1845 and was accepted into full connection in 1846. He married Mary A. Phillips from Marion, Alabama, and pastored churches in western Alabama and eastern Mississippi until 1865, when he was appointed by Bishop William May Wightman to work "in Central America or Brazil." According to Judith MacKnight Jones, Newman left the United States because he could not reconcile the new social order with his reading of the Bible.[15] James L. Kennedy gives a more pragmatic explanation: Newman had lost almost everything during the war and decided to follow along with friends to Brazil in order to regain his fortune. He also hoped to be able to help spread the gospel.[16] According to Newman's own account, he had only $100 when he arrived in Brazil.

Although Kennedy does not name the friends whom Junius E. Newman followed to Brazil, he probably was influenced by Col. Charles Grandison Gunter, who brought many Alabamians to Rio Doce, north of Rio de Janeiro in Espírito Santo, by promising good land for twenty-two cents an acre.[17] Newman probably was also influenced by Daniel P. Kidder and James C. Fletcher's book *Brazil and the Brazilians*, which was first published in 1857.[18] It is also probable that Newman was already acquainted with the Norrises, and others who ended up in Santa Bárbara, before reaching Brazil. Col. William Norris was the state senator from Dallas County, Alabama, right next to Marion, the homeplace of Mrs. Mary Newman, and both Norris and Newman were active Masons. Colonel Norris, in fact, was the grand master of the Grand Lodge in Alabama in 1861–62, and both Norris and Newman were founding members of the Masonic lodge in Santa Bárbara.[19]

When Newman reached Brazil, he settled near Rio de Janeiro in the suburbs of Niteroi, where his house became a meeting place for Southerners who were relocating to Brazil. Apparently, he had planned to open a school and a church,[20] but he was unable to do so. After a few months, Newman brought his family from the United States (April 1868). The fam-

J. M. Dawsey

ily stayed in Niteroi for one more year and then moved to Saltinho, near the Norrises. The reasons for this move are not clear but might have been tied to the drought of 1868 and the beginning of the dissolution of the Rio Doce colony.[21] By 1869, many of the Alabamians were abandoning that area north of Rio de Janeiro, and according to Judith MacKnight Jones, the emperor himself counseled at least one colonist to move to the area near the Norrises, where Newman eventually settled.[22]

In two books, *Histórias da historia do Metodismo no Brasil* and *Pioneiros e bandeirantes do Metodismo no Brasil,* Isnard Rocha claims that the real reason why Newman settled first in Rio de Janeiro and then in Saltinho was that he was foremost concerned to reestablish Methodism in Brazil.[23] The thesis is certainly overstated, but in a letter written October 10, 1869, and printed in the *Nashville Christian Advocate,* Newman seems anxious to carry on with the Methodist work among the colonists, to whom he was preaching twice a month. He is concerned to maintain his standing in the Mobile Conference and also wishes that young missionaries be sent to preach to the Brazilians.

It is now more than two years since I became resident of Brazil—a country almost exclusively occupied by Roman Catholics, as you are aware—and during this time I have been almost entirely cut off from the privileges so dear to the heart of every true Christian minister, seldom, until quite recently, having opportunity to preach, or hear preaching from others, but little access to Christian associations, and but seldom seeing a religious paper.

There are some American families scattered in various parts of this province; in all they number between 500 and 600 souls. More than half this number are settled within 35 miles of the town of Limeira, and compose small settlements of from 3 or 4, to 10 families near each other. . . .

From what I have just written, you will see that at our preaching places our congregations must be small—even when a part of those present have ridden 10 or 12 miles to hear preaching—yet most of the Americans in this part of this province, hear preaching at least once a month.

. . . It is strange to me that neither of the two great divisions of the Methodist Church in the States has ever attempted to plant a permanent Mission in Brazil. . . .

Some Brazilians express a strong desire to hear Protestant preaching, and I think if our Church would send two or three young men to this province, of good talents and pure piety, they would be eminently useful. . . .

The Methodists

But perhaps you are ready to ask, "Why do not you, and the other American ministers in Brazil, preach to the Brazilians?" Alas! We have found by hard experience, that when a man has reached his 50th year, it is too late for him ever to become so familiar with a foreign language as to preach it with fluency. I still hope to be able to preach in the Portuguese language, but never as if I had learned the language when young.

. . . I have not written this letter for publication, but because I wanted you to hear from me, and want you to be kind enough to let my brethren of the Mobile Conference know of it at Conference, if this is received in time. I request this, as Brother Heard writes me that they did not hear from me at last session. I wrote to the Conference in September of last year, and have written to Brother J. T. Heard and to the Conference by the last steamer.

I preach twice a month now, and will preach oftener soon, as I am now confined at home with clearing and planting land for a crop.

I have written to one of my sisters to send me a few Sunday-school books, etc. We need books and papers badly. . . .

Pray for me and my family. With much Christian love, I remain, as ever, yours in Christ.

J. E. Newman

Limeira, Province of S. Paulo, Brazil, Oct. 10, 1869[24]

We can see the same general interest in establishing Methodist work in Brazil in a letter written one and a half years later. In this letter, Newman indicates that he is able to devote more time to preaching than before. He asks to be recognized as a missionary to Brazil but sees his work "on the borders" of the field, preaching to the Americans. Again, he laments his inability to preach in Portuguese and expresses his love for the Brazilian and the Methodist church.

I have recently received the two copies of the Advocate containing your editorial letter, detailing the proceedings of the Alabama Conference, as reorganized, and I have read the letter with the most lively interest; indeed, I cannot express the deep emotion with which my heart was moved. The holiest and the happiest memories. . . .

I have often said that the loss of Christian and brotherly association with my brethren of the Conference was the greatest sacrifice I made when I left my native land. . . .

I was at first much restricted in my ministerial labors in this country, but I am now so situated that I can leave home to preach almost as much as I did when I was "in the regular work." Hence I indulge the hope that my name may be restored at your next Conference. If it is

J. M. Dawsey

proper, let me be recognized as a missionary in Brazil. I ask no compensation as such, or in any other way, at the hands of the Conference; and whether I preach in English exclusively, or in future in English and Portuguese, I intend to devote all the time I can to ministerial labor, and to be self-supporting.

The Americans in this country generally manifest a strong desire to hear preaching, and I have been very cordially received among them. They are generally very kind to each other, and many of them are members of some orthodox branch of the Church. Nearly all of them are industrious, and are doing well. I feel a deep interest in preaching to them, and I now feel that I am in the right work. It is that kind of work in which I have often felt a desire to be engaged. I have never thought that I was suited for strictly missionary work; yet I have long felt a desire to work on the borders of such a field—and here is such a work. While I preach Christ to these Americans—who are here scattered over the country—in English, all around me is one grand missionary field, ready for the laborers; but alas! they are not here. O how my heart is moved by the scenes around me! Could I only preach Christ to this kind people, in their own tongue, I should make it the work of my future life. But as yet I can only leave a Bible, or Testament, or tract, with the prayer that God may save the reader.

Thus far I have made no attempt to organize a Methodist Church in this country, chiefly because the few Methodists here are so much scattered. . . .

J. E. Newman

Limeira, Province of San Paulo, Brazil, April 28, 1871[25]

However, it was not long thereafter, on August 17, 1871, that Newman in fact organized a Methodist church among the colonists. The congregation began with nine members, counting Newman's wife and one of his daughters, but increased gradually to number "29 or 30."[26] Newman set up a circuit with five preaching stations and took up his ministry among the American colonists full-time. He continued to appeal to the Methodist Episcopal Church, South, for help for the Brazilians and for recognition of his work among the colonists. In May 1875 the board of missions "recognized the Rev. J. E. Newman, of Saltinho, District of Limeira, Province of San Paulo, as our missionary at that point."[27]

J. J. Ransom and the Southern Response to the Brazil Mission

Newman expressed great appreciation for Brazil and the Brazilians. For instance, in 1871 he wrote that "the Brazilians are almost universally kind and hospitable. There is no kinder people in any land. Their kindness makes me love them, and feel at home in Brazil."[28] But his ministry was among the colonists. What was to be done to bring Methodism to the Brazilians?

Upon hearing that he had been recognized as a missionary, Newman immediately hatched a plan by which the Board of Missions of the Methodist Episcopal Church, South, could send a missionary to Brazil to help the Brazilians at very little expense to the Methodists in the United States. A young Methodist preacher of German descent could be sent to minister to the many Germans who lived in that area. While the German and American colonists supported the young man, he could learn Portuguese and soon preach to the Brazilians too.[29]

Newman's long letter describing the potential for Methodist labor in Brazil was published in the *Nashville Christian Advocate* on June 12, 1875. The letter was followed in the *Advocate* by an open request by David C. Kelley, secretary of the board of missions, for money to send two young men.

Brother Newman encourages us to send to certain points, which he mentions, young men, thoroughly educated, who are competent to teach; gives a plan by which they can be employed in teaching while they are acquiring the Portuguese language, and getting ready for preaching. He further indicates that a limited number of such men, carefully selected, could be supported almost at once. We are very fortunate in having a man such as brother Newman on the ground, with seven years of residence, and fine opportunity and capacity for observation. Here is a field on our own continent, of favorable climate, on whose sympathy we of the South have the strongest claims—a stable government strongly inclined to education and progress. A people who, as education increases, are growing out of Romanism into infidelity. The call upon the Church has the Macedonian ring. There are two young men ready to go. Can the Board, with pledges out beyond collections of previous years, dare to make an advance? Who will cut the knot? Who will say here is five hundred dollars, send the two men? If you make the pledge for one year, make it for three, and the Board will take into favorable consideration the offer.

D.C.K.[30]

This appeal by D. C. Kelley in the June 12 issue of the *Advocate* for support for Brazil, following upon the board of mission's recognition of Newman as a missionary, marked a new attitude in the Methodist Episcopal Church, South. American Methodists were beginning to appropriate Brazil as a mission field.

A response to the secretary's appeal came within a few days. On June 16, there was a called meeting of the board of missions, and after a discussion concerning the urgency of Newman's call, the Reverend John J. Ransom of the Tennessee Conference offered to go to Brazil as a missionary. Bishop John Christian Keener, who had joined the Alabama Conference in 1843 and thus knew Newman well, had been placed in charge of the Brazil Mission, was present at the meeting, and accepted Ransom's offer on the spot.[31] Ransom was twenty-two, a graduate of Emory and Henry College, and was at that time serving the North Nashville Station.

But even before this meeting on the sixteenth, Methodists had begun to respond to Secretary Kelley's appeal for support. On June 14, the Reverend J. T. Curry, one of Newman's colleagues from the Alabama Conference, had written to Dr. A. H. Redford, the board's treasurer, proposing "to be one of a hundred persons who will pledge ourselves for the required amount, by paying each $5 a year, for three years, payable on the 1st of August." Two other signatories joined him in the pledge.[32]

Curry's letter, which was printed in the *Nashville Christian Advocate*, was soon followed by others, each pledging $5 of support a year for three years: P. H. McCullough from Huntington, West Virginia (July 5, 1875);[33] B. B. White, Jr., from Jacksonville, Alabama (July 11, 1875);[34] and an anonymous widow, through the Reverend H. Urquhart of Greenville, Alabama (July 31, 1875).[35] By August, D. C. Kelley wrote that "there are now reported 36 responses" to the proposition "to be one of one hundred to pay $5 each to pay the expenses of the Rev. J. J. Ransom."[36]

Although it is very likely that the first responses came from former friends of Junius Newman and that some of the responses were generated by sympathy for relatives or friends who had moved to Brazil, one should not underestimate the growing zeal at that time of the Methodist Episcopal Church, South, for evangelism and foreign missions. At a meeting in Nashville in late 1875, the board of missions expanded Article 15 of its constitution in order to allow any conference to "propose the support of a single missionary" in Mexico, Brazil, or China.[37] Women's auxiliaries were also becoming more active. Mrs. M. L. Kelley, who had first begun organizing women's support for the Lambuth Mission in Shanghai in 1858, joined with other Methodists to organize the Woman's Bible Mission of Nashville in 1873 for the support of foreign missions. Mrs. Kelley, who was the mother of D. C. Kelley, corresponded frequently with Mrs. Juliana Hayes of Trinity Church in Baltimore, credited with having formed the first Woman's Missionary Society in the Methodist Episcopal Church, South, in 1868.[38] Mrs. Hayes's society had originally supported only home missions, but in 1872 it had expanded its operations to embrace foreign work as well, and in 1873 it was busy raising support for the China mission. In 1875 some of that growing interest in missions in general was translated into interest in Ransom's mission in particular.

The connections that Ransom established with these groups of women and other supporters in the South later proved very significant to the growth of Methodism in Brazil. Ransom seems to have had a gift for garnering good will for missions, for procuring financial support, and for recruiting fellow workers.[39] Soon before his departure for Brazil, Ransom wrote a letter to the secretaries of the board of missions which gives us insight into his efforts at cultivating support for his work.

> Drs. J. B. McFerrin and D. C. Kelley—Dear Brothers:—I have now to write you a few facts in regard to what I have been doing since my last. At Emory and Henry College I spent a gracious time, and two or three young men mentioned to me a desire to study with a view to missionary work. At Danville I assisted in organizing a society similar to that in the Holston Conference, but not for Brazil—at least, it has not yet been decided that the funds shall take that direction. I am convinced that you will, during the year, have young men of the Virginia Conference to offer themselves for mission-work. My thanks are due Drs. Bennett and Edwards, and various other persons, for a donation of $100 to myself at the Virginia Conference, and also to other friends in Knoxville and Emory for a donation of $17.
>
> I enclose you a copy of a circular which I have addressed to the conferences, and which appears in this week's *Episcopal Methodist*. Would it be presuming on your goodness and judgment to ask you to present my letter to the Tennessee Conference? I have received assurances of help for my school from the Baltimore Churches, though these assurances have taken no tangible form, nor has any society been formed, nor the amount of help indicated. . . .
>
> In New York . . . I visited the Bible House, and obtained a consignment of Portuguese and English Bibles.
>
> I have been very agreeably situated in this city [Baltimore]; have spent most of my time at the hospitable house of Dr. S. K. Cox, pastor of St. Paul's M. E. Church, South. . . . I have preached four times in his Church to excellent and attentive congregations. . . . Part of my time has been agreeably passed under the roof of Miss Melissa Baker, a woman of missionary spirit. I have also met Dr. Kelley's old friend, Mrs. Hayes. Brother Blogg, our German Mission Superintendent, has been very kind to me, and, indeed, paid me every possible attention.
>
> I have been so exceedingly busy that it has been impossible for me to

write any thing for the *Advocate*. I desire Dr. Kelley to insert my address (Santa Barbara, Prov. San Paulo, Brazil) in the *Advocate*, with a suggestion that those expecting replies enclose stamps for return postage. Some 200 persons, and more, have asked me to write them, and say they intend to write first. Also ask the other Church papers to copy the address.

J. J. Ransom

Baltimore, Dec. 11, 1875 [40]

Ransom thus made preparations for his trip and raised support for the mission throughout the fall of 1875, until he departed for Brazil on December 13, 1875. The December 25 *Advocate* ran a full account of Ransom's departure, including a report by D. C. Kelley, Ransom's letter to the secretaries, in part repeated above, and a graphic description of the embarkation written by Mrs. Hayes, who helped see him off at the port.

Annie Ayres Newman Ransom and the Beginning of Methodist Education in Brazil

John James Ransom is often described as the pioneer most responsible for taking Methodism to the Brazilians. He is given credit for beginning work in Portuguese in Rio de Janeiro in 1879, for receiving the first Brazilians into the Methodist church, for battling to open the first Methodist school in Brazil, and for urging the translation of Methodist works into Portuguese. The tendency among historians clearly has been to separate the work of Newman "among the southerners who migrated to Brazil after being defeated in the Civil War" from the work of Ransom, who was sent to work among the Brazilians.[41] In truth, however, the work of Ransom cannot, and should not, too easily be separated from the Methodist work already begun among the colonists. Judith MacKnight Jones is quite right in her claim that "in a way, the life of the American missionaries is very much connected to the life of the Southerners who lived here. The friendships that they formed and the ambience offered by their countrymen did much to ease the life of these servants who dedicated their lives to the work of giving others the inner joy that they themselves felt."[42]

Ransom disembarked in Rio de Janeiro on February 2, 1876, and by the sixteenth he had made his way to Junius Newman's house outside of Santa Bárbara. He did not start Methodist work immediately but instead studied Portuguese at the Colégio Internacional in Campinas, where he also taught English and Greek. As we have seen in chapter 5, this college had been founded by the Presbyterians in order to provide adequate education for the sons and daughters of the colonists. In 1876 the school was "perhaps the most beautiful building in the town" and had approximately 100 students, serviced by three Presbyterian missionary families.[43] Ransom's first Portuguese teacher when he arrived at the school was Junius Newman's daughter, Annie Ayres Newman.[44]

Annie Newman had been born in Livingston, Sumter County, Alabama, on December 25, 1856. She was only eleven when first arriving in Brazil and thus had learned the language well. Later, Ransom would write with admiration of Annie's ability to speak as educated Brazilians spoke. It was actually Annie Newman who first began translating Methodist literature into Portuguese. She was the person who translated the first hymns into Portuguese. She also translated Bishop McTyeire's *Catechism on Church Government* and the *Wesleyan Catechism, No. 3* into Portuguese. Although J. J. Ransom is the name most often associated with the beginning of Methodist publishing in Portuguese, for instance with the *Compêndio da Igreja Metodista* (1878), it was actually Annie Newman who did the earliest writing.[45]

Annie Newman's role in starting the Methodist school in Piracicaba has often been overlooked. This is a significant point, because Methodist inroads into Brazilian society were made through the schools. By 1926, Methodism in Brazil counted 1 school for every 3.5 churches and supported approximately twice as many professors as preachers.[46] Both Junius Newman and John Ransom, independently of each other, had plans for starting a mission school, but it was Annie Newman who really opened the door for Methodist education in Brazil.

Annie Newman had been one of the first students of the Colégio Internacional and, as already mentioned, taught Ransom Portuguese there when he first arrived from the United States. As we have seen, the school had been founded by George Nash Morton and Edward Lane (who had arrived from the United States in 1869), working with progressive elements of Brazilian society interested in coeducation and in the pedagogy of Horace Mann.[47] Emperor Dom Pedro II had visited the school in August 1875,[48] soon before the arrival of J. J. Ransom from the United States, and in January 1876, soon after his arrival, F. Rangel Pestana, one of Brazil's most famous educators, gave the commencement address at the college.[49] Others interested in the American system of education were the brothers Prudente and Manuel de Moraes Barros.[50]

Annie Newman was such a gifted student and teacher that upon graduation she was sought after by several Brazilian schools. She accepted a position teaching at the Colégio Rangel Pestana, which was an elite women's school in São Paulo serving some of the outstanding families of the province. While she was teaching at this school, the Barros brothers approached the Reverend Junius Newman about opening a school in Piracicaba. Ransom later related the story in the following way: "It was then [1878] that Collegio Newman in Piracicaba began to be talked of. The citizens of the place knew of Miss Annie Newman through their daughters who had been at Collegio Pestana, and they urged the matter.... In July, 1879, the Collegio Newman was opened."[51]

Annie Newman opened the school in Piracicaba with the help of her sister, Mary Newman, three regular assistants, and a temporary art teacher. Her father, the Reverend Junius Newman, had hoped, from his first years in Niteroi, to open a school and had urged Annie ahead with the project. In order to support the project, he actually moved his family to Piracicaba in 1879. The Reverend J. J. Ransom had also urged the project and had directed an appeal to the first annual meeting of the Woman's Board of Foreign Missions (then, the General Executive Association of the Woman's Missionary Society of the Methodist Episcopal Church, South) meeting in Louisville on May 16–17, 1879, which, in response, had promised $500 toward "Miss Newman's school."[52] The next year, the Woman's Missionary Society appropriated $1,000 for "school purposes" in Brazil.[53]

Annie Newman had not been anxious to open the school in Piracicaba, but as Ransom related, "with some reluctance, acceded to her father's plans." Ransom did not explain the reason for Newman's reluctance, but one can speculate that it had to do with her desire to get married, because on December 25, 1879, she married J. J. Ransom and took on "the work that would be hers as the wife of a Methodist missionary."[54]

Ransom had restarted Methodist work in Rio de Janeiro in January 1878, and soon after their marriage Annie Ayres Ransom left Piracicaba and moved to Rio de Janeiro with her husband. By that time, the end of 1879, the Catete Methodist Church in Rio was well established with both Portuguese and English services, and a strong Sunday school. Ransom had started satellite congregations in Santana and Niteroi. Preaching was on Thursday, Friday, Saturday, and twice on Sundays. Ransom had also begun to publish Methodist materials in Portuguese, had organized a library with 200 volumes, and planned to open a school. Annie became a full partner in all of the work.

Annie Ayres Newman Ransom was a key to solidifying Methodism and Methodist education in Brazil. Her connections with the Barros brothers were important. Also the models of education that she brought together from the Colégio Internacional and the Colégio Pestana were significant, for they set the pattern of Methodist education in Brazil. Just as significant,

The Methodists

however, was her death. She died tragically just a few months after her wedding, in July 1880. J. J. Ransom had contracted yellow fever for a second time in March 1880, and after nursing him back to health, Annie too contracted the disease and died. Ransom was heartbroken and returned to the United States to recover. Much seemed lost, as the Newman school in Piracicaba had been forced to close without Annie and as the school in Rio might not start without her. But Ransom was a gifted speaker, and as he traveled throughout the South of the United States and spoke of needs and opportunities for the gospel in Brazil, Ransom personalized his appeal by narrating the story of his wife. (See Appendix below.)

Ransom's heart-rending account of his wife's death was largely responsible for solidifying the interest of the Methodist Episcopal Church, South, for the mission in Brazil. As a result of this appeal, Ransom was able to garner tremendous support for the work that he, Annie, and Junius Newman had already started. Thus, two Southern conferences and the Woman's Missionary Society decided to support missionaries to Brazil, and in 1881 the missionaries James W. Koger and family, James L. Kennedy, and Martha Hile Watts, after hearing Annie's story, volunteered to go to Brazil and were appointed to do so.[55] Watts's specific mission was to restart the school at Piracicaba, which she did with the financial support of the Woman's Missionary Society and the local help of the Barros brothers.[56] There, she became the close friend of Prudente de Moraes, who later, as governor of São Paulo, took Martha Watts's school as the model for the state school system that he was trying to develop, and who still later after becoming Brazil's first constitutional president, offered Martha Watts the position of minister of education, which she refused to accept.[57] Koger and his wife and small child also worked in Piracicaba, close to Newman. Meanwhile, after learning some of the Portuguese language, Kennedy accompanied Ransom to Rio, where for a third time Methodism began work.

Ransom's appeal of 1880 in memory of his wife also bore fruit in the 1883 adoption by the Woman's Missionary Society of the Centenary Fund drive to raise money for a school in Rio de Janeiro to provide education for young women of influential families in Brazil.[58] Property for the Rio College, as it was initially called, was bought in 1887.

Conclusion

To my knowledge, the Reverend Junius Newman never preached a sermon in Portuguese. After Annie's marriage and death and the initial failure of the Colégio Newman, he moved back from Piracicaba to the *Campo*, near the other colonists. Newman's first wife had died in 1879, and he remarried a widow from the colony, Mrs. Lydia E. Barr. He continued to be an active pastor to the Americans until 1887, when he decided to return to the United States. By that time, his health was failing, and the Mobile Conference had changed his status from clerical to lay member. In 1889 he returned to Point Pleasant, West Virginia, where he died in 1895.

J. J. Ransom accompanied Martha Watts, Kennedy, and the Kogers to Brazil in 1881. He immediately took these new missionaries to the Norris colony, where they remained until they had adapted to the climate and the language. The first congregation to which Kennedy and Koger spoke was the congregation of the Americans at Santa Bárbara, and their first church conference took place in the house of Alfred I. Smith, "our music director."[59] Ransom picked up, as best he could, where he had left off with the Methodist work in Rio de Janeiro, spending most of his efforts on the mission in Portuguese. Soon he, with the help of Kennedy, expanded the Methodist work to Juíz de Fora, Minas Gerais. But in 1886, after he began publishing the first Portuguese-language Methodist periodical, *Metodista Católico*, and opened what became the Methodist Publishing House of Brazil, Ransom left Brazil, returning to the United States for good.

In *Cincoenta annos de methodismo no Brazil*, Kennedy wrote that "from the first days of its work in Brazil, the Woman's Board of Foreign Missions (in the United States) understood the great importance of a boarding school for females in the country's metropolis."[60] It took many years for the idea of a women's college in Rio to become a reality, but it finally did so in the form of Bennett College, the place where government officials and generals sent their children to school. In 1887 money from the Centenary Fund was used to purchase land and a school was opened, but after an outbreak of yellow fever in Rio, the boarding part of the school was moved to Juíz de Fora. A few years later, the property was sold, and the money from the sale was used to open another school in Petrópolis, which at that time was the city where the leaders of the nation and the foreign diplomats had their summer residences. From 1895 until 1920, the Colégio Americano de Petrópolis served approximately 2,000 young ladies, some of them the children of Brazil's most influential families. Meanwhile, the Colégio Americano Fluminense, a day school, was maintained in Rio on rented property. Later, after Dr. Oswaldo Cruz rid Rio of yellow fever and the bubonic plague, several attempts were made to purchase new land and reopen a boarding school in the capital. Belle H. Bennett and other leaders of the Woman's Missionary Society took on the project in 1913, and Colégio Bennett opened in 1921. At that time, the boarding school in Petrópolis and the day school in Fluminense were closed, and the missionaries and professors from those schools were consolidated into Colégio Bennett.[61]

Meanwhile, the school at Piracicaba had been reopened in 1881 under the direction of Martha Watts, who, with the help of Manoel and Prudente de Moraes Barros, made the school into what has today become a major university. As Kennedy related the school's early success, "Soon, children started filling the school, and it was quickly recognized as the best school in town, frequented by the children of the best families of the place. The two brothers Moraes Barros were great admirers of Miss Watts and always remained firm friends and protectors of the school."[62] The institution begun by Newman was solidified by Watts as the Colégio Piracicabano, which more recently has developed into the Universidade Metodista de Piracicaba (UNIMEP).

When attempting to explain the Methodist dedication to missions, denominational literature often points to the intrinsic missionary spirit that Methodists imbibed from Wesley's view that the world was his parish.[63] This is often accompanied in Methodist denominational literature by the tendency to view missionaries as heroes, true Christians filled with "sacrificial devotion to the service of Christ and the world."[64] Isnard Rocha's two books published by the Imprensa Metodista, *Pioneiros e bandeirantes do metodismo no Brasil* and *Histórias da história do metodismo no Brasil*, surely fit this mold. They are nothing less than "lives of Methodist saints." To read these books is to read about how courageous and dedicated Christian individuals overcame great difficulties in order to evangelize Brazil.

A competing tendency of denominational literature has been to explain the Methodist missionary effort in terms of church programs. For instance, at the time that the Methodist Episcopal Church, South, began its efforts in Brazil, it was common for the *Nashville Christian Advocate* to devote its entire second page to missions. The paper printed letters from missionaries, information concerning missionary programs, and requests from D. C. Kelley and J. B. McFerrin, mission secretaries, and A. H. Redford, the missions treasurer, for support. Although this tendency to understand Brazilian missions by looking at church programs has been more prevalent in North American Methodist literature, it also is present in the first history of Brazilian Methodism written in Portuguese, James L. Kennedy's *Cincoenta annos de methodismo no Brazil*, completed in 1927. In this book, Brazilian Methodism was treated not as a compendium of aretalogies but as a church movement.[65]

The tendency to credit the beginnings of Methodism in Brazil both to the work of heroes, on the one hand, and to church programs, on the other, fit with what we can see through the lives of Junius Newman, John Ransom, and Annie Newman Ransom and through the efforts of the Methodist Episcopal Church, South, and its Woman's Missionary Society auxiliaries. Neither heroes nor programs, however, fully explain the implantation of Southern Methodism in Brazil. The American missionaries and the church programs were effective to the extent that they fit within a context already provided by the post–Civil War migration to that area around Santa Bárbara. The role that Junius Newman played in urging missionaries to Brazil, the role that John Ransom played in recruiting support from the mother church for Brazil, and the role that Annie Newman played in establishing the pattern of Methodist education among the children of influential Brazilians were possible because of multiple personal connections between the colonists, Methodists in the South of the United States, and progressive Brazilians who were interested in the education of their children.

Appendix

The following account of the life and death of Annie Ayres Ransom appeared in the September 25, 1880, issue of the *Nashville Christian Advocate:*

Mrs. Annie Ayres Ransom
By Rev. J. J. Ransom

Mrs. ANNIE AYRES NEWMAN RANSOM, daughter of the Rev. Junius E. Newman and Mary A. Newman, his wife, was born in Livingston, Sumter county, Ala., Dec. 25, 1856. In 1867 she accompanied her father's family to Brazil, where, after residing one year in the suburbs of Nitherohy, Province of Rio de Janeiro, their residence was fixed for some years at Saltinho, District of Limeira, Province San Paulo. When the *Collegio Internacional* was opened under auspices of the Southern Presbyterian Mission in Campinas, 1873, she entered that institution, and there she remained as pupil and teacher from July, 1872, to December, 1875. In 1876 she was my first teacher of Portuguese, and during the few months of my acquaintance with her in this capacity, I formed a high estimate of her intellectual worth, and learned to admire the simplicity and purity of her spirit. In the "Cyclopedia of Methodism" there is a reference to her translation of Bishop McTyeire's "Catechism of Bible History," begun at this time, a task she executed faithfully and well. She also translated "Wesleyan Catechism, No. 3"; but neither of these works has yet been published.

In 1876 she received communications from various persons and institutions of learning, requesting her services as teacher. As it seemed unlikely that our Church, to which she was devotedly attached, would make any immediate educational move, she finally accepted a situation in *Collegio Pestana*, in San Paulo City, at that time undoubtedly the worthiest and most popular girls' school in the Province of San Paulo. Here she remained for two years, not only teaching, but by patient study fitting herself for more extended usefulness.

In 1878 *Collegio Pestana* passed from the direction of its founder, Dr. F. Rangel Pestana, into the hands of a woman, doubtless worthy; but although the most flattering conditions were proposed, Miss Annie Newman felt that her work in San Paulo was done. She returned to the home of her father at Saltinho.

It was then that *Collegio Newman*, in Piracicaba, began to be talked of. The citizens of the place knew of Miss Annie Newman through their daughters who had been at *Collegio Pestana*, and they urged the matter. With some reluctance she acceded to her father's plans; but before taking upon herself the direction of the school, she returned to San Paulo to pursue, under the best masters, certain studies in which she was interested. In July, 1879, the *Collegio Newman* was opened, the two Misses Newman, three regular assistants, and a temporary teacher of Art, forming the teaching corps.

Miss Annie Newman's connection with the *Collegio Newman* was severed Dec. 25, 1879, by her marriage with the writer. And six days later, on the last evening of the old year, we climbed one of the eminences of the city of Rio de Janeiro, overlooking the mouth of the harbor, and part of the far-famed bay, and she crossed the threshold of her new home. Let it be permitted to musing sorrow here to recall her gentleness and love, that shed over less than seven short months the sweet fragrance of an undreamed of happiness.

In person she was very attractive. Small and low of stature, she was of almost faultless proportions. Her fair face, large, dark eyes, and dark hair, soft and abundant, formed a striking picture. Her beauty was not simply a feature, but borrowed its chiefest charms from a quick and penetrating intelligence, and a soul full of all gentleness and love. Her attire, always simple, modest, and faultlessly neat, was an index of her unaffected, yet truly refined taste. Said one of her, while we watched beside her dead body: "She was beautiful, very beautiful; there was something so refined in every expression of her countenance."

From the time of our first acquaintance she had manifested a sympathetic appreciation of the work in which I was engaged. After I had won her promise to be my wife she often referred to the work that would be hers as wife of a Methodist missionary. We were married. Her heart was thoroughly committed to the work upon which we fondly hoped she had now entered for many long and useful years. And surely few have undertaken such labors with better qualifications of mind or heart than she. Speaking the Portuguese language with an elegance and precision equaled only by the more cultivated Brazilian ladies, familiar with the images of the best society of one of the gayest and most fashionable of the provincial capitals, she was eminently fitted for commanding respect and winning sympathy socially. But she could never, under any circumstances, have so failed of her mission as to become a mere child of fashion. Her reading had been careful, her observation was minute, both of events and of persons, and she had formed for herself a high ideal of wifely and womanly excellence, and of Christian devotedness. She was scrupulously exact in all that pertained to the arrangement of her home. But she saw in every thing a Christian duty. We paused a moment to kneel and pray God's blessing on our union, while the assembled guests were waiting to witness our marriage; we asked that blessing again when left alone; and one of our first acts on entering our new home, while yet the tears of joy were wet upon her cheeks, was to kneel and consecrate that home to God. And thus it was ever, so that I may confidently affirm, she undertook no social or household task without recognizing in it a religious duty. Her desire for usefulness was consuming. As her strength permitted, and beyond her strength, did she give herself to the great work that lay before us. She planned for herself broad and severe studies, and had God seen fit to spare so lovely a flower, she would have executed them with the same steadfastness with which she adhered to them until she lay down to die. She earnestly desired to aid in perfecting the Portuguese translation of the Holy Scriptures; her studies for some time before her death had been directed to this end, though no one beside myself knew of the fact, nor of the tireless industry she brought to bear upon the mastery of the original tongues of Scripture. The variety, the multitude, and often the complexity of her engagements, would appall a weaker or less orderly mind; but through it all she bore herself not only with ladylike composure, but with so sunshiny and so equable a spirit as could only be found in one whose every inspiration was at the Throne of Grace.

Says the Rev. A. L. Blackford, the oldest Protestant missionary in Brazil: "Dear Brother Ransom: Perhaps a word in regard to my appreciation of your lamented wife may not be ungrateful in your deep sorrow, although you already know it well. I first remember her in 1874, when I met her in Campinas, where she was studying and teaching in *Collegio Internacional*. The cordial frankness of her manners rendered us friends from the first. Our subsequent acquaintance, and what I learned of her from others, confirmed and increased my high regard. Her vigorous

The Methodists

mind, carefully cultivated by all advantages within her reach; the prompt decision of her character, and the steady energy in her plans and efforts to do good, won my admiration; crowning all was her Christian faith, and earnest, trustful, consecration of all to her Redeemer and his service here."

Her father writes, Aug. 1, 1880: "I am fully convinced that Annie was soundly converted before she was 6 years old. Her mind was precocious, and her mother always took special pains with the religious instruction of our children when yet very young—and I can truly say she was the best child I ever knew, and when she was only 7 years old she was so gentle and so good as to have become a great favorite with all our family, and with all others who knew her. I do not suppose she was ever reproved in school. When 7 years old she wrote and composed as well as most children at 15, and the sweetness, gentleness, and brightness of mind and heart at that time was just as marked as in later life. Of course I am a partial judge, but the innocency and beauty of her young life made a profound impression on my heart years ago, and I am sure I never saw its equal in any other one. Many years ago, in West Virginia, I knew a Mrs. Miller, of whom Annie reminded me so much. The same quiet spirit, and soft voice, and gentle manners. Mrs. Miller was a rarely gifted woman, and better than all else, a holy woman. I knew her when she was about 36 years old. A cool, clear-headed preacher said of her once: 'She is the best woman in this world;' and when I became acquainted with her I thought so too. The traits of resemblance to her in Annie were very striking indeed. Take it all in all, Annie's life from early childhood was the most lovely and the most beautiful I ever hope to see in this world."

In March, 1880, I had yellow fever a second time, and under God's blessing my recovery was due to the care and devotion of my wife. But she was in turn prostrated by a low remittent fever, which left her only in May, when it was necessary to visit her father's home in Piracicaba.

On the evening of July 5 she began a letter to my father, but on account of the lateness of the hour, and her own illness, wrote only about a page; she was never to write to him again, and was indeed to pen but one other letter. That last letter of all was to her father some days later. In it she said: "I can well understand how you must have disliked to give up the work at Piracicaba. I regret very much that it had to be done—especially since the Woman's Missionary Society seems really interested in the matter. I wish the school might have been saved, but that was impossible, and it remains to be seen whether our Church will ever establish a Mission there. At any rate, I think that your and our work in that place is sure to produce good results sooner or later." And then she laid aside her pen forever; but with its last use she gave her sisters of the M. E.

Church, South, a proof of how deeply and tenderly she loved the work for which a few days later she was in some sense to lay down her life.

For ten days she was in constant pain, but touchingly patient throughout. Two nights before she died I was watching alone by her bedside; the opiates she had taken inclined her to talk, though as yet we hardly doubted her recovery. She told me her Christian experience—how that when a child she had trusted in God with such a child-like faith that she hesitated not to ask him for any needful thing. When at Campinas she realized her lack of that faith; but while at home on a visit, as she walked alone and thought on the matter, she had resolved simply to return to God as of old. She did return. "And," added she, very quietly and solemnly, "though I have kept it in much weakness and imperfection, that faith has been with me ever since." At one time she desired to know her condition, and said: "Doctor, you need not be afraid to tell me just what you think; I am not afraid to die." After a moment's pause, she added: "You know, Doctor, it must be hard to leave all we love in this world; but I am not afraid to die." And then the end drew near, and we knew her days were numbered; though, looking back, I perceive that even against hope I hoped. The night but one before she died, she said that she had no fears, no doubts; "but I do not realize the presence of my Saviour as I desire." For that we prayed, and during the last day that, too, was granted to her. I presume that in dying the supreme victory of faith will be gained when we become resigned to lay aside our plans and leave our unfinished work; it was so with her, and affecting was it to see her wrestle with the temptation to regret the incompleteness of her life. Beautiful was the triumph of divine grace; and then naught was left but to send the last messages of deathless love, and compose herself to die. Among her pupils in Piracicaba were some in whom she had become especially and hopefully interested, and she remembered to say, calling their names, "Tell ———— to love the Book, the Book." Habitually she was the calmest, the most undemonstrative of Christians; but as she knew that death drew near her soul flamed with a holy ecstasy. As I read to her one by one those precious words with which God's book has soothed so many dying pillows, she repeated the sentences after me until her lips grew rigid in the stiffness of death. Amid the shadows of the early dawn some vagrant strains of distant music were borne in at the open window of her chamber. She assumed a listening attitude. "Did you hear it?" said she. "Yes," said I; "but you, dear wife, will soon hear sweeter music in the heavenly city." "O how sweet!" said she. Often she extended her arms, and cried: "Come, Lord Jesus; come now!" Often, "O death, where is thy sting? O grave, where is thy victory?" Before the destroyer had made his last sad ravages, she sang, with a clear, sweet voice:

The Methodists

Just as I am—without one plea,
But that thy blood was shed for me,
And that thou bidst me come to thee—
   O Lamb of God, I come, I come!

Just as I am—and waiting not
   To rid my soul of one dark blot,
To thee, whose blood can cleanse each spot,
   O Lamb of God, I come, I come!

Just as I am—thou wilt receive,
   Wilt welcome, pardon, cleanse, relieve,
   Because thy promise I believe;
   O Lamb of God, I come, I come!

She asked me to sing, and I began the hymn, "How firm a foundation," but in one place my voice failed, while she caught up and sustained the air to the end. Her speech failed; but toward the last she recovered her voice, though the attendant physician said that circulation
had ceased in the brain, and her speech was incoherent. But even so,
she always knew her name, she always recognized me, and always answered the question, "Is Jesus precious to your soul now?" with "Yes, precious, precious; more than every thing else."

And thus she passed away. At 7 1/2 A.M. Sunday, July 18, 1880, I
closed reverently the sightless eyes, and turned away from the yet warm
corpse. She was my earthly all. God had asked that which was dearer
than life, and with a bruised heart I had commended her spirit to his
gracious keeping.

Kind friends had been with her in her illness; they and all the pastors
of Protestantism in the city, excepting one who was not advised in time
and one who was unavoidably detained, attended the funeral-service at
what had been our home. On Monday morning we buried her amid
the graves of strangers of every nation under heaven in the cemetery of
S. Francisco Xavíer, at the Ponta de Cajú. Her body awaits the resurrec-
tion; but I labor on yet a little while for the salvation of the people in
whose behalf, like our Lord Jesus, she was ever ready to offer up her
soul unto death; yet a little while, and then beside her, or elsewhere, as
it pleases God, I too shall sleep in the dust. Beyond the grave her spirit
is forever at peace in the blessed country that grows dearer as we grow
older, and afflictions come thicker.

Her collapse was brief, and marked by no dazzling deed to recommend her to the Church's regard; and if I claim for her a place in the
memory of the Church among the heroines of our faith, I vindicate the
claim by the rich aroma of the offering she gladly brought to our common Lord—she gave her life.

Eight

A Community Center
Evolution and Significance of the *Campo* Site in the Santa Bárbara Settlement Area

Cyrus B. Dawsey

In 1928 Mark Jefferson wrote an article for the *Geographical Review* entitled "An American Colony in Brazil."[1] He described his contact with a group of descendants of Americans who left the southern United States immediately after the Civil War and migrated to Brazil. Jefferson characterized the people whom he met at Americana, São Paulo, as having maintained racial purity, the English language, and many elements of the material culture carried from Georgia and Alabama. After describing features of their rural economy, Jefferson concluded his article on a negative note. He wrote: "They raised their food easily enough and something for a money crop but were apt to become Brazilianized, as they put it, which seems to mean lazy, shiftless, and content to get along on little. The colony is not expected to endure. It may be said to be passing away. . . . Economically and socially they had been better off in Georgia than most of them ever were in Brazil."[2]

Jefferson's 1928 comments portrayed a bedraggled group of descendants on the verge of abandoning the cultural traits that had been taken to Brazil by their ancestors. However, his description failed to account for the colony's remarkable resiliency during the previous sixty years. Though three generations had grown up in a society where few used anything but Portuguese, many of the residents spoke English as a first language. Their manner of dress, food preferences, construction methods, farming techniques, and religious practices still reflected much of the North American heritage.

Over sixty additional years have since gone by, yet some of the older surviving individuals continue many of the ways of their ancestors, including a knowledge of Southern English. The generational transfer of the language is not likely to go much further, but the descendants' respect and veneration of the transplanted heritage remain strong. As I will show in this chapter, the community possesses certain institutions that have helped preserve the ties to its history.

Perhaps no more than 2,000 or 4,000 people made the journey to Brazil in the years immediately after 1865, and many who went soon returned to North America.[3] Most of the immigrants originally went to the formal colonies that were established under special agreements between group organizers and the Brazilian government. With the debatable exception of the group led by Maj. Lansford Hastings to Santarém in the Amazon region, all of the colonization efforts failed.[4] Immigrants who followed the Reverend Ballard S. Dunn, Dr. James M. Gaston, and Frank McMullan to the Ribeira de Iguape region of coastal São Paulo, and those who went with Charles G. Gunter to the valley of the Rio Doce to the north of Rio de Janeiro, were quickly disillusioned.[5] Among the difficulties leading to the collapse of these formal colonies were unsuitable soils, excessive rainfall, rough terrain, limited access to transportation facilities, diseases, and conflict among leaders.

By 1870 almost all of the people who had gone to Brazil had either returned to the United States or relocated to what became the most viable agglomeration of Americans in Brazil. The group was made up of families who were drawn to the vicinity of the town of Santa Bárbara, fifty-four kilometers beyond Campinas in the interior of the state of São Paulo. They gathered near the property of Col. William H. Norris, who in 1866 had purchased a portion of the Machadinho *fazenda* fronting on the Quilombo stream.[6]

Though it never included more than 100 families, the group had a very significant impact on Brazilian society. As described elsewhere in this volume, the Americans from Santa Bárbara shaped elements of Brazilian agriculture, religion, and education in important ways, and the effects have persisted well into the twentieth century.

The community also proved to be remarkably durable. The European immigrants, who arrived in far greater numbers during the late nineteenth century, usually adopted, within one or two generations, most of the Brazilian cultural traits. The Americans, however, remained separate. For decades they influenced the surrounding society while preserving a way of life that was completely different.

The persistence of the cultural traits of the Americans can be attributed to many factors. First, their rural-agricultural occupations and the location of reasonably priced farm land that was available for purchase carried the Americans to a sparsely populated area. Few contacts were made with those outside of the community.[7]

Second, much of Brazilian farm technology was less efficient than that of the Americans. The Americans' plows, wagons, seeds, tools, and ability to handle animals were superior, and their fields were more productive. The Americans and their descendants were often contracted by *fazenda* owners to manage estates and to teach farming methods.[8] The Americans did not readily adopt practices from a culture that some perceived to be deficient and less developed.

Third, the Americans actively communicated with friends and relatives in the United States. The correspondence conveyed information about people and events back home, and the contacts constantly reinforced many of the Old South beliefs and practices. Furthermore, the letters and news clippings were tangible evidence of the importance of being able to communicate in English.

Fourth, the Americans were able to purchase moderate-size parcels of land, and they established owner-occupied family farms. In contrast, most of the European immigrants took jobs on coffee *fazendas* or in city factories, where they were placed in everyday contact with Brazilians.

Fifth, the differences between Brazilian and American institutions were greater than between Brazilian institutions and those of the Mediterranean countries that supplied most of the late nineteenth-century immigration to the state of São Paulo. A familiar religion a similar language were encountered by many of the Europeans who arrived in Brazil. Their assimilation into local society did not require as great a change in established practices as it did for the Americans.

Sixth, the purposeful nature of the American immigration and the Broad River roots shared by many of the participants probably promoted group solidarity.[9] The Americans held common political beliefs and similar motivations for relocating to Brazil.

Additional factors may have contributed to the preservation of American traits among the group at Santa Bárbara. The political climate of the era and the group's associations with members of the republican movement may have been important.[10] The process of urbanization and political consolidation in interior São Paulo may have created environments that excluded, and therefore isolated, the Americans. These and other hypotheses might serve as a basis for further investigation.

The purpose of this report is to propose an additional factor, one that may have had a more unifying and preserving effect on the American group than any of the conditions previously mentioned. Soon after the arrival of the Americans in the Santa Bárbara area, a specific site became associated with important community functions. Simply known as *Campo*, the location was at first a simple graveyard, but later it was also an interdenominational church and community center. The contention of this chapter is that *Campo* was established in response to critical community needs and that it in turn served to strengthen interfamily ties and intragroup solidarity. Significantly, none of the failed colonies possessed a similar unifying focal site.

The remainder of this chapter will examine the evolution of *Campo* through four stages:

1. The spatial pattern of the settlement as a precondition.
2. The consolidation of religious activity in the Campo population cluster.
3. The establishment of the *Campo* site and its early role as a community center.
4. The later role of *Campo* as a cultural shrine.

Settlement near Santa Bárbara

The Americans who arrived in interior São Paulo in the mid-1860s established their farms in an area that had been explored by the Portuguese *bandeirantes* (explorers) as far back as the sixteenth century. During the early decades of the nineteenth century, the land had been settled by Europeans and cultivated by their African slaves. By 1865, few Amerindians remained, much of the original forest had been cut, urban centers had been established, and the region was recovering from the collapse of an earlier sugarcane cycle.[11]

Settlement of the exiled confederates began when Col. William Norris purchased approximately 400 acres of the Machadinho *fazenda*, a plantation carved out of the Costa Machado *sesmaria* (land grant).[12] Whereas the colonization ventures in the Ribeira de Iguape River area had involved special agreements granting to the colony leaders the exclusive rights to distribute land owned by the Brazilian government, property in the Santa Bárbara area was acquired in a conventional manner. The parcels were privately purchased by the Americans from Brazilians or, sometimes, from other Americans. Consequently, the property holdings of the Americans were of different sizes and varying soil quality. The settlers purchased what was available at the time of their arrival in the area.

Most of the Americans arrived in groups during the 1866–70 period.[13] The earliest families, such as those of William Norris and Hervey Hall, acquired choice plots, but later settlers were often forced to pay more for

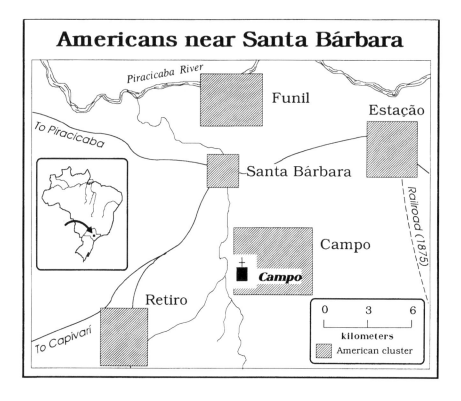

Americans near Santa Bárbara

lesser quality. By the early 1870s the coastal colonies had collapsed, and the core of the American community had arrived in the interior of São Paulo.

The Americans in the vicinity of Santa Bárbara did not settle in a single area but were scattered across approximately 400 square kilometers of what are presently the *municípios* (counties) of Santa Bárbara and Americana. A clustered residential pattern evolved because groups of people arrived at different times, and the property available to the newcomers was not usually contiguous with sites already settled by others. Individuals who arrived together or who were linked by family ties would often, but not always, settle in the vicinity of each other.

As shown above, five population clusters emerged: Estação (station), Retiro (retreat), Campo, Funil (funnel), and Santa Bárbara.[14] Except for those residing in the village of Santa Bárbara, most lived and worked on their own private farm holding, so the clusters featured a dispersed distribution of home sites. Some settlers, such as the Dumas family, whose home was midway between Santa Bárbara and Estação, were not located exactly within any of the clusters.[15] Some of the immigrants, especially single men, moved from one site to another.

The area here defined as Estação was the first to be settled. After completion of the railroad in 1875, Estação (station) was the name used to refer to the area around the depot.[16] Previously, the site had been called Fazenda do Machadinho or Bairro do Recanto, and later it was known as Estação de Santa Bárbara and Vila dos Americanos. Today, it is simply Americana. Col. William Norris and his son Robert purchased land on the Machadinho *fazenda* in 1866, but the rest of the family did not reach the area until one year later.[17] Arriving with the Norris family in 1867 were the families of son Robert and sons-in-law Willie Daniel, Edward Townsend, and Joseph Whitaker.[18] All located near William Norris's property.

By 1868 the cluster at Estação had increased substantially. Among the new arrivals was Winston Broadnax, a dentist whose parents returned to the United States after two years in Brazil.[19] Christopher Ezelle, another dentist, and Alabamians William Presteridge and Benjamin Yancey also joined the cluster.[20] Others who moved into the vicinity were the Moores, the Triggs, the Mills, the Scurlocks, the Coles, and the Carltons.[21] Around 1870 the group was increased with the arrival of the Fenleys from Florida, the Beasleys, and the Seawrights.[22] Baptist ministers Ratcliff and Thomas were prominent members of the cluster, and another resident, Michael C. Hawthorne, was an Irish national who had come with the group and was considered to be a part of the community.[23]

William Pyles, son of the Reverend Samuel M. Pyles, lived just to the north of the main Estação group, and his parents eventually moved in with him.[24] William's brothers, Ezequiel and Judson, later married into the McKnight family, and they settled at Retiro in the late 1870s.[25] Also associated with Estação were the Terrell family, who lived to the northeast at the old Salto Grande *fazenda*, and three bachelors named Anderson, Brownlow, and Provost.[26] In 1876 the Demarets, who had originally gone from Louisiana to the Ribeira de Iguape area, also moved to Salto Grande.[27]

Retiro was the second largest concentration. Sometimes called Bom Retiro, this cluster was located approximately twenty-two kilometers from Estação and twelve kilometers southwest of Santa Bárbara on the road to the city of Capivarí. Hervey Hall, who in 1866 purchased a farm already in operation, was the community's first settler.[28] The Halls were soon joined by the Weissinger brothers, the Crisps, the Cullens, the Hollands, the Steagalls, and the Perkins.[29] In 1868 several families arrived from the failed Ribeira de Iguape colonies. Among them was the family of Jesse

Wright, who would later kill Hervey Hall, and the Johnsons, the Crawleys, the McKnights, and Bony McAlpine.[30] Methodist minister Junius Newman, who had lived in Rio de Janeiro and later at the Saltinho community near the neighboring town of Limeira, moved to Retiro after his second marriage in the late 1870s.[31]

The cluster known as Campo (Campo identifies the settlement cluster, while *Campo* refers to the chapel and cemetery compound built in the Campo area) included a group of families that purchased land in the open country south of Santa Bárbara between Retiro and Estação. Though characterized as pasture land and perhaps used for grazing animals, the cleared areas most likely were the result of earlier agricultural cycles.

Col. Anthony T. Oliver bought a piece of property that was to become very significant to the Americans because on it the focal *Campo* site would evolve.[32] Others settled near Colonel Oliver. The James Miller family, referred to as the "sour" Millers to distinguish them from the Irving L. Millers who came from Charles G. Gunter's colony on the Rio Doce (*doce* means "sweet" in Portuguese), arrived in 1868.[33] The McFaddens and the Fergusons appeared one year later.[34] Other settlers who arrived in 1868 were the Orville Whitakers (different from the Joseph Whitakers at Estação) from Louisiana and the Carrs, who had also first gone to the Rio Doce.[35] Alfred I. Smith and his family, including daughter Sarah Bellona, arrived in 1870 from their homestead at the McMullan colony on the Juquiá in the Ribeira de Iguape area.[36] Baptist parson Elijah H. Quillin, also from the Juquiá, moved in approximately three years later after spending some time at Estação.[37]

Another location that received residents from the failed coastal colonies was the cluster sometimes referred to as Funil. The name was applied to a stretch of the Piracicaba River, just to the north of Santa Bárbara, where the stream narrows in the shape of a funnel. Maj. Robert Meriwether, famous for his precolonization exploration with Dr. Hugh A. Shaw, lived for a time at Funil before moving on to the city of Botucatú.[38] In 1867 Henry Strong purchased the Barrocão *fazenda*, a few kilometers to the south of the river.[39] The Strongs had also been at the Rio Doce colony, and they were accompanied by son-in-law Warren Ellis and by Irving L. Miller and Frank Bankston.[40] Others arriving in the area were William Brown, who loved but never married Sally Strong; Thomas L. Keese, who purchased the Jamaica *fazenda* to the west of Barrocão; and Col. Peter Hardeman, a relative of Keese.[41] Rev. Ballard S. Dunn, the author and orator who attracted many to his Lizzieland colony in the Ribeira de Iguape region, also lived at Funil for a time before eventually returning to the United States.[42]

A relatively small group settled in and around the town of Santa Bárbara. Included among them were John Domm, a Dutchman who had moved to Texas and who was the metalworker who helped initiate the manufacture of steel plows in Brazil, and the Tarvers, the Tanners, the Capps, and the Kennerlys.[43] The modest daub and wattle house of the Dumas family was located near Santa Bárbara, along the road to Estação.[44]

Finally, various sources mention individuals and families without a geographic reference. Among the names of people whose residential location is unknown are Beaseley, Britt, Ward, Cherrie, Currie, Harrison, Turner, White, Shippy, Pierce, Thorn, Gates, Freleigh, Mura, Blackburn, Bowen, Grady, Peacock, A. P. Smith, and Barr.

Unfortunately, the residence of Presbyterian minister William C. Emerson is also not known. He was an eloquent speaker, an important member of the community, and one of the founders of the first official church among the Americans. He lived in the Santa Bárbara area during the late 1860s and then moved to Tatuí, where he died after a few years. For one year he served as editor of the *Emigration Reporter*, a journal of events about the Americans in Brazil.[45]

By 1870, therefore, the members of the American community near Santa Bárbara had settled into the clustered pattern that was to persist for decades. Families usually occupied sites adjacent to other Americans within the same cluster, but they were separated from fellow expatriates in the other clusters by a substantial distance. Furthermore, most of the people in the general region, especially in the town of Santa Bárbara, were predominantly Brazilian, so the immigrants comprised a minority within the total population.

The Emergence of Campo

The community of Americans scattered across the area included a high percentage of farmers, but a variety of other occupations were represented. Not speaking Portuguese and accustomed to a way of life that was very different from that of the Brazilian, most in the community relied on fellow Americans for necessary professional services. Machinists, dentists, doctors, educators, and religious leaders actively pursued their occupations. Most of the families supplied many of their own necessities by producing food, shelter, and clothing.

While dentists and doctors provided services by traveling to their patients' homes, some types of activities brought members of the community together. Childhood education was one example. Though many of the young began their studies at home, not all farmers (and wives) had the skills necessary to teach beyond an elementary level. Eventually, educators from the United States were contracted, and schoolhouses were established at Estação and Retiro.[46]

Other activities that brought people together were the preaching services and religious ceremonies overseen by the local ministers. These events exerted a unifying effect on the community. Many considered religious practice to be a critical necessity, and establishing conditions that would promote a regular schedule of worship was given a high priority. Perhaps because of the contrast with the prevalent Roman Catholic rites encountered in Brazil, differences among the Protestant denominations of the Americans appear to have assumed lesser importance than had been true in the United States. Services were attended by most, regardless of the sect of the orator.

Related to the preaching services were the rites conducted to mark important life events. Baptisms, marriages, and burials brought people together, and they also required the services of a minister. These religious functions demanded an additional feature—a fixed site. The first American graves were on private property because Brazilian cemeteries were controlled by the Roman Catholic church, and Protestant burials were not permitted. Most Americans, however, believed that proper funerals should be conducted at a cemetery and that religious worship should occur in a church. During the decade following the first arrivals in the Santa Bárbara area, the American community was impelled to create a specific site that would meet these needs. It was to become a focal center for the people scattered in the separate clusters, and it served purposes beyond those for which it was initially designed.

The evolution of a community religious center was due to the occurrence of certain specific activities that took place at a centralized location. At first, *Campo* was on a one-hectare square parcel of land set aside on the property of Colonel Oliver in the Campo cluster south of Santa Bárbara. On a hill overlooking the Toledo Creek, the site had been selected as the final resting place for Mrs. Oliver, who had died soon after arriving in Brazil. Because of the exclusion of Protestants from the local cemeteries, Colonel Oliver allowed others from the community to be buried nearby, and the American cemetery was thus begun. In time, some of the bodies interred elsewhere, such as William Norris's daughter Nancy Angeline Daniel, were transferred to the cemetery on the Oliver land.[47]

The events that led to the centralization of religious worship at *Campo* were not as specific. The earliest church meetings among the Americans appear, in fact, to have been held at Estação, where Baptist ministers Robert P. Thomas and Richard Ratcliff resided. Ratcliff presided over services in 1869 at the homes of John Cole and Joseph Moore.[48] Years later, a wooden structure was built on Moore's land, and it became an alternate place of worship as well as a schoolhouse.[49]

The Presbyterians were the first to establish a formal congregation. In June 1870, in the home of William McFadden, who was a resident of the Campo cluster, the Hopewell Church was constituted, with thirteen new members in attendance.[50] The church was placed under the direction of Rev. James R. Baird, who also resided in the Campo community. Rev. William C. Emerson preached as often as his health permitted, but around this time he moved away from the Santa Bárbara area.[51]

When the Methodist church began in 1871, it was also in the Campo area. At the time, Rev. Junius Newman lived at Saltinho, but in the tradition of the American Methodist circuit riders, he regularly visited and ministered to the communities around Santa Bárbara. The first meeting place was a "room of about 14 square feet with a dirt floor and constructed of mud. The same room had served as a store where alcoholic drinks were sold."[52] Sarah Bellona Smith identified the site as being on the road between Santa Bárbara and Campo.[53] Sometimes men would clear a meeting area under the trees, and Newman would hold all-day gatherings that included preaching, hymn singing, and a meal of food prepared the day before.[54] The Methodist church was established at one of these events in 1871, and Newman was designated as the pastor. The preserved early attendance rolls included forty-five family names representing the community clusters of Estação, Retiro, Funil, and Campo. The record identified the location of the meeting as *Campo*.[55] The Methodists continued to meet regularly, and in 1875 the congregation numbered around thirty members.[56]

The Baptist church was also officially begun around 1871. Preaching services at Estação had been initiated earlier, but by the mid-1870s the location of regular meetings, as occurred for Methodists and Presbyterians, had shifted to *Campo*. The reason for the move is not evident, for Baptist ministers Ratcliff, Thomas, and perhaps Quillin resided near the Norris cluster at Estação. Rev. Samuel Pyles was also a Baptist minister who lived northwest of Estação with his son William, but he apparently settled there later than 1871.[57] There is no doubt that *Campo* was the primary Baptist religious site by the late 1870s. When the *Campo* chapel was finally erected in 1878, it was said to be used by all three denominations.[58] Furthermore, a baptismal depression was dug in the Toledo Creek behind the church, which would have been necessary only for the Baptists.[59]

The occurrence of various events, therefore, led to the evolution of *Campo* as the religious center for the community. Official records list the Campo area as the founding site for two denominations, and the third may have started there as well. The use of the cemetery on Colonel Oliver's land was an important attractant, but it was not the only factor. Burials on private property elsewhere, including the Norris farm, had taken place. Campo was also the location of the former *venda* (store or bar), mentioned by Sarah Bellona Smith and Junius Newman's daughter, where he began conducting religious services. Little information about the physical structure is available, and its selection by Newman may have been due to chance. It was, however, definitely located in the Campo area.[60]

Finally, some evidence suggests that the families who settled in the Campo cluster may have placed greater value on religious tradition than those who lived elsewhere. The Presbyterians organized in the McFadden home in the Campo area, and he became an elder in the Hopewell Church.[61] Alfred I. Smith, also a Campo resident, hosted the first Methodist conference in an orange grove, and he was the church song leader. Colonel Oliver, on whose property the chapel was later constructed, was said never to miss services, and he was dressed for church on Sunday morning in 1873 when he was murdered by an intruder.[62]

The residents at the Campo cluster may have been more pious than those living at Retiro, where the first and leading settler, Hervey Hall, never attended church.[63] Family names tied to Retiro were identified with *pinga* (rum) manufacture, and some were expelled from the church for drunkenness.[64] No references to such activity or expulsions have been found for members of the Campo community.

Several specific, sufficient conditions thus combined to produce a religious center at *Campo*. The use of the Oliver property for burial and the already-established patterns of religious activity were the most important. But a more general, and necessary, precondition existed: *Campo* was strategically located with respect to the American community scattered across the landscape in the various clusters around Santa Bárbara.

Community Unifier

The twenty-two kilometers that separated the immigrant clusters of Retiro and Estação may seem a short distance if traveled by automobile, but in the nineteenth century a full day's journey was needed for the round trip. Any meeting place that was to serve the total population of Americans would best be established at a location accessible to all clusters.

The Santa Bárbara village might have provided a central location, but few American families lived in the town itself. Furthermore, most of the Americans were farmers accustomed to all-day meetings with dinner on the grounds, so the rural Campo region was more favorable than the urban Santa Bárbara. The completion of the railroad in 1875 brought a population boom to Estação, and its character also became more urban. During the 1870s the Americans in the growing villages of Santa Bárbara and Estação were a minority within the Brazilian majority, but the Campo area was theirs almost exclusively.

In 1878, over a decade after the first Americans moved to the region, the chapel at *Campo* was finally constructed. As Jones reports:

> An old dream is realized. For some time the trees had been cut and the wood prepared for their church. Anyone who had a skill worked on her. . . . The new church was so plain! All made of boards, so rustic, and not painted. The roof was of wood tied to the frame. There were several steps out front and two small rooms, one to keep the belongings of the church and the other for the ladies to change out of their riding skirts and take care of small children. The meeting room was of good size, and on one side sat the men while on the other were the women. It was so ridiculous when a man sat on the wrong side.[65]

The dream that had finally been realized was an old one. The first collection of money to support the construction had been taken in 1870, eight years earlier.[66]

Built by the community and used by three Protestant denominations, the chapel belonged to everybody. When Colonel Oliver died in 1873, James Miller bought the property, and the land continued in the hands of Miller's descendants, Leroy, Anna, and Mary Bookwalter until 1954.[67] Though the *Campo* chapel and cemetery remained on privately owned land during this period, the family kept it available for all to use. The one-hectare compound that included the cemetery and chapel was deeded to the Fraternity of American Descendancy in 1954, and since then families of deceased descendants have continued to seek burial for their loved ones.

Regular church services continued at *Campo* during the decades of the 1880s and 1890s. With the passage of time, however, Junius Newman returned to the United States, Parson Quillin died, and the remaining pastors became too old to lead regular meetings. By 1894 the Methodists and Presbyterians were actively founding churches and schools throughout southern

Brazil, and in that year the official records of these denominations at *Campo* came to an end.[68] For the Methodists, *Campo* became an infrequent stop on the circuit of a pastor Dickson who lived in Capivarí.[69]

Campo continued to be an important center, however, even as funerals and church services became less frequent. The role of *Campo* was broader. In addition to being a religious site, it was the community's social center. In the southern United States in the nineteenth century people regularly came together primarily in churches, whose meetings were especially significant to rural populations. The *Campo* church, with its Southern roots, was even more important in Brazil because of the limited interaction and lack of commonality with the Brazilian neighbors. Sunday meetings were more than worship services; they were times for joint meals, fellowship for all ages, catching up on news and gossip, exchanging information about work, and meeting or being met by new members of the community.[70]

During the first decades, most of the Americans' friendships and romances were forged within the group itself. "When a meeting occurred at Campo, everybody got together, the boys from Retiro would be transfixed as they watched those strange young ladies, their faces peppered with freckles and such beautiful pigtails the color of copper."[71]

The majority of the original immigrants spoke only English, and almost all of the early courtships and marriages occurred between Americans. A compilation of first-generation marriages as listed in the genealogy tables of the major families indicates that only 17 percent of the unions were with people outside the American community, and intercluster marriages were common (see table 8.1).[72] Many of these relationships must have been initiated and nurtured at *Campo.*

Campo was also the site where the community's identity was preserved. Here, English was spoken, American-style clothing was worn, Southern fried chicken was shared, and Protestant hymns were sung. Outside of the home, *Campo* was the site where children and youth were most strongly exposed to the culture imported by their parents and grandparents. *Campo* was the only institutional center where people of all ages and from all clusters came together on a regular basis. Other centers such as the schoolhouses at Retiro and Estação or the Masonic Lodge were limited to subgroups within the total population.

The persistence of activity at *Campo* long after the passage of its role as a burial ground and religious center suggests a broader reason for its existence. Cemeteries in Brazil were opened to non-Catholics in the early 1870s, yet the Americans continued to use *Campo.* In 1921 it was given legal status by the Município of Santa Bárbara when the American group voted

A Community Center

Table 8.1
Marriages Involving First-Generation Americans
in the Clusters near Santa Bárbara

Nationality and Home Cluster of One of the Marriage Partners	Home Cluster of the Other Marriage Partner				
	Estação	Retiro	Campo	Santa Bárbara/ Funil	TOTAL
American, from:					
Estação	14	5	5	5	29
Retiro	5	4	8	3	20
Campo	5	8	2	3	18
Santa Bárbara/Funil	5	3	3	4	15
(residence unknown)	9	7	8	6	30
Brazilian	5	9	0	9	23
TOTAL	43	36	26	30	135

Source: Jones, Soldado descansa, 235–40, 273–80, 313–15.

to upgrade the facilities, and at that time several bodies were exhumed from private plots for reburial within the compound.[73]

Though church services were held only sporadically after the 1890s, the grounds and chapel were continually maintained and improved. The building was refurbished in 1893, and the first brick chapel was constructed in 1903.[74] The present structure was raised in 1962.[75]

Cultural Shrine

At present, *Campo* is a tree-shaded one-square-hectare compound separated from the surrounding cane fields by a low wall. The enclosure includes three buildings. A covered patio is located near the entrance, and off to the side stands the modest house of a caretaker family. The small brick chapel dominates the center of the compound, and the cemetery stretches over the back portion of the grounds. The sidewalk leading up to the church entrance is flanked by an obelisk-shaped monument that is decorated with the stars and bars of the Confederate battle flag. The monument features the engraved names of the families who moved to the Santa Bárbara area in the 1860s.

The cemetery contains the remains of many of the original settlers and their descendants. Gravestones are inscribed with references to the old

Interdenominational Church at the Campo Compound Near Santa Bárbara (*Photograph by William C. Griggs*)

country Confederacy and comments about their new home in Brazil. The
sign of the Masonic Lodge, to which several Americans belonged, is prominently displayed on some of the markers.

The Fraternity of American Descendancy was established in 1954, and
ownership of the compound was passed to the fraternity by the Bookwalter
family.[76] The organization oversees the maintenance of *Campo* and sched-
ules quarterly and yearly reunions that draw descendants from across Brazil.
These gatherings harken back to the old days by featuring dinner on the
grounds and nineteenth-century America-style clothing. Most participants
speak in Portuguese, but many of the older generation still use English.
Pageantry abounds, some of the youth dress as Confederate soldiers and
ladies, and the conversations are laced with stories of the past. The festivities conclude with a church service that according to the fraternity bylaws,
must be held in a religion of the original founders, and the hymn "There
Is a Happy Land" is sung in unison by all.[77]

Campo, still a community unifier, now plays a new role. The site origi-
nated as a stopgap solution to the immediate necessity of burying the dead,
and over the years it became a social and religious community center for

A Community Center

the scattered families near Santa Bárbara. During the early years it was a site of ceremony and pleasant fellowship. It provided a familiar setting in a foreign land, as if a small bit of Alabama territory had been transported to São Paulo. It was neutral ground where intracolony political or religious differences were put aside. At *Campo* the individuals in the group again became one colony of displaced Americans far from their native soil. *Campo* developed in the location that was most accessible to all of the settlers in the clusters scattered around Santa Bárbara.

Today, the role of *Campo* is different. It is now, in many respects, a shrine to the memory of the adventurers who left their defeated state and created a new home in Brazil. As with other shrines, it has no other function. Though a blood descendant can still petition for burial in the cemetery, funerals are rare. Regular church services are no longer held, and most descendants live elsewhere.

During recent years *Campo* has become hallowed ground. There the heritage is nurtured, and the descending generations are instructed in its importance. The displayed artifacts and symbols recall that heritage. The battle flag and uniform of the Confederacy have quite a different meaning from their significance in the United States. The symbols are not strongly associated with the battles of the Civil War, nineteenth-century political controversies, a slave-based economy, or contemporary racial discrimination. To the American descendants born in Brazil, the signs of the Old South evoke memories of founding origin more akin to North American recollections of the arrival of early European pilgrims. Similarly, the gravestones in the cemetery recall the heroes of the early years and provide stark evidence of the hardships they faced.

Campo is a shrine with special meaning only to the descendants. Though reunions are sometimes reported in the local or national press, the behavior of the descendants is viewed with no more than mild interest. *Campo* is not marked on maps, and it can be reached only by traveling over a pitted narrow dirt road through the cane fields. No signs show the way, and few local residents can provide directions.

In summary, *Campo* is a present feature on the landscape that has no importance other than to serve as a repository for the shared symbols that identify the American descendants as a distinct group within the larger Brazilian culture. It is at the site, on the occasion of the quarterly and yearly reunions, that the articles and traditions that identify the group are reviewed and renewed. Located on private property until 1954 and on community land since, it has always functioned as common ground not linked to any specific faction within the group.

The periodic gatherings, first out of necessity but later for pleasure, were a mechanism for preserving the common culture. Though English as a first language will disappear with the passage of the current generation, other traits are being continued because of the periodic reunions. The old stories of valor, the physical artifacts, the Southern recipes, the festival traditions, and the religious practices are recalled and passed on to the next generation. Of the many settlements started in Brazil by the Americans, only the clusters around Santa Bárbara had a separate site for maintaining the cultural heritage. And only there have the Americans remained connected to their history.

The current state of good maintenance and attractiveness of the *Campo* site and the well-attended reunions indicate that the heritage is being preserved. A museum celebrating the early Americans in Brazil has recently been opened in downtown Santa Bárbara, but the soul of the group remains out at the chapel and cemetery. Were Mark Jefferson alive and able to visit interior São Paulo in 1995, he would be surprised to see that the descendants of the old Confederates still cherish their heritage and maintain some elements of their original culture. Its future survival may be questioned, but traces of the Old American South have persisted in Brazil far longer than he would have guessed possible.

Nine

Constructing Identity
Defining the American Descendants in Brazil

John C. Dawsey

At the time that Judith MacKnight Jones was writing *Soldado descansa!* (Soldier rest!) in the 1960s, designs of the Confederate flag could be found on ceramic pieces produced by Indians on the Island of Marajó in the Amazon basin, a discovery that suggested a twentieth-century vestige of Confederate exiles in the Hastings colony.[1] Marajoara Indians are not the only people who preserved Confederate symbols in Brazil. William Griggs mentioned Harold Barnsley Holland, a respected manufacturer in Jacareí, who kept a set of instructions for making a Confederate battle flag in an old family trunk.[2] More intriguing might be the sight of 200 or more people gathering at an old cemetery in the interior of the state of São Paulo, Brazil, where three flags are raised—the Southern Cross, the Stars and Stripes, and the Confederate battle flag.[3]

Toward the end of the Civil War various efforts were made, with encouragement of the Brazilian emperor, to organize Confederate colonies in Brazil. As a result, nine different settlements were established. The settlement in Santa Bárbara, in the state of São Paulo, survived, even prospered, then largely dispersed during the early twentieth century. Until this day, descendants meet four times a year on the church grounds next to the *Campo* cemetery.

Identity Construction

Much of the literature relating to the persistence of the Confederate or American heritage in Brazil seems to be based on the notion of passivity, of a cultural tradition adapting to new sociophysical environments and perpetuating itself as best it can in the face of the new obstacles which are encountered. As time goes by, the old culture proves to be increasingly irrelevant. Things such as raising the Rebel flag, making biscuits, dressing in Confederate uniforms, parading in *Gone with the Wind* dresses, and meeting at the old cemetery serve no real purpose. They constitute cultural "survivals" which should not really have survived. Even in the United States, the sight of a few hundred people appearing to relive the Confederacy might lead some to raise doubts concerning the mental health of the group. *Don't they realize that the Civil War ended more than a century ago?*

The preservation of American symbols also raises questions. *If they want to be American, why don't they pack up and move to the States? Isn't that what many of their Brazilian neighbors are doing?* This group of descendants would make things easier to explain, according to some, if, during their reunions and celebrations, they used only American symbols. *After all, doesn't everybody want to be American?* Maybe not, for, to complicate the matter, some descendants are likely to make emphatic statements such as, "I'm a Southerner, I'm Brazilian, I'm not American!"

The temptation is to say that these people have an identity problem. *Why do they go to so much effort to preserve relics of Confederate or American culture? They obviously have not adapted to their Brazilian environment. They are living in the past.*[4]

There is another aspect to this. Not only is one tempted to question the validity of holding on to relics, but one is enticed by the idea that all of this is just pretense. Many of the descendants are Catholic, many have Italian or Syrian names, and many no longer speak English.

Recently the Fraternidade Descendencia Americana (Fraternity of American Descendancy) promoted a celebration at Santa Bárbara in which young couples danced according to Old South styles. The couples seemed to be relieved when the presentation was over and the *lambada* (contemporary Brazilian dance) music got under way. Indeed, the Old South dances had not even been taught to the youth by their parents. Researchers from Campinas had assisted the group.

Likewise, the *Gone with the Wind* outfits worn once a year were not handed down from one generation to the next, nor were the patterns for making them. Researchers assisted. An outside observer has the impression that much, if not all, has to do with theater.[5]

"Under Erasure"

In trying to deal with the identity of these descendants, one gets the feeling of walking on slippery ground. Are they "Confederate" descendants or "American" descendants? Do they descend from an American or from a Confederate colony? Did their ancestors, or did they themselves, attend Confederate or American schools in Brazil? Even those who emphasize that they are Southern and Brazilian, but not American, are oftentimes stalwart members of the Fraternidade Descendencia Americana.

Other terms have an unclear meaning. Were those people who left the United States and went to Brazil after the Civil War "exiles" or "immigrants"? Were they "self-imposed exiles," or were they "American pioneers"? Given the heterogeneity of the group, in what sense could they be called Confederate or Southern? Considering that a number of them had only recently arrived in the United States from Europe, before leaving for Brazil, should they even be called American?[6]

The first problem one must deal with, then, is what to call these descendants and their ancestors. As a way of approaching problems pertaining to the instability of language, Derrida developed the idea of *sous rature*. Sarup described Derrida's use of the phrase by stating that *sous rature* is: "a term usually translated as 'under erasure'. To put a term '*sous rature*' is to write a word, cross it out, and then print both word and deletion. The idea is this: since the word is inaccurate, or rather, inadequate, it is crossed out. Since it is necessary it remains legible. This strategically important device which Derrida uses derives from Martin Heidegger, who often crossed out the word Being (like this: B̶e̶i̶n̶g̶) and let both deletion and word stand because the word was *inadequate yet necessary*."[7] Sarup elaborated: "In other words, Derrida argues that meaning is not immediately present in a sign. Since the meaning of a sign is a matter of what the sign is *not*, this meaning is always in some sense absent from it too. Meaning is scattered or dispersed along the whole chain of signifiers; it cannot be easily nailed down, it is never fully present in any one sign alone, but is rather a kind of constant flickering of presence and absence together."[8]

Likewise, the identity of the people whom I have chosen to write about is difficult to nail down. Instead of speaking simply of Confederate or American descendants, I will occasionally make use of Derrida's and Heidegger's device and cross out the words. In these cases, I will let both words and deletions stand because these words are inadequate yet necessary (like this: C̶o̶n̶f̶e̶d̶e̶r̶a̶t̶e̶, A̶m̶e̶r̶i̶c̶a̶n̶). The similarity between the crossed bars of the deletion and the bars of the Confederate flag is mere coincidence.

This might suggest that indeed these descendants have an identity problem. However, I believe that the problem itself is an illusion. We are the ones who, having entered into the business of dealing with categories, have a problem regarding how to view the construction of identities. Putting it simply, just like being Italian during a Columbus Day parade in the United States is a way of being American, so also being American or Confederate at the *Campo* cemetery in Brazil is a way of being Brazilian.

Old Trunks

Research conducted by Carneiro da Cunha concerning the Brazilian community of Lagos, Nigeria, gives us another perspective regarding construction of ethnic identity.[9] This community was formed during the nineteenth century by Yoruba descendants who, having been freed from slavery, returned to the African homeland. What is particularly interesting about this group is that, once in Africa, instead of returning to the ancestral areas and adopting home-grown religions, they stayed in Lagos, converted or strengthened their ties to Roman Catholicism, and made efforts to maintain the Portuguese language and other Brazilian cultural traits. Why?

Developing some of the presuppositions worked out by Abner Cohen, Carneiro da Cunha argued that Brazilian (and Catholic) traits were used as diacritical signs, that is, as signs which differentiated the group from others in Lagos and in Nigeria.[10] This in turn was tied to the group's effort to control trade between Lagos and Brazil.

According to this line of thought, ethnic groups are viewed as forms of organization adapted to their immediate environment. They share an identity; they also share economic and political interests. They organize themselves into larger groups and vie for resources with other rival groups.

Following these presuppositions, a cultural tradition is not to be viewed as something which determines behaviors so much as a reservoir of traits which can be used selectively according to context. It is like Harold Barnsley Holland's old trunk, where one might go to find cultural elements. The trunk may include instructions for making a Confederate battle flag, which can then function mainly as diacritical symbols of ethnic identification.[11]

When viewed in this way, the original culture of the group will tend to acquire a certain rigidity, reducing itself to a number of traits which will mainly be used to differentiate the group from other groups.

Objectives

I intend to indicate in this essay, on the basis of secondary sources, some of the ways in which this line of reasoning might be applied to the *confederados*. Regarding the sources, two books are of particular interest, both written by descendants. Each author, writing in a different context, has chosen to remember different aspects and periods of the group's history. Most interesting is how each has viewed the identity of the group.

Judith MacKnight Jones published her book, entitled *Soldado descansa! Uma epopeia norte americana sob os céus do Brasil* (Soldier rest! A North Ameri-

Constructing Identity

can saga beneath the skies of Brazil) in 1967. Most of her material relates to the years preceding World War I. It is the story of Southern Americans who over the years also became Brazilian.

Eugene C. Harter published his book, *The Lost Colony of the Confederacy: The North-American Immigration to Brazil Following the War of Secession*, in 1985. He drew extensively on family memories and other sources relating to the late 1920s and early 1930s. His story is about how an early generation of Americans was followed by a second generation of Confederate Brazilians, or *confederados*.

Relying on materials from these and other sources, I will sketch two ways of the many possibilities by which the descendants have constructed their identity, particularly during the periods mentioned above.

American Farmers

Most of the people who left the South and other areas of the United States to go to Brazil were farmers. In encouraging the emigration, the Brazilian Empire was interested in accomplishing two things: "purifying the Brazilian race" and introducing "progressive agricultural techniques," particularly for cotton production. The continued presence of slavery in Brazil may have also attracted Southern farmers more than other professions.

Indeed, in keeping with expectations of the Brazilian government, the Americans who settled the Santa Bárbara and Americana area achieved early successes as farmers, mainly because of the moldboard plow which they carried with them. The agricultural implements and techniques used by these settlers gave them distinction. According to Goldman: "There is no doubt that, given the heterogeneity of the group which came to Brazil, there would be isolated professions and occupations. However, what united the North-Americans and gave them status (at a time when this was still possible in agriculture), providing them also with the opportunity to contribute to the progress of their new land with their knowledge and techniques, undoubtedly, was agriculture."[12] By the end of the century, members of the group would distinguish themselves not only as farmers but also as schoolteachers, engineers, doctors, and dentists.

They became identified as Americans. According to Harter, representatives of the Southern Colonization Society who came to Brazil in 1865, under the leadership of General Wood, were enthusiastically greeted by cheers, "Long live the Confederados!"[13] However, by the end of the century, those who settled in the Santa Bárbara area would be called, not Confederates or *confederados*, but Americans.

The moldboard plow, the basic technological implement of the Southerners, became known as the American plow (*arado americano*). Various schools which were associated with this group became officially called American schools. Those who became dentists were known as American dentists.[14] The railroad station, which was of vital interest to the farmers, grew into a town, and in 1900 this town was officially baptized "Americana."

In many respects, this development is surprising because the group called themselves Southern and Confederate. Harter pointed out the close ties between Col. William Hutchinson Norris, the first settler and leader of the community, and Sen. William Lowndes Yancey, "the voice of secession." Two of Yancey's sons were members of the group, and speeches of their father were recited by memory on commemorative occasions.[15] Jones wrote that Colonel Norris's son Robert, who fought under Stonewall Jackson, refused to swear allegiance to the American flag after the Civil War, saying, "I'll give my allegiance only to the flag of the South!"[16] DeMuzio presented a similar version regarding the colonel himself: "At the close of the [Civil] War, Colonel Norris was ordered to take the oath of loyalty to the Yankee government. He replied in the strongest possible terms, telling the Yankees what to do with their oath and their flag. It was shortly after this, and mainly because of this, that the Colonel and his companions decided to leave for Brazil."[17] Many children were given names of Confederate generals, particularly those of Robert E. Lee and Wade Hampton.[18] The name Yancey was also very popular.[19] Much of the press in the United States criticized those who went to Brazil for being unpatriotic and un-American. Even General Lee counseled Southerners to remain in the United States. During the 1890s, abruptly getting up from the dinner table, Dr. Robert Norris is said to have told a Yankee, "I'm not an American anymore!"[20]

It might be argued that the "American" identity, rather than being constructed by the group itself, was conferred on the group by outsiders. Indeed, Jones asserted that "they were called Americans."[21] Harter pointed out that the people who began referring to the town that developed around the station by the name of Americana were not the settlers themselves but were their neighbors. Up to the twentieth century, the settlers themselves continued to call the place simply the Station. Nonetheless, Harter also noted that, although Brazilian authorities arbitrarily baptized the city Americana, the *confederados* (Harter's term) did not oppose this choice.[22]

Yet, some of the evidence appears to be contradictory. Tellingly, Harter claimed that "first-generation Confederates like Colonel Norris continued to consider themselves Americans. They were from the C.S.A. not the U.S.A.; but still they were Americans, linked firmly to George Washington, Thomas Jefferson, James Madison, and the colonial heritage. The Fourth of July holiday was the major event of the year."[23] The Masonic lodge which Colonel Norris and other settlers founded was named after a general—not Robert E. Lee or Wade Hampton, but George Washington.

These accounts and others suggest that the settlers were engaged in a process of manipulating, or selectively using, elements of their heritage. Were they de-emphasizing Confederate traits and emphasizing American ones, at least in their relations with outsiders? If so, for what reason?

Republicans

The emigration of Protestant Southerners from America had been sponsored by the Brazilian emperor himself, Dom Pedro II, the Roman Catholic grandson of a Portuguese king. Although the Brazilian Empire maintained official neutrality during the American Civil War, sentiment in Brazil was mainly pro-South. Like the Old South, Brazil was an agricultural economy founded on slave labor. If many Confederate Americans hoped to be able to maintain Southern lifestyles in Brazil, Dom Pedro II hoped that Brazil could take over the international role of the Old South as the major cotton supplier to Britain. Early reports by members of colonizing societies stressed similarities between Brazilian and Southern ways, building a Brazilian identity consisting of such values as generosity, grace, and honor.[24]

However, political conditions were changing. The Republican party was formed in the 1870s, and the abolitionist faction was growing. Both movements were intent on distinguishing themselves from the old Brazil.

The Roman Catholic church, guardian of the official religion of the Brazilian Empire, controlled schools and cemeteries. Many of the important leaders of the Republican party, such as Prudente de Moraes Barros, his brother Manoel, and Luiz de Queiroz, lived in the city of Piracicaba, thirty miles from Santa Bárbara. In order to emphasize their opposition to state religion, the Republicans of Piracicaba had also founded a Masonic lodge.

The Santa Bárbara settlers ran into difficulties with the Roman Catholic church. Cemeteries were Catholic, and so were the schools. The settlers had trouble finding ways to bury their dead and educate their children. The Republican party of Piracicaba took up their cause. Why?

Sign Warfare

The Republicans communicated their opposition to the power structure in key ways. They were involved in sign warfare. North American culture served as a source of key cultural elements. The Brazilian Empire itself had encouraged the emigration of Americans. America was identified with "progress."[25] The Republicans used the American identity for their own purpose, to mark their opposition.

The Brazilian Empire fostered Roman Catholic schools; Republicans promoted Protestant schools. The empire was based on the technology of the hoe or of the old-fashioned plow; Republicans promoted the "American plow." The Brazilian Empire was Roman Catholic; Republicans defended separation between church and state and supported Protestant interests. The empire was governed by the grandson of a Portuguese monarch; Republicans defended principles of the American Constitution. Republicans were opposed to the Brazilian Empire; Americans had successfully confronted the British Empire.

By supporting Santa Bárbara settlers who were being harassed by the Roman Catholic church, the Republicans dramatized their support of "progress." They showed how the Roman Catholic Brazilian Empire was impeding development of new forces of progress. The Fazenda Modelo, owned by the Republican leader Luiz de Queiroz and administered by Lee Ferguson, one of the Americans, was meant to be a model, as its name points out, for farmers throughout the state. It served purposes of political drama.

Santa Bárbara settlers and leaders of the Republican party in Piracicaba became allies. The symbolic efficacy of this alliance, however, depended on one important condition: that these settlers be seen, not as Old South supporters of slavery and Yancey-style opponents of industry, but as progressive Americans.

Prudente de Moraes Barros, his brother Manoel, and other Republicans allied themselves with Santa Bárbara settlers and helped establish American schools. One of the first students of the Methodist school in Piracicaba, the Colégio Piracicabano, was Pedro de Moraes Barros, son of Manoel and nephew of Prudente. Years later, during school commemorations, Pedro honored the memory of Martha Watts, the Methodist missionary from Kentucky who helped found the school. He said: "[She] came from the land of Jefferson, the philosopher of American democracy, from the land of freedom of worship, of separation between church and state, of secularization of cemeteries, from a nation where, more than sixteen years before, slavery had been abolished. She came to the only existing monarchy in the three

Americas . . . where his Majesty Pedro II was protector of and protected by the Catholic religion, which was the religion of the State."[26] The Colégio Piracicabano, which Harter calls a Confederate School, was being publicly identified not with the Confederate South, which had fought to preserve slavery, but with America, which, in contrast to the Brazilian Empire, had abolished slavery.

Abolition

In his analysis of the so-called failure of the Hastings colony near Santarém, in Amazonia, Vianna Moog suggested that the colonists would have succeeded had they been Yankees rather than Southerners.[27] Darcy Ribeiro, a Brazilian anthropologist, once stated that Brazil is what the United States would have become had the South won the Civil War. In the battle of signs, the inverse of Brazil was not the South but America and the Yankee.

An alliance between progressive Republicans and Confederate settlers may certainly point to the need to explicate what is being meant by "progressive" in Brazil. Indeed, the term may have served Republicans primarily as a diacritical sign of their own.[28] In any case, one would expect some crossed signals. According to Harter, when a pro-abolitionist senator was killed in 1888, Santa Bárbara settlers were the first suspects.[29] Nonetheless, they were allies of Republicans, some of whom were proponents of abolition.[30] According to Jones, Abolition Day in Brazil (May 13, 1889) went by almost unnoticed by Santa Bárbara settlers.[31] Siqueira Costa wrote: "Paradoxically, they preserved a mythic project involving privileges such as those associated with Southern plantations, therefore attributing high value to institutions of slavery. At the same time, compelled by real necessities presented by the new environment, they acted through their institutions in such manner as to perpetuate liberty, individuality and democracy, forthrightly supporting the Republic when it was proclaimed."[32] They had good reasons to support the Republic.

Rewards

Upon arrival in the Santa Bárbara area, the first settlers called attention to themselves by their successful use of the moldboard plow. Skillfully applying the tool, these farmers distinguished themselves from other groups in Brazilian society. The "American plow" was compared advantageously to the "Brazilian plow," as well as to the "heavier European plow," such as the one brought over by Lithuanians. Not only did the moldboard plow give these settlers an advantage of increased production, it opened up other opportunities for income.

The first American plows in the Santa Bárbara area were made by John Domm, a Dutchman who had lived in Texas.[33] Companies for importing plows from the United States were started by people who belonged to or were closely associated with the Confederate Americans.[34]

Colonel Norris supplemented his income by giving plowing lessons to other farmers in the state of São Paulo.[35] Santa Bárbara settlers acquired a reputation as agricultural experts, and many were hired as farm administrators on large Brazilian *fazendas*. As in the case of Lee Ferguson, who was hired by Luiz de Queiroz to administer the Fazenda Modelo, support given by Brazilian Republican elites had much to do with the job opportunities that became available for the Americans.[36]

Dr. Carlos Botelho, secretary of agriculture under a Republican administration, gave incentives for farmers to use the American plow. Botelho "required farmers to come to Americana to learn the new methods of working the land, which involved, of course, using plows which were made there. He arranged for sons of Americans to give demonstrations for using plows in various areas of the State [of São Paulo]. . . . The reputation of the plows and methods employed by Americans was so widespread that many important people visiting the state went to Vila Americana to see firsthand."[37]

In 1915 one of the American settlers, Cicero Jones, wrote: "[The Americans] introduced the plow for the first time in Brazil . . . which enabled them to buy lands and reclaim them that were lost to the Brazilian except for grazing purposes. At present the [Republican] Federal Government has twenty of our American boys teaching plowing, one in each state."[38]

During the period known as the First Republic (1890–1929), the federal government hired American descendants to direct topographical research and other operations related to the Works against Droughts (*Obras contra as secas*) program in the northeast of Brazil. According to Jones, many of the American descendants became involved with this program.[39] Apparently, the descendants were able to control key positions. When William Lane died, Robert Miller took his place as director of the topographic research.[40] David McKnight was also hired by the state of São Paulo as topographer, and he developed what would become one of the main state highway projects, the Via Anhanguera.[41]

During the Republican period, special incentives were given to American schools. The Colégio Piracicabano practically started in the dining room of Republican leader Manoel de Moraes Barros. In 1883, with Republican support, work began on the two-story school building, which was constructed according to principles of North American architecture. The first student, Maria Escobar, was the daughter of the liberal journalist Antonio Gomes de Escobar, whose newspapers maintained an ongoing battle with the Roman Catholic church. "These schools provided employment opportunities for descendants. In 1898, after a vacation period in the United States, Martha Watts returned with orders to start the school in Petrópolis, and Leonora Smith, daughter of T. D. Smith, assumed the direction of the *Colégio Piracicabano*. The following year, Miss Smith was sent to Ribeirão Prêto to start another school, the *Colégio Metodista*."[42] According to Jones, teaching became a "board of salvation" for many women among descendants.[43]

"Southern Aristocracy"

If it made sense to ally themselves with Republicans and emphasize their American heritage, then why did the descendants hold on to elements of Confederate and Southern culture? Traits linked to such notions as Southern hospitality, generosity, and honor may certainly have been adaptive in Brazil. The question one raises, however, is Why did they continue to identify this honor and hospitality as particularly Southern or Confederate? Why did they still display the Confederate flag on occasion and recite the speeches of Senator Yancey, "the voice of secession"? Goldman wrote: "It is believed that the immigrants constituted a Southern 'aristocracy.' . . . [But] evidences demonstrate an extremely heterogeneous group. . . . There were many northerners, as well as foreign residents in the United Sates and naturalized Americans."[44] According to Bellona Smith Ferguson, the first trolleys in Brazil were made by a Yankee by the name of Sampson.[45] Griggs mentioned "fellow Texan" John Domm, who made many of the early plows used in Santa Bárbara.[46] Domm was in fact a Dutchman who came to Brazil with the Southerners,[47] and Niels Nielsen, who became a part of the American community and also made plows, was Danish. Franz Muller, sometimes called Miller,[48] was a German who became the owner of the Carioba textile mill near Americana and was often identified as an American.[49]

Horace Manley Lane was considered by some to have been a Southerner from Louisiana. Lane, who had arrived in 1858, later started a business importing plows, apparently through his close ties with the Santa Bárbara group.[50] In 1894 he became director of Mackenzie College, formerly called the American School in São Paulo. He was said to have been a close friend and frequent guest at Retiro, one of the Santa Bárbara settlements. Despite other reports, Lane was from Readfield, Maine, not Louisiana.[51]

The picture is complex. This is a heterogeneous group which is being identified as American as well as being a "Southern aristocracy." As already seen, they had good reasons to present themselves as Americans. Were there advantages to presenting themselves as a "Southern aristocracy" as well? Perhaps. Confederate symbols were used to constitute an exclusive group in Brazil. The question I am posing is not whether they were descendants from a decadent or progressive aristocracy in the United States South. More interesting is the question of whether and why they were forming a "Southern aristocracy" in Brazil.

For the most part, the Santa Bárbara settlers worked with their families on their own land or worked for others until able to purchase their own land, like the yeomen in the United States. Properties of the American immigrants (exiles) averaged between 17 and 18 hectares. In contrast, large cotton plantations were considered to average around 95 to 121 hectares.[52] Whatever the nature of the "aristocracy" that the group was forming in Santa Bárbara, it appears to have been an aristocracy of yeomen. Their greatest status symbol was the moldboard plow and, as Jones noted, their ability to train mules.[53]

Although "they were called Americans,"[54] it was apparent that during the late nineteenth century and early twentieth century, at least, this was a close-knit group. Referring to the 1890s, at a time when they had switched from cotton to watermelon production, Jones quoted a contemporary observer: "The planters and sellers of watermellons of Villa Americana . . . form a layer apart from other planters of the neighboring district."[55] In 1899 they formed the Farmers' Club (Clube da Lavoura) in Santa Bárbara, the first in that city. All of the officials had "American" names.[56]

Perhaps the desire to control the limits of the group also explains some of their religious behavior. The chapel which was built next to the *Campo* cemetery served to unite them. "The church belonged to all: Methodist, Baptist or Presbyterian."[57] That is, it belonged to all who belonged to the group. According to one source, preachers of this period were accustomed to saying that the second coming of Christ would occur when all of Catholic Brazil became Protestant.[58] This was another way of saying that if there were any Brazilians or other immigrants thinking of becoming members of the group, most would have to wait for the second coming. Indeed, as Jones wrote: "They were neither bent toward religious proseletizing, nor to the imposition of their customs."[59]

There is evidence that, besides setting itself apart from Brazilians and other immigrants, the group was also trying to differentiate itself from other Americans. Jones delighted in collecting annecdotes about Santa Bárbara Americans who got into conflict with "Yankees." She also portrayed in great detail the anguish and suffering inflicted by Yankees on Southerners during the Civil War. Although she entitled her book *Soldier, Rest*, she was not eager to lay down her defenses against the Yankees. Nor did the Santa Bárbara Americans of the nineteenth century whom she portrayed seem eager to lay down theirs.

The apparent paradox is that they were representing themselves and being represented in public as Americans while defining the conditions for belonging as Southerners or Confederates. In order to be classified as American in Brazil, with the connections controlled by the Santa Bárbara group, being Confederate made things easier. Being Confederate was a way of controlling those connections and membership in the group. It was a way of defining, at least in certain areas, who could be an American. The Confederate flag was their exclusive sign. It marked boundaries in ways which an American flag could not.

One does not get rid of old clothes until being pretty sure that one will not be wanting to use them again someday. Indeed, as we will now see, descendants would find new reasons to wear their old clothes (or new Confederate outfits) well into the twentieth century.

Nationalism and Soil Depletion

Harter's book provides us with insight into the ways in which descendants constructed their identity during the late 1920s and early 1930s. This was a critical moment in Brazilian history. In 1929 international markets crashed; coffee prices tumbled. The Old Republic (now "old"), based on coffee exports, also collapsed. In 1930 Getúlio Vargas from Rio Grande do Sul took control of the government in Rio de Janeiro. Nationalist sentiment, accompanied by increasing criticism of the United States, had increased since World War I, and during the 1930s, with government incentive, this nationalism surged.[60]

The American descendants were being affected by changing conditions. Massive influx of Italian and other European immigrants, soon after the arrival of the Americans during the later part of the nineteenth century, altered the structure of rival groups in ways which threatened the ability of the Americans to maintain control. "In the beginning of this century, the production of plows and agricultural implements was transferred to the Nardini family. Already in 1908, Nardini agricultural machines dominated the field."[61] Political control was wrested from ~~Americans~~ and passed to the Italians. In Americana, it would later pass to the Syrians.[62]

During the 1920s, as soil depletion hampered the ~~American~~ farmers, another Italian would build an industry:

> The planters of Santa Bárbara, after almost fifty years planting cotton, found that their land was not producing the abundant harvests like before. They decided to strengthen their land with fertilizer. . . . In Vila Americana, Achilles Zanaga, who had come from Italy at the end of the previous century, started an industry for making buttons from bones. In 1919, influenced by Americans who were using fertilizer, and by their neighbors who were seeing its advantages, Achilles started to grind the leftovers from his button factory. Slowly he began to add elements to enrich the fertilizer. . . . His largest consumer was John Cullen.[63]

In an article published in 1928 in the *Geographical Review*, Mark Jefferson described the ~~American~~ descendants as overburdened with debt, disheartened, and hating their Italian neighbors.[64] The descendants started leaving the land and the region of Santa Bárbara and Americana, and they moved to the big cities.[65]

American Businesses

Many descendants worked as interpreters and executives in United States and English companies. Harter wrote: "Confederados were often employed by U.S. banks and industrial firms with offices in Brazil. . . . It felt as though the English language was the key to success."[66] Jones illustrated this point:

> The career of Richard [Pyles] was brilliant, for he became head of the entire electrical department of Light [and Power]. . . . English-speaking companies absorbed many American descendants. . . . São Paulo Light and Power kept American names on its pay sheets for many years. They were employed in jobs which required knowledge of both languages, something which came naturally to descendants. Other new companies which were installed in Brazil needed this type of help and countless people offered their services. There were many opportunities for bilingual secretaries.[67]

Some, like Eugene Harter himself, who became a U.S. consul in São Paulo, worked in the diplomatic services. Mary Miller, the granddaughter of Mary Thomas Norris, was heard regularly throughout Brazil as she reported from New York on the Voice of America radio network.[68] Ben and Dalton Yancey, whose father had defied the industrial interests of the North during the Civil War, became connected to American business interests in Rio de Janeiro.[69]

Jones characterized the second generation of Americans, those born in Brazil, in the following way: "[They] came to live in two worlds at the same time, serving as a binding element between them."[70] Descendants were carving out an economic niche for themselves as interpreters and intermediaries hired by U.S. and other English-speaking businesses.

According to Harter, "[These] last Confederates, who once again challenged the frontiers, were culturally Latinized over time, and became 'os Confederados.'"[71] If they were being hired by American companies, many of which would have been from the North, why would descendants still call themselves *confederados*? In order to explore some of the meanings which the term *confederado* held for the descendants, it is necessary to investigate some of the term's opposites. Who were those who called themselves *confederados* differentiating themselves from? Two moments in Harter's recollections provide insight.

Diplomats

In a discussion concerning the Hastings colony, Harter took issue with the view that this settlement failed. He suggested that the fact that Southerners (*sulistas*) blended into the Brazilian population demonstrated, rather than disproved, the success of *confederado* migration. Harter wrote:

> Such assimilation is difficult to achieve. In sixteen years in the foreign service [the author is writing from the United States], I have seen hundreds of American diplomats try to transplant themselves for a mere two-year stay in a foreign land. Many of them have barely made it through their tours. Even though these diplomats—**unlike the Confederados**—were expensively housed, some in baronial surroundings, they seemed lost, unable to adapt. Few of them learned the language, and almost none understood the culture of the country they were living in.[72]

Notice the distinction which Harter made between "American diplomats" and *confederados* (or *confederado* diplomats, such as the author himself had been). By way of contrast, *confederados* are seen as those who understand local culture, speak the language, and know how to adapt. Also, *confederados* do not live in expensive residences or elite districts.

J. C. Dawsey

The Spinach Rebellion

A second moment refers to the efforts of the Ford Motor Car Company to establish itself in the Amazon region in 1928. The area chosen by Ford was located eighty kilometers from the Confederate colony and the frontier city of Santarém.

As it turned out, the Confederados in Amazonia had not seen the last of the Yankees. In 1928 the peaceful scene was ruffled by the arrival of a large contingent of Americans, an advance party representing the Ford Motor Car Company of Detroit. . . . [Henry Ford], like the Confederate migrants of 1867 [who established themselves near Santarém], considered the Amazon area an untapped treasure, needing only the application of North America know-how and sufficient working capital to bring forth riches—in Ford's case, riches in the form of rubber.
. . . As the Rikers, Rhomes, Jenningses, Vaughans, Henningtons [founders of the Confederate colony near Santarém], and their children watched from the shores of the Amazon, expecting to be called upon to supply the timber, the foodstuffs, and supplies needed to set up the grand scheme, they saw the loaded ships pass them by. . . . Cleverly, the Yankees from Detroit, following their time-saving habit of making their products on the assembly line, had decided to build everything back home. . . . Ford placed an entire American city smack on top of the jungle. . . . [This] was the Confederados' and their children's first view of post–Civil War America, albeit transplanted.
They [the confederados] were not left out of the operation. Some of the Confederados leased their lands to Ford at profitable rates, and others were recruited into a variety of white-collar jobs. Over three thousand Brazilians were employed to gather the rubber, plant the trees, and run the machinery to process the product. Riker, still vigorous at age seventy-five, worked as an interpreter and even supervised some of the operations. His three sons, too, were given jobs that they kept when they followed the Ford Company back to Detroit.
Unhappily, the endeavor was run by remote control directly from Detroit, where everything was done according to American standards. . . . Ex-Confederate Riker, years later, couldn't help laughing when he described the costly venture and how Ford had "attempted, from Michigan, to govern eating habits and table manners among Indios and tropical tramps. . . . Tried to give those people patent breakfast food and tinned milk. Fed them at sit-down tables, with waiters and napkins." Uncle Sim's [the author's uncle's] comment from his São Paulo base far to the south was, "They tried to do to these Brazilians what northerners

had always wanted to do to the South—Yankeefy it!—and it didn't work there either."[73]

Harter also cited Vianna Moog's description of a rebellion of *caboclos* (i.e., people from the countryside) against Ford Company:

Suddenly, in the midst of this idyll, the first unexpected trouble. The caboclos, those meek, humble half-breeds, turn into wild beasts. They start by smashing up the whole cafeteria, they tear everything down. A riot. The officials of the Ford Motor Company run with their families, all terrified, for the freighters anchored in the port. The caboclos, armed with clubs like the French in the taking of Bastille, march on the strongholds of the directorate and management, roaring something unintelligible to the listeners aboard ship. What can they be shouting about so angrily? Can it be "Down with Mr. Ford!"? Can it be "Down with the Ford Motor Company!"? Nothing of the sort. It appeared that it was a personal disagreement with Popeye the Sailor. What the half-breeds were yelling was "Down with spinach! No more spinach!" . . . the caboclos were full of boiled spinach and well-vitamized foods; they could not even look at spinach any more. As for the corn flakes, better not even mention them. . . . enough is enough.

And in one night the officials of the Ford Motor Company learned more sociology than in years at a university. . . . They learned that the caboclos detested the tiled houses in which they lived and the Puritan way of life the officials wished to impose upon them. . . . the houses were veritable ovens, as is easily imaginable when one considers how hot the majority of American houses are in summer. . . . Mr. Ford understood assembly lines and the designs of Divine Providence. He did not, absolutely could not, understand the psychology of the caboclo.[74]

Thus, Ford Motor Company returned to Detroit. Harter's final comment: "The Confederados, who had learned how to come to terms with the Amazon and its people and who invested, not millions of dollars, but their own hearts and minds in the area, are still there, Brazilianized."[75]

This example clearly shows how a "Yankee-Confederate" mind-set is not merely used as a way of interpreting the past. It is used to structure and interpret relations in twentieth-century Brazil. The way in which the past is constructed indicates how the present should be constructed. In this sense, past and present are contemporaneous. They mirror each other. "*Confederados*" are contrasted with "Yankees" from Detroit and, perhaps even mor' tellingly, with the Confederate immigrants of 1867. The Yankees come : representatives of "America": "This was the first vision which *Confederados* and their descendants had of post–[World War I] America."

"*Confederados*" also stand apart from "the Brazilians," the ones who were contracted to harvest the rubber, plant trees, and operate machinery. Occupying an intermediary ground between two cultures, the *confederados* serve as interpreters, supervisors, and executives.

The Ford project failed, according to the *confederado* version, when the American company tried to turn Brazilians into Yankees. By contrast, *confederados* "had learned how to get along with Amazonas and its people."

The question which had been posed was, If during the 1920s and 1930s the descendants were being hired by American companies, why were they emphasizing a Confederate identity? Part of the answer may lie in the fact that American companies were hiring other Americans. As Harter noted, the *confederados* had not seen the end of the Yankees. In 1928, the peaceful scenario was shaken by the arrival of immense numbers of Americans, an advanced detachment representing the Ford Motor Company.[76] Constituting themselves as *confederados*, the descendants differentiate themselves from the competition—in this case, from other Americans. Their specialty, perhaps, was to serve as cultural brokers, helping these companies during a period of increasing nationalism, to become Brazilianized. *Confederados* could play essential roles in preventing these companies from acquiring an "ugly American" image.

Brazilians were concerned, and some still are concerned, that Americans would try to control the Amazon region. There were concerns regarding American "Manifest Destiny."[77] Hastings evidently participated in designs to incorporate the Amazon into an empire which would also include the Gulf of Mexico and the Caribbean.[78] McMullan had taken part in the Walker expedition, which had attempted to overthrow the Nicaraguan government.[79] Southerners as well as Northerners gave Brazilians reasons to fear imperialism. Dr. Barnsley, a member of the McMullan colony, once wrote in his diary:

> The Anglo-Saxons are completely ignorant of amalgamation of thoughts and religion. Naturally egotistical, they do not admit superiors, nor do they accept customs which are in disagreement with their pre-formed ideas. They think that it is their right to be boss. In my opinion, and it seems to be proven by history, English and American colonization of lands which they are not allowed to dominate, has been useless. Despite the desire of Brazilians and Argentines to receive Anglo-Saxons, it will be useless unless there are sufficient numbers to take over the country. When American immigration was at its peak, it was the desire of many of them to occupy the country and they even learned the language. The Anglo-Saxon and his descendants are birds of prey, and woe to those who get in their way.[80]

Constructing Identity

Table 9.1
Terms of Identity of the *Confederados*

Period	Economic Group	Political State
Civil War, U.S. (1865)	Agriculture	Confederate
Santa Bárbara, Brazil (1890–1910)	Agriculture	American
Rio, São Paulo, etc. (1920s–1930s)	Industry	Confederate

Jones commented: "These are hard words to hear, but time has proven that, in part, [Barnsley] was right."[81]

Harter also assimilated the first generation of Confederate immigrants with Americans and Yankees. He distinguished *confederados* from both. Why choose the *confederado* image? The answer may lie in the tendency of Brazilians to equate imperialism with Americans first, particularly Yankee Americans. Most industries have come to Brazil from the American Northeast. One of the battle cries of nationalists in Brazil, as well as elsewhere, has been "Yankee go home!" This is a battle cry which a *confederado* could surely retrieve from his own cultural trunk.

Symmetrical Inverse

In this essay, I have explored some secondary sources in order to suggest possible lines of research. I might even suggest the following thesis: The identity of descendants during the 1930s, which served as a mirror for Harter in the late 1970s, was being constructed in such a way as to constitute the symmetrical inverse of the basic terms of identity outlined by Jones during the 1960s in her portrayal of the late nineteenth-century generation. Both identities constitute transformations of a mental structure attributed to the Old South.

Whereas Americans living in the South during the Civil War were seen by both authors as farmers and Confederates, the groups living in Brazil during the late nineteenth century were seen as farmers and Americans. A second generation, some of whom would come to maturity during the 1930s, were viewed by Harter as industrial employees and Confederates. These transformations can be coded and represented as in table 9.1.

Cultural items are selected and given meaning according to the manner in which they are used or positioned within a system of oppositions. Though an analysis of secondary sources does not allow for much speculation about further transformations, there are some important clues which could be pursued.[82]

Confederate Motif in the Seal of the City of Americana, São Paulo, Brazil
(*Courtesy of Judith M. Jones*)

Racism and the Confederate Flag

It may come as a surprise to some readers in the United States that I could have written about the Confederate flag and other Confederate symbols without mentioning matters of racism. Of course, as might be expected, the documents do reveal tremendous forces of racism which impregnate not only this particular group but both American and Brazilian societies.[83]

Rather than focusing on the matter of racism, this essay has explored the processes of ethnic and regional identity construction. A certain arbitrariness of ethnic and regional categories is demonstrated throughout the chapter, however. These categories are socially constructed.[84]

It seems that the Confederate flag has come to mean something quite different among descendants in Brazil than whatever meanings it might have in the United States. There is little evidence that Confederates of the nineteenth century fought against abolition of slavery in Brazil.[85] Contrary to what may occur in the case of some low-income white Americans in the U.S. South, the groups with whom these settlers were competing were not primarily characterized as being black, but as being Brazilian, Italian, Syrian, German, Spanish, Portuguese, Lithuanian, Yankee, or American.

Within the structure of these relations, the Confederate flag gave American descendants in Brazil an exclusive symbol. Other Americans were coming to Brazil as educators, missionaries, engineers, and business people. As a way of demarcating boundaries in respect to these "outsiders," the Confederate flag served descendants well.

Now, perhaps, it may not seem so strange to see the interest with which some descendants still talk about the Civil War. Nor will it seem strange to know that a descendant such as Harold Barnsley Holland would hold on to an old family trunk containing instructions for making a Confederate battle flag. Indeed, as Griggs pointed out, "A relic of the Old South may be more significant in Brazil than in the United States."[86]

The Fraternidade Descendencia Americana was formed on December 4, 1954. The statutes define members as "the descendants of the old American colony." At the center of the fraternity symbol, there are two hands shaking. According to Harter, the handshake symbolizes the union of two cultures, Brazilian and American.[87] Nonetheless, the handshake is encompassed by the design of the bottom triangle of a Confederate flag. The descendants seem to have done like Derrida and put their American and Brazilian identities "under erasure." The fraternity might call itself American Descendancy and the two hands might symbolize Brazilian and American cultures, but the crossed bars which help form the angles of the triangle are definitely Confederate.

Ten

The Language
The Preservation of Southern Speech among the Colonists

Michael B. Montgomery and Cecil Ataide Melo

For more than 120 years, descendants of the Confederates who migrated to the region near Santa Bárbara have remained a tiny English-speaking Protestant minority in a Portuguese-speaking Catholic nation. They maintained English-language schools; used English in their homes, churches, and community life; and kept alive memories of their former country. Over the years the principal settlement developed into the city of Americana, and the *confederados*, as they were known, gradually integrated into Brazilian society. For those born after World War II, Portuguese became the first and dominant language, and there are no longer monolingual English speakers in the region.

Still living in the environs of Americana are several hundred older descendants of the original settlers for whom English is their first language and who speak in soft, slow voices quite reminiscent of people of the same age in the Lower South of the United States today. While their accents are unmistakably Southern American, they have a definite Portuguese ring also. Given the isolation of the Americana community, cut off from other English speakers for over a century (although some Americana residents occasionally visited relatives back in the South), the *confederados* today and their speech patterns appear to represent a lost cousin to Southerners in the United States.

It turns out that studying Americana English is far more than a genealogical exercise of locating a faraway relative and determining where he or she belongs on the family tree, because the speech of the *confederados* also represents a time capsule. Analyzing it can help us understand what Southern American English sounded like in the third quarter of the nineteenth century. There is much about Southern speech—particularly the pronunciation—of that period that linguists have been able only to guess at. It was only in the 1930s, three to four generations later, that recordings began to be made which can be analyzed for clues to these questions.

The Language

As a result, linguists have little more than speculated about how similar Southern English a century and more ago might have been to its modern-day counterpart, or about whether or how Southern speech has become more different from other types of American English since the Civil War. Assuming that isolation has permitted present-day speakers of Americana English in Brazil to preserve the pronunciation of Confederate immigrants of over a century ago (there is, as we will see, good reason to assume this), recordings of them enable us to begin documenting many details of an earlier stage of Southern speech than has hitherto been possible. Americana English thus offers the key to answering two of the most fundamental questions about the history of Southern American English: Has it always been distinctive from the rest of American English? And how much has it changed in recent generations? Without a kindred variety like Americana English, these would be very difficult indeed to answer.

Recently, interviews with eleven mostly older members of the Americana community have been recorded and then excerpted on the public television program *The Last Confederates*.[1] This paper examines how these individuals use six patterns of pronunciation that are well-known in Southern speech today. These include the lack of "r" after vowels in words like *car* and *bird*, the use of "n" as the final consonant in words ending in *-ing* like *singing*, and the pronunciation of the vowel in words like *my*, *kind*, and *right*. Analyzing these features will help us assess the character of Americana English and determine its resemblance to present-day Southern American speech.

As described elsewhere in this volume, both psychological attachments and geographic separation helped the *confederados* hold onto the culture and speech of their ancestors. The questions at hand in this paper concern how similar their English is to that in the Southern United States, and what this tells us about the development of Southern speech over the past century and a quarter. We use the term "Southern American English" to refer to a generalized version of the traditional speech of the Lower South recognized by writers like Raven I. McDavid, Jr., as used by whites in the former plantation belt, which extends from Eastern Virginia southwestward to Georgia and then westward to Texas.[2]

Data and Speakers for This Study

Of the eleven individuals on whom this study of the pronunciation of Americana English is based, ten (five women, five men) were born around the turn of the twentieth century or shortly thereafter, and the eleventh was a boy of about ten years old. Their names—such as Sonny Pyles, Sara

Bell Matthews, Robert E. Lee Conti—certainly make them sound like Southerners. All of them were middle class, and most were college educated. Among the men were prosperous farmers, a physician, and a dentist. One of the women was a local historian, and others were public school teachers and professors. These individuals apparently had little contact with speakers of English outside Americana; two of them mentioned a sentimental visit in recent years to Alabama—the home of their immigrant ancestors—"after a hundred years' absence." It is clear from the interviews that some of these speakers had known their ancestors well. At least two of them were the children of immigrants, and several others were grandchildren. For these reasons, the English of these Americana residents is likely to be quite close to those who left the former Confederacy well over a century ago.

The Pronunciation of Americana English

The eleven Americana speakers are quite similar in the six features of pronunciation examined in this chapter. While comparisons between generations of Americana English speakers are not possible from these interviews because of the closeness in age of these individuals (the young boy who was interviewed spoke briefly, using only four clauses), further research should address how much and how quickly this fascinating variety of English is changing. Such work must be done quickly, because younger members of the Americana community no longer have English as their dominant language, and Americana English is steadily losing ground.[3]

More important, however, Americana speech offers clues to how Southern American English was pronounced over a century ago, about which we know little because there are no recordings of Southerners who reached adulthood at that period. It provides a baseline against which to identify and measure subsequent changes in Southern speech and then to determine the extent to which it may be converging with other varieties of American English.

Listed below are the six features of pronunciation, two involving consonants and four having to do with vowels, that are analyzed in Americana English. They are chosen because they are well known to vary along regional lines in the United States and to have variants typical of Southern English in the twentieth century.[4]

1. The pronunciation of "r" after vowels (what will henceforth be called postvocalic "r") in several different types of words. In traditional South-

ern speech, this consonant is often not pronounced, making *bear* sound like "be-uh."

2. The final consonant in words ending in -*ing*; in the South, this sound is frequently "n" rather than "ng."

3. The pronunciation of what is popularly called "long i." For many speakers of American English, but less so in the South, this is actually a combination of sounds (a vowel and a semivowel, or glide, pronounced together like "ah-ee"), and for this reason linguists call it a diphthong and represent it phonetically as [ai]. In Southern American English today, the vowel is frequently pronounced as one sound—the vowel [a] without a following glide, as if *ride* were spelled "rahd."

4. The pronunciation of consonants "l" and "r" between vowels in the middle of words, as in *hellish* and *Sara*. In Southern speech, these consonants are sometimes sounded only with the following syllable, which approximates the pronunciation of "he-lish" and "Say-ra." Most speakers of American English pronounce such words as if the consonants are spread across both syllables—"hel-lish" and "Ser-rah," in which case the consonant sounds as if it were doubled.

5. The length of short vowels in words like *man* and *bed*. In Southern speech today these vowels are frequently stretched or drawled to produce pronunciations like "ma-uhn" and "be-uhd."

6. The pronunciation of "en," particularly in one-syllable words, as "in" (thus making *pen* and *pin* identical in sound). This pattern is extremely common in modern Southern American English.

Methodology

Although all six features vary, sometimes in complex ways, within the South, at least one pronunciation of each is widespread in traditional Southern speech and is recognized as either more typical of or as almost entirely restricted to the South. In analyzing these features, each one was viewed as a binary variable, with variants being classified on a dichotomous basis (i.e., whether or not, in each case, evidence of the Southern variant was present). For instance, postvocalic "r" was considered present whether it was weakly or strongly articulated, and any degree of a glide, or second vowel, for [ai], was sufficient to consider it a diphthong. A given case was ignored if the pronunciation was ambiguous or if (for features 5 and 6) it occurred in an unaccented syllable (which usually made it difficult to assess in any case). The data were classified independently by each author of this paper, who subsequently compared assessments and consulted the recording together until a consensus of interpretation was reached. The resulting quantitative calculations, based on the percentage of Southern variants, can be used for comparisons with other varieties of English.

The general, subjective impression of the modern-day hearer of Americana English is that it is distinctly akin to modern-day Southern American English, although it also has some of the rhythm and accent of a member of the Romance language family like Portuguese. A closer, quantitative examination confirms this impression to be true to some extent, but as we will soon see, several of the above-mentioned pronunciations that typify Southern American speech occur rarely or not at all in Americana English. This suggests that Southern American English has undergone considerable change in the century and a quarter following the war and has become, somewhat surprisingly, more unlike other varieties of American English in some ways than it used to be.

At least for the eleven speakers featured on the television program, the pronunciation of Americana English is quite homogeneous. There is variation only in the first four features. Table 10.1 gives a summary view of this, and a detailed look at each feature follows below.

Postvocalic "r"

The lack of "r" after vowels has long been a hallmark of Southern American speech (it is found elsewhere as well—for example, in Great Britain and Boston). More has been written about whether or not Southerners of different types and in different areas do or do not articulate this consonant than any other aspect of the region's pronunciation. McMillan and Montgomery's bibliography lists no fewer than fifty-eight studies dealing with the historical, geographic, social, and linguistic dimensions of postvocalic "r."[5] With regard to its history, George Philip Krapp states that the lack of "r" came "to be generally omitted in Eastern and Southern American speech at the end of the eighteenth century," and Edward Stephenson concludes that "r"-lessness was a prestigious pronunciation that had spread through much of North Carolina from Virginia by 1800.[6] Apparently because of this prestige, it spread from coastal areas, including cities farther south like Charleston and Savannah, across the Lower South all the way west to Texas in the nineteenth century. By the early twentieth century it typified the speech of middle- and upper-class whites, as well as all blacks, in this territory.

More recent evidence indicates that postvocalic "r" has been returning to Southern English. For instance, a recent study of the white speech of

Table 10.1
Pronunciation of Traditional Southern English versus Americana English

Phonological Feature	Traditional Southern Pronunciation	Americana English		
Postvocalic "r"	without "r"	generally without "r"		
		without "r":	182/212	85.8%
		with "r":	30/212	14.2%
Diphthong [ai]	without glide	generally with glide		
		pronounced [ai]:	98/112	87.5%
		pronounced [a]:	14/112	12.5%
Final -ing	pronounced "n"	either "ng" or "n"		
		pronounced "ng":	19/34	55.9%
		pronounced "n":	15/34	44.1%
Doubling of "r" and "l"	not doubled	generally doubled		
		doubled:	40/56	71.4%
		not doubled:	16/56	28.6%

Tuscaloosa, Alabama, found that "the oldest informants show no ["r"] 24% of the time. This figure drops to 5% for the middle age group and to 0% for the youngest age group."[7] Another study, by Feagin and Bailey, of five generations of speakers in South Alabama, finds that the older generation (born around 1900) does not pronounce "r" at all, while the youngest generation (born in the 1970s) uses it most of the time.[8]

The settlers of Americana were most likely "r"-less or nearly so, since they were middle class, and the nonuse of "r" until recently was considered more fashionable and cultured than the use of "r." Older Americana speakers today are largely "r"-less, with the consonant occurring overall at about 14 percent (30 cases out of 212), although this rate rises to nearly 20 percent if we count only those words (such as *were* and *where*) in which it could have occurred in an accented syllable (see table 10.2). Where it is pronounced, the "r" is weak. It occurs sometimes as a "linking r," a bridge between vowels as in the phrase *more or less* (otherwise the consonant is not pronounced in *more*). In other cases the articulation of "r" exhibits Portuguese influence in that it is uvular (pronounced at the back of the mouth), rather than alveolar (pronounced behind the upper teeth), as in English. This inflates the rate of occurrence of "r" somewhat.

Table 10.2
Influence of Linguistic Context on the Presence
of Postvocalic "r" in Americana English

Linguistic Context	Contexts	"r" Pronounced (Number)	"r" Pronounced (%)
Type of preceding vowel			
Front *(year, where)*	44	0	0.0
Central *(were, part)*	133	17	12.8
Back *(port, sure)*	30	12	40.0
Diphthong [ai] or [au] *(fire, our)*	5	1	20.0
TOTAL	**212**	**30**	**14.2**
Type of syllable			
Accented *(where, were)*	141	28	19.9
Unaccented *(later)*	71	2	2.8
TOTAL	**212**	**30**	**14.2**

Table 10.3
Individual Variation in Pronouncing Postvocalic "r"

Speaker	Contexts	"r" Pronounced (Number)	"r" Pronounced (%)
James Jones	49	5	10.2
Charles McFadden	47	5	10.6
Esther Smith	18	2	11.1
Arlindo Thomas	13	2	15.4
Judith MacKnight Jones	24	4	16.7
Sonny Pyles	21	5	23.8
Lilian Smith	21	6	28.6
Others (4)	19	1	5.3
TOTAL	**212**	**30**	**14.2**

None of the Americana English speakers always pronounced postvocalic "r"; they used it from 10 to 29 percent of the time. Table 10.3 shows that "r" occurred for seven Americana speakers (four others were combined under "Others" because they had fewer than ten words in which it could have been pronounced—considered the minimum for calculation). There was more variation in the occurrence of "r" by linguistic context, that is, according to the preceding vowel and the type of syllable, as we see in table 10.2. This table shows that postvocalic "r" occurred for Americana English

The Language

speakers in all contexts except after front vowels in accented syllables in words like *year* and *where.*

What could it signify that Americana speakers do not entirely lack post-vocalic "r," other than that the influence of Portuguese encourages the occurrence of it? Since postvocalic "r" has been shown to be returning to Southern English today and the figures in table 10.2 suggest that its occurrence when the Confederate exodus took place was variable and probably quite limited, there are two possibilities: it was either still being lost at the time of migration, or it had begun to be reestablished. We can discern which was more likely the case by comparing the pronunciation of the eleven Americana speakers with those in South Alabama studied by Feagin and Bailey (many migrants to Brazil came from the same area). A similar rate of "r" in different phonetic contexts in the two varieties supports the view that the consonant was already being reestablished in Americana English. A dissimilar patterning implies that nineteenth-century ancestors of Americana speakers were still losing "r." This answer brings us closer to understanding how long ago "r" began to return to Southern American English.

In Feagin and Bailey's research older speakers (born around 1900) do not pronounce "r" at all; younger speakers pronounce it to some extent after central vowels (*were, car*) and front vowels (*there, hear*) and to a less extent after back vowels (*sure, more*). But Americana speakers differ from the older generation in South Alabama in that they pronounce "r" 40 percent after back vowels, 12.2 percent after central vowels, but not at all after front vowels.[9] Because the patterning of "r" in Americana English is strikingly different from that in the American South, this implies that it was still being lost by at least some Confederates at the time of immigration to Brazil.

Americana speech does resemble that described by Feagin and Bailey in one regard—the type of syllable in which "r" occurs. In Americana speech "r" is most likely in accented syllables as in *were/where* (28 out of 141 cases, or 19.9 percent) and less likely in an unaccented syllable (2 out of 71 cases, or 2.8 percent) as in *later* and *center.* Feagin and Bailey find that in the twentieth century "r" has been restored first in accented syllables and then in unaccented ones (their youngest speaker, born in 1970, had "r" exclusively in all types of syllables). There is probably a phonetic reason for this similarity, however, in that sounds are intrinsically weaker in syllables that are not accented.

On the whole, then, postvocalic "r" occurs at a rather low level in Americana English. This supports the view that it was marginal in nineteenth-century Southern English and probably still was being lost by former Confederates when they left for Brazil. With respect to this feature, modern-day Southern speech is converging with other varieties of American English.

Pronunciation of [ai], "Long i"

Almost as well known and maybe a more salient feature of contemporary Southern American speech is the tendency to pronounce the diphthong [ai], popularly called the "long i," either by centralizing the second part of the vowel, the glide, making it sound like "uh," or by eliminating it entirely. This makes *ride* sound like "ra-ud" or "rahd" rather than "ra-eed." Hans Kurath and Raven I. McDavid, Jr., in *The Pronunciation of English in the Atlantic States* state that in the Atlantic states surveyed by the Linguistic Atlas project the glide tends to disappear "before voiced consonants [such as "b," "d," and "g"] and finally [at the end of a word] throughout the South and the South Midland, except along the coast of South Carolina, Georgia, and Florida"; the lack of a glide before voiceless consonants [such as "p," "t," and "k"] in *ripe, night,* and *like* is prevalent primarily in South Midland (or Upper South) areas.[10] Thus, today in the Lower South one can hear *ride* and *side* pronounced as "rahd" and "sahd," but *night* and *like* pronounced as "naht" and "lahk" does not occur as often.

There is little comment on this diphthong in the history of Southern English. Neither Eliason in *Tarheel Talk: An Historical Study of the English Language in North Carolina to 1860* nor Krapp in *The English Language in America* mentions it as typical of the nineteenth century, and Americana speakers show little evidence of complete absence of the glide.[11] This indicates that the pronunciation of *ride* as "rahd" is either an innovation in twentieth-century Southern English or was marginal in nineteenth-century speech. As seen in table 10.4, in only 14 of the 112 cases (12.5 percent) was there no glide for the eleven Americana speakers. When they do use the glide, it is often weak, especially in unaccented syllables (these include 67 instances of *my* and *I,* words that tend to occur in unaccented positions).

The lack of the glide in Americana speech, although limited, does conform to the general pattern noted by Kurath and McDavid above and by other studies that find glideless pronunciation more common before voiced consonants than before voiceless consonants.

The dominance of the pronunciation with the glide in Americana speech certainly contrasts with modern-day Southern English, but the variation in the glideless pronunciation in the latter makes its status not altogether clear. Recent work by Bailey suggests that the lack of a glide is in-

Table 10.4
Influence of Following Segment on the Use of Glide [ai] in Americana English

Following Segment	Contexts	No glide (Number)	No glide (%)
Voiceless consonant	41	4	9.8
Voiced consonant	55	9	16.4
Vowel or glide	16	1	6.2
TOTAL	**112**	**14**	**12.5**

creasing in Texas, while in his Tuscaloosa study Crane finds variation by social class rather than age, with lower-class speakers having much higher rates of glideless [ai] for all age groups.[12] The history of this feature is complex, but data from Americana speech clearly indicates that the glideless pronunciation is almost certainly more common now than a century ago. If this was the case, Southern speech in 1870 was less different from the rest of American English then than it is today.

Final Consonant in Words Ending in -ing

Although also found in other varieties of American English, the use of "n" for "ng" in words with final -ing "occurs more regularly in the South and South Midland than elsewhere," according to the *Dictionary of American Regional English*.[13] Dating back at least to the eighteenth century and found in varieties of British English then as well as today, the use of "n" in -ing seems to have been maintained for two centuries as a stable pronunciation in Southern speech.[14] Frequent misspellings in nineteenth-century letters reveal that the strictures of schoolteachers not to "drop the final g" were "apparently unheeded by cultivated Southerners."[15] (This admonition actually involved a misnomer, in that the "ng" represents a single consonant pronounced at the back of the mouth, not the two consonants "n" + "g.")

Americana speakers vary more in pronouncing final nasal consonants "n" and "ng" than in any other feature discussed in this paper. This may represent a stable variation between the two pronunciations, the general pattern found in much of the South today, although the low number of contexts (only thirty-four) prevents definitive statements about this variation with the confidence we could have for postvocalic "r" and the diphthong [ai]. The "n" pronunciation occurs at a rate of 44.1 percent (fifteen

Table 10.5
Influence of Linguistic Context on the
Occurrence of "n" for Final -ing in Americana English

Linguistic Context	Contexts	Pronounced "n" (Number)	Pronounced "n" (%)
Following phonological context			
Consonant	21	11	52.4
Vowel	9	2	22.2
Pause	4	2	50.0
TOTAL	**34**	**15**	**44.1**
Grammatical category			
Gerund	16	8	50.0
Progressive	5	4	80.0
Participial adjunct	8	3	37.5
Attributive adjective	2	0	0.0
Indefinite Pronoun	3	0	0.0
TOTAL	**34**	**15**	**44.1**

out of thirty-four cases, seen in table 10.5), more often before a consonant than before a vowel or a pause, most often with a progressive verb (*was doing*) or a gerund (*cotton picking*), and less often with grammatical forms like a participial adjunct (*having met on the ship*) or an indefinite pronoun (*nothing*).

Doubling of "r" and "l" between Vowels

The fourth feature concerns whether either of two similar consonants, "l" and "r," is spread or "doubled" over two syllables (when the first syllable is an accented one). In traditional Southern pronunciation this often does not occur, so that names like *Helen* and *Sara* are pronounced without the consonant affecting the sound of the preceding vowel. In phonetic terms, this means *Helen* and *Sara* are pronounced in the South like [hɛlən] and [serə] rather than [hɛtlən] and [serrə] in most of the country.[16] In Americana speech, the lack of doubling of [l] is complete (fourteen cases of this, although thirteen are for the word *Brazilian*, and Portuguese influence is probably at play here). Almost the reverse is true for "r," where doubling occurs in forty of forty-two cases (see table 10.6). Why Americana English, which largely lacks postvocalic "r," so strongly doubles the consonant on accented vowels of words like *parents*, *very*, and *Americans* seems something

Table 10.6
Frequency of Doubling of "r" and "l" in Americana English

Consonant	Contexts	Doubling (Number)	Doubling (%)
"r"	42	40	95.2
"l"	14	0	0.0
TOTAL	**56**	**40**	**71.4**

of a paradox (of course, these words were not considered as having contexts for the occurrence of postvocalic "r"). This is a point that space does not permit us to examine further, because it would lead to a detailed exploration of the influence of Portuguese on Americana English, a topic for another essay. From the evidence at hand we cannot determine at this point how strong the doubling of "l" and "r," or the lack of such doubling, was for the Confederate immigrants to Brazil.

The Southern Drawl

Another prominent feature of modern Southern speech is the so-called Southern drawl, which Feagin says is characterized by the lengthening of vowels, the addition of glides after vowels, and "remarkable change of pitch," that is, its falling off at the end of a phrase or sentence.[17] Thus a word like *bid*, when drawled, is pronounced "bi-ud" [biəd], or sometimes as "bi-yud" [bijəd]. Whether the drawl occurred in Southern speech in the third quarter of the nineteenth century is open to doubt, because there is no comment on it in early literature. The first description of it by Claude Merton Wise in 1933 is consistent in all details with recent accounts.[18] This would lead us to speculate that it existed earlier but did not show up in misspellings, which usually provide the clues to nineteenth-century pronunciation. The pronunciation of Americana English is crucial here, because there is no evidence at all of the drawling of vowels for the eleven speakers, consistent with the lack of mention of the drawl in earlier literature.[19] It appears that the Southern drawl, along with the glideless pronunciation of [ai] and the next feature of pronunciation to be discussed, have all either developed or become far more common in the speech of Southerners since the Civil War.

Montgomery & Melo

Pronunciation of Vowel in pen/ten

The shift of the vowel [ɛ] (popularly called "short e") before "n" and "m" to become the vowel [I] (the "short i") makes the words *ten, hem,* and *pen* sound like *tin, him,* and *pin.* This is a common and distinctive feature of modern-day Southern American English, although apparently a recent one. In a recent paper, Vivian Brown argues that this homophony of words like *ten* and *tin* has spread from the Upper South, especially North Carolina and Tennessee, into the Lower South only in the last hundred years. She speculates that this "was affected by the wave of urban migration that followed during the Post–Civil War period."[20] Scattered earlier evidence for this pronunciation comes from misspellings in antebellum documents, according to Eliason, and Krapp argues that it was brought by Ulster Scots in the eighteenth century and was once "a general feature of popular American speech."[21] But the homophony of *pen* and *pin* has undoubtedly increased rapidly in the twentieth century and has become a mark of many varieties of contemporary Southern speech. For instance, in a study conducted in Charleston, South Carolina, in the 1960s, O'Cain finds that it occurred 6 percent of the time for speakers in their seventies, but at a rate of 60 percent for speakers in their thirties.[22]

In Americana speech, there is no evidence of words like *pen* being pronounced as *pin,* based on thirty-five contexts in accented syllables. This provides further evidence of the recentness of this pattern and argues that the homophony of *pen* and *pin* in modern-day Lower Southern speech developed largely in the twentieth century.

Conclusions

Our study finds that although Americana speech lacks several of the hallmark features of twentieth-century Southern English pronunciation, it is clearly Southern speech, particularly in the patterning of postvocalic "r" and the occurrence of "n" in words ending in *-ing.* The combination of these linguistic similarities, along with demographic and psychological factors, supports the view that Americana English is conservative and represents or closely approximates the speech of Southerners who arrived in Brazil in the third quarter of the nineteenth century. This helps us understand how Southern speech has changed in the past century and a quarter and how much it has become both similar to and different from other varieties of American English during this period.

Specifically, the lack of homophony of *pen* and *pin,* the lack of drawling, and the relative lack of the glideless pronunciation of [ai] in Americana all indicate that Southern English was closer to other varieties of American English in the nineteenth century than present-day Southern speech is. Changes in pronunciation have apparently taken place that represent a divergence of Southern English from American English in the twentieth century. In short, Southern speech is in some ways more distinctive today than ever before. The differences between it and Americana speech indicate that the two should more appropriately be considered linguistic cousins than siblings.

Attempting to explain this with our current knowledge of the social history of Southern speech is a considerable challenge. One possibility is that the divergence is connected to the isolation of the defeated South in the two generations after the Civil War. Historians have often cited the solidification of regional identity and a barricade mentality that were fostered by the Civil War and its aftermath. For instance, Wilson states that "the late 19th century was perhaps the age of the most cohesive regional culture and an identifiable, distinctive southern way of life."[23] This suggests that the linguistic changes in the period in part reflected the evolving consciousness of the region's distinctiveness. While it is premature to make a more specific claim about how influential this was on Southern speech, such a possibility may usefully guide future research.

More likely, though, the divergence of Southern English is related to the spread of Upper Southern pronunciation into the Lower South as many Southerners have migrated out of the hills and into the towns and cities of the Piedmont and beyond, beginning a generation after the war and continuing until recent times. For over a century, Upper South pronunciation has been marked by the glideless version of [ai] and the homophony of vowels before "n" and "m." Raven McDavid has emphasized the increasing size and prominence of urban areas like Nashville, Charlotte, Birmingham, and Atlanta over the past four generations, pointing out that such shifts were "bound to increase the importance of the South Midland component of Southern speech, at the expense of coastal Southern."[24] He cites as an example that "as early as 1946 [he] noticed that upland vowels were common among native Savannians."[25] The spread of the homophony of front vowels and of glideless [ai] has in the past two generations reached even into other bastions of traditional prestige, such as Charleston, South Carolina, where O'Cain found Midland pronunciations much stronger in the 1960s than McDavid did a generation earlier.

It is crucial for future research to take the linguistic patterns presented in this chapter from older Americana speakers and to compare them with the speech of younger members of the Americana community, with speakers recorded by the Linguistic Atlas of the Gulf States from the areas of the Southeast from which ancestors of Americana settlers derived, and with older historical data, such as examined in Norman Eliason's *Tarheel Talk* in North Carolina. This is necessary to pin down further both the conservativeness and the stability of the pronunciation represented by the speakers in this essay. To explore the grammar and vocabulary of Americana speech, the data and methodology used in this paper are inadequate, but happily, research based on interviews to elicit such specific items has recently begun to collect data for further addressing questions about the nature of Americana English.[26] It is now safe to say that, linguistically speaking, the Americana colony is no longer a lost relative at all; rather, it is becoming a crucial link in reconstructing the history of Southern American English.

Eleven

Conclusions
Currents in *Confederado* Research

Cyrus B. Dawsey and James M. Dawsey

The preceding chapters of this book reflect the efforts of scholars independently pursuing unique research interests. Yet their common subject is the Confederate emigrant and Brazilian *confederado*. Beyond adding to the overall body of historical knowledge, each contribution points the way to further investigation of independent and particular topics. Besides expanding isolated and separate research frontiers, however, the chapters also trace several common themes. We believe that three of them are especially important and represent significant new insight.

The first theme relates to the motivation of the migration in the 1860s. In the second paragraph of his inaugural 1927 study of the emigration to Brazil, Lawrence Hill wondered what impelled the Southerners "to desert their native land and begin life anew in a strange country." Without hesitation he answered: "Although they [i.e., the reasons] varied greatly with the different individuals and with diverse groups, in general they can be placed under one heading—a desire to get out from under a government controlled by Brownlows, 'niggers', and Yankees. It was felt that a government in such hands could not protect 'life, liberty and property', much less 'conserve honor, chivalry and purity', that inestimable trinity without which life is not worth living and without which no community can be termed Christian."[1]

But perhaps Hill himself thought that he had answered too quickly, without proper reflection. For in 1935, eight years later, he no longer wrote about Confederate "exiles," but rather about the Confederate "exodus"; and he subtitled the first part of his more mature study on the subject "Romance and Strife," showing that he was keenly aware that there were other reasons driving the Southern exodus to Latin America besides the émigrés' desire to flee reconstruction.[2]

In fact, since the 1930s there has been a growing realization among scholars that there were numerous, complex reasons leading Southerners to emigrate after the war. Several of the chapters in this book shed new light on what motivated the *confederados* to go to Brazil. Chapters 1, 3, and 4 recapitulate earlier research by summarizing many of the conditions that pushed Southerners from one homeland and pulled them to another. Chapter 2, written by *confederado* Smith, confirms Hill's second opinion and indicates that the call to adventure was a powerful motive. Already in the 1980s, Daniel Sutherland had focused on the key role that economic factors played in the Southern emigration.[3] Wayne Flynt begins chapter 6 by acknowledging the new poor of the South; and Laura Jarnagin in chapter 4 relates the migration to world economic forces. Chapters 5, 6, and 7 remind us that several of the Southerners were driven by evangelical zeal and the goal of spreading the "pure religion" to Brazilians.

But perhaps the greatest contribution of the essays to our understanding of what led the *confederados* to go to Brazil is the identification and exploration of the role played by personal linkages. Thus, Griggs in chapter 3 examines the relationship between Alfred Iverson Smith and Frank McMullan. Jarnagin in chapter 4 looks at the multiple family connections: on the one hand, among the emigrants and, on the other hand, among the Brazilians; and she traces linkages between the two groups—the business interests, Protestant ideal, Masonic lodges, and so forth. Furthermore, Wayne Flynt and also Cyrus and James Dawsey examine how these personal connections helped propagate the religious beliefs and educational values of the Southerners. Thus, the influence of personal linkages in the emigration to Brazil deserves further study. These essays represent a promising current of inquiry.

A second theme that marks the book and will likely be a rewarding area of study concerns an improved picture of the *confederados'* influence on Brazilian society. As mentioned in chapter 5, Blanche Clark Weaver set the agenda for present-day research in this area by looking at the ways in which the Southern émigrés contributed to the establishment of the Presbyterian, Baptist, and Methodist denominations and the missionary schools in Brazil.[4] Following Weaver's lead, Jones and others gradually shifted attention away from the technological innovations introduced in the nineteenth century and focused on the American churches and schools as the important aspects of *confederado* culture whose influence would persist into the twentieth century.

The tendency here has been to claim too much by letting the large scope of American influence color our perception of the specific contributions of the *confederados*. Nowhere is this clearer than in Frank Goldman's book *Os pioneiros americanos no Brasil*, which acknowledges but does not really distinguish the influence of non-Southern Americans like Dr. Horace Manley

Lane, who arrived in Brazil from Massachusetts in 1858, and Ella Kuhl, from Cooper Hill, New Jersey, from the contributions of Confederate emigrants like Gaston and Barnsley.[5]

Chapters 5, 6, and 7 present a balanced view and help correct the *confederados'* appropriation of missionary and Brazilian accomplishments in religion and education. In chapter 5, in particular, James and Cyrus Dawsey demythologize the emigrants' contributions to the establishment of Presbyterianism in Brazil and to the foundation of the Colégio Internacional in Campinas.

Wayne Flynt in chapter 6 and James Dawsey in chapter 7, however, are careful to give the Southerners due credit. The *confederados* did make important contributions to the beginnings of the Baptist and Methodist churches in Brazil, contributions for which they have sometimes not received proper acknowledgment in denominational literature.

In chapter 7, James Dawsey examines the role of Annie Ayres Newman Ransom in establishing Methodism in Brazil. In fact, *confederado* women have probably contributed more than the *confederado* men to the spread of American religion and education in Brazil, as approximately twenty of the female immigrants and their daughters married Protestant missionaries, and many others became schoolteachers.

Confederado women have also played a critical role in preserving a record of the immigrants' accomplishments. It should be remembered that Julia L. Keyes wrote an important diary of her stay at Lake Juparanã[6] and that Jones and Guilhon have been the principal historiographers among the descendants. Thus, it is fitting that Sarah Bellona Smith Ferguson's narrative is featured in this volume. The study of the specific contributions made by women to preserving the Southern heritage in Brazil is an important area of research which should be pursued more energetically, leading to the proper recognition of other important women.

A third current of scholarship running through the essays in this book can be traced to a 1947 article by José Arthur Rios, who asked about the assimilation of Old South emigrants in Brazil.[7] Rios discovered several social obstacles to the acculturation of the Southerners, including their isolation, different religion, racism, and different understanding of work. But the assimilation of the emigrants had nonetheless taken place gradually, and at the time when Rios wrote, Vila Americana was "the only remaining settlement of all those founded by Southerners."[8] He argued that the community presented "all of the features of marginality which are characteristic of the process of assimilation" and thus concluded that the community was "of singular importance for the study of the process of assimilation."[9]

Several of the essays in this book have taken a clue from Rios and explored topics that he mentioned but failed to develop. For example, in his article Rios surmised: "The endurance of the American colony at Santa Bárbara, later called Vila Americana, perhaps is due to the fact that its inhabitants were able to overcome the great obstacles and construct a school and a church."[10] In part, this is the subject of chapters 5, 6, and 7 on the Presbyterians, Baptists, and Methodists. But it is specifically the topic of chapter 8, in which Cyrus Dawsey examines how the *Campo* site helped the *confederados* preserve their identity as a distinct group of people. Again, Rios's observation of both "evidences of loyalty to the country of origin" and "others which bring out an advanced stage of deterioration in the original culture patterns which are no less important" is pursued by John Dawsey in chapter 9.

However, the essays in this book go well beyond Rios, by asking a set of new questions concerning the *confederados'* self-awareness. Thus, the real focus of chapter 9 is not on the assimilation, or lack thereof, of the Southerners into Brazilian society but on a better understanding of those characteristics purposefully preserved by the *confederados*. Furthermore, the book includes two instances of what could be called insiders' views: chapter 2 written by an immigrant, and a postscript written by a descendant.

The contributions of the book, then, carry on the scholarly dialogue started by Rios, but with fresh questions and from a fresh perspective. Here then, also, is a rich area of research to be explored.

The stories that regularly appear about the *confederados* in the popular media have often been misleading. For example, a 1992 article in *Parade Magazine*, entitled "A Continent Away, Confederates Flourish," focused on what appear to be oddities of a culture frozen in time.[11] But the descendants who gather periodically near Santa Bárbara are not die-hard Old South apologists or advocates of antiquated values such as racial segregation. The customs of the people who meet and sing the old hymns have evolved in a fascinating manner and result from a complex interaction between two very different societies.

The title of this chapter is "Conclusions," which means ending. The story of the *confederado* immigrants has not ended, however. Some things have passed, but others have not. Time is fading the old manuscripts and the memories of the descendants, but for many, a sense of identity remains. The ethnically homogeneous—or "racially pure," as the immigrants might have said—communities near the Brazilian towns of Santa Bárbara and Santarém no longer exist, but the mementos, the regular traditional ceremonies, and a preserved location where the heritage is passed on are very evident. Although few of the descendants are still fluent in English, most are proud to claim a connection to the nineteenth-century adventurers who sailed to an unknown future in a strange land.

To use an analogy from the landscape that became home to Hastings's followers, the black waters of the Rio Negro and the silt-laden yellow waters of the Amazon flow for miles as separate currents after the streambeds merge near Manaus. Far downriver, the light and dark colors begin to mix, not in a uniform blending, but as swirls and eddies of one flow advancing on and penetrating into the other. Eventually the Negro, laden with tannic acid from the north, becomes part of the great Brazilian Amazon, and combined, they meander to the sea.

Today, the descendants of the proud Confederate Southerners are unmistakably part of mainstream Brazilian society. The assimilation has almost been completed, but traces of the group's unique origin can still be identified. Significantly, we possess a record of the many years of contact between the newcomers and the host society. Collections of old letters, newspaper reports, firsthand accounts, and secondhand compilations preserve the history of the group in Brazil. Because communication with friends, relatives, and religious organizations in the United States was maintained for over a century, the trials and triumphs of the "lost colony of the Confederacy" have become widely known. As the cultural currents flowed at first beside each other and later intermixed, the process was documented and the record preserved.

For many, the history of the Americans in Brazil is of personal interest, for among the Brazilians are relatives and namesakes of families in the United States South. Others are motivated by remnant ideas and fervent ideals from the time of the Civil War when the United States of America was a divided nation. Of greatest interest to the scholar, however, are the generic issues of what motivates migration, how newcomers survive in an alien setting, what elements of group identity are preserved over time, and how one culture impacts another. The historical record of the Americans in Brazil is a rich source of information pertinent to these and other questions.

Several hundred miles east of Manaus, where the Amazon flows sluggishly past Santarém, the river's color is yellow, and the contributed waters of the Negro cannot be easily identified. Yet the load of sediment and debris from the north is still present, thoroughly incorporated in the current of the total stream. Similarly, North American cultural traits were taken to Brazil, and they have affected the flow of the mainstream host society. The extent of the influence is subject to debate. The Americans are sometimes credited with introducing the steel plow, but it would have appeared in Brazil in any event. Similarly, other innovations such as the buckboard wagon or new varieties of crops would have been invented or imported by others.

Not as obvious but more permanent was the Americans' influence through churches and schools. The Brazilian Baptist and, to a lesser extent, Methodist churches began with the arrival of the immigrants in the 1860s. The missionary effort of these denominations and the Presbyterians, a group whose Northern branch was already active in Brazil, were greatly boosted by the arrival of the settlers at Santa Bárbara. Though the membership of these three Protestant churches was never more than a minute fraction of Brazil's total population, they exerted a telling influence on the country. The denominations established several of the country's leading private schools and universities. The schools became channels through which liberal Western ideas about government, society, economics, and ethics were exposed to large numbers of Brazilians. The children of the elite, most of whom were Roman Catholic, were often educated in the Protestant institutes, and many of these youth went on to positions of influence and power. The current president of Brazil, Itamar Franco, is a graduate of one of the Protestant schools, Granbery of Juíz de Fora. The American influence, therefore, has not reached a conclusion, for it remains an active part of the evolving Brazilian society.

"Conclusions" can also mean final opinions. But the essays included in this volume are not conclusive in that sense, as if they were the decisive, irrevocable, last words to be written about the *confederados*. The contributions are threads of scholarly interest, pursued and studied but not concluded. The efforts of the scholars cover common topics, and as shown above, common themes emerge. The threads of interest often intertwine and appear to run in the same direction. The research does not always lead to a set of common ideas, however, so the threads do not come together in a neat and final knot. The pursuit of inquiry is unique to the individual investigator, and each quest uncovers as many new questions as answers.

Though different in scope, each chapter above makes an important contribution to our understanding of the *confederados*. The volume includes in chapter 2 the Sarah Bellona Smith Ferguson manuscript in its entirety with an introduction by the editors and notes on original spelling and grammar. Though widely referenced, the complete account has never before been included in a scholarly publication.

The account is invaluable to the scholar and fascinating to the layperson. Similar to Jennie Keyes's diary, it is an adventure tale experienced by a child. Bellona Smith's narrative is also the story of a colonist who perse-vered. And it is a story told by a proud last Confederate. Bellona Smith Ferguson's story is one of only a few eyewitness reports of the migration and settlement in Brazil. To our knowledge, it is the only extant account that sees the events experienced by the child through the eyes of a colonist who endured. It adds perspective that is not otherwise readily available to the historian and serves as a bridge between the first generation of South-erners who left the Old South and the second generation of descendants who were brought up in a new land.

Bellona Smith's narrative also is a significant social symbol. The story of the trip to Brazil and settlement there has played an important role among the colonists in Brazil. As already noted, to this day the Southerners in that area where the Smiths settled maintain their identity as a community. They think of themselves as *confederados* and see themselves as people with a spe-cial heritage who share a common past. Bellona begins her narrative with her reason for writing: "I have been just lately asked by several persons and acquaintances, both old and new friends, to give an account of the Southern families who emigrated to Brazil soon after the Civil War." The descendants of the Southern immigrants in Brazil wanted to preserve the story of their families' migration. The same force urging Bellona to write her account in English would lead later, in 1967, to the publication in Portuguese of Judith MacKnight Jones's *Soldado descansa!* In a very simple way, Bellona Smith's account is like Virgil's *Aeneid*. It is more the formative story of a new people than one of flight by war-torn refugees. The tale of the difficult passage from one homeland to another is a powerful symbol that has helped bind the colonists of the Santa Bárbara area into a common community. As Bel-lona's story is preserved and repeated, it helps the descendants identify themselves as a distinct group of people.

The Bellona Smith Ferguson account also is of interest to linguists. Bel-lona's father, Alfred I. Smith, had been a music teacher at one point in his life—and the Smiths valued education. Bellona's narrative betrays the Southern English of a girl who learned at home. The spellings are quaint, and the grammar hints at a mixture of old Southern and Brazilian idioms. For the benefit of linguists, Bellona Smith's language has been preserved where appropriate.

The essay by William Griggs in chapter 3 places Bellona's account in historical perspective as it provides the context for the saga of the migrants who left the war-ravaged South and set off for Brazil. Griggs provides details of the early explorations, the preparations, the journeys, the founding of the colonies, and the subsequent collapse of those in the coastal areas. In addition to tracing the story succinctly, the chapter provides illuminating details of the experience, such as the stored metal skirt hoops causing the Norris family's ship to stray off course.

One of the most important contributions of this chapter is that it shatters any facile attempt to make a caricature of the emigrants. Griggs begins the chapter by recounting the life story of Alfred I. Smith, Bellona Smith Ferguson's father. In the process, he reminds us that his, and other emigrants', reasons for moving to Brazil were more complex than simply the desire to escape reconstruction and preserve the Old South. Smith did not own slaves, nor did he wish to purchase slaves in Brazil. He did not come from a plantation background. He was not even a farmer by trade. Although his close friendship with Frank McMullan helped persuade him to go to Brazil rather than to Mexico, Smith already had decided to leave Texas before being approached by McMullan. Apparently he was a person "on the move." He was an independent sort who sought a new frontier.

This chapter strongly indicates that the colony organizers also were not all cut from the same cloth. While McMullan was loyal to his followers and was beloved by Smith and the others in his group, Dunn abandoned his supporters. Wood also proved to be an embarrassment to those who put their trust in him. Hastings was an adventurer. Though the Southern Colonization Society of Edgefield, South Carolina, made elaborate plans and generated much interest, and though Meriwether and Shaw wrote a detailed report about Brazil, few South Carolinian families actually emigrated to that country. The most successful colony was not organized as a colony at all. William Norris bought land and settled near Santa Bárbara, and others followed.

Besides a feel for the diversity of the emigrants and the organizers, Griggs's essay adds significantly to our understanding of the level of support for immigration from the Brazilians, and the initial enthusiasm for emigration of the Southerners. Furthermore, Griggs presents us with enough details of the hardships faced by the McMullan, Gunter, and Hastings groups to let us understand why much of that initial enthusiasm waned.

Laura Jarnagin in chapter 4 carefully documents how the movement to Brazil was one of a sequence of dislocations by a restless and courageous group. She shows that the selection of Brazil as a destination was not accidental and meticulously traces some of the personal linkages between important Brazilian families and the Americans. The chapter delves into themes that have only begun to be explored, and they warrant further research.

Conclusions

Jarnagin shows that there was a groundwork laid by Brazilian liberals, English manufacturers, American naval explorers, and Protestant missionaries. But most important were those kinship networks of Southerners and Brazilians, and the personal contacts between them. Jarnagin identifies the socioeconomic class of the principal migrant families. She then traces the family and business connections linking many of them to each other and to the Broad River group of the Georgia–South Carolina border region. Among the Brazilians, she traces connections through Tavares Bastos and other liberal reformers who wished to duplicate the American model in Brazil and who were linked to Freemasonry and to the Protestant movement in Brazil.

Laura Jarnagin's chapter provides a needed counterbalance to chapters 2 and 3 in that it views the migration of the Southerners to Brazil in large scale. It also breaks new ground in the academic study of the emigration to Brazil by highlighting the role played by personal and kinship connections. This important theme recurs in chapters 5 and 7.

Wayne Flynt and James and Cyrus Dawsey examine the religious connections. In chapter 5, the Dawseys take a fresh look at the Southerners' influence on Brazil. Following the suggestion of Jarnagin in chapter 4, the authors place the agricultural innovations within the framework of nineteenth-century economic development and show that the kind of technology that the Southerners took to Brazil was appropriate to the development of the periphery. The Southern émigrés provided the know-how and the tools that the Brazilians were seeking. Thus, Cyrus and James Dawsey argue that the Southerners' influence upon Brazilian agricultural technology was immediate but perhaps not as important as the impact in other areas.

They then examine the beginning of Southern Presbyterianism in Campinas and discover that the influence exerted by the *confederados* on the establishment of the Presbyterian church and the Colégio Internacional was different, and in some ways more complex, than asserted by earlier scholarship. Here, Cyrus and James Dawsey add to our understanding of how the *confederados* influenced Brazilian religion and education. They discern a more complex picture than allowed by Weaver and other emigration scholars who often have misrepresented the origin of Presbyterianism in Brazil by tying it too closely to the history of the Methodist and Baptist churches there. Introducing a theme that was examined again in chapter 7 in regard to the Methodists, the authors conclude that the greatest influence that the *confederados* exerted on Presbyterian religion and education occurred through personal linkages. The chapter also uncovers the role played by Brazilians in founding the so-called American schools in Brazil. This role has been largely ignored by *confederado* and missionary publications.

Tapping a rich documentary record of letters and articles, Flynt in chapter 6 describes the establishment and growth of the Southern Baptists. The Baptist ties to the community near Santa Bárbara were strong, and local services were started soon after arrival in Brazil. Baptist ministers Ratcliff, Pyles, Thomas, and Quillin were among the original settlers.

Flynt's character sketch of Quillin and quick references to the other early Baptist clergymen help us perceive why the Baptists did not initially grow as rapidly as did the Presbyterians and Methodists. The author also focuses more closely on the missionaries Daniel and Puthuff, who arrived from Texas in 1885. The story of these two illustrates the complex connection between the mother denomination in the South of the United States, the emigrant community, and the desire to evangelize the Brazilians that led to today's Baptist church in Brazil.

This chapter, like the essay by Griggs, reminds us of how complex the motives were driving the migrants to Brazil. An important contribution of the chapter is that it closely ties the missionary activity of the Baptist church in Brazil to the migration following the Civil War. Although the Southern Baptist Foreign Missionary Board had wished in the 1850s to open work in Brazil, the mission did not come to fruition until after the arrival of the Southerners. In fact, the first missionaries were not sent to evangelize Brazilians but rather to supply the community of American immigrants. The motives of the Baptists, therefore, were very different from those of the Presbyterians as described in chapter 5.

James Dawsey in chapter 7 explores the early days of Methodism. In the first part of the chapter, Dawsey explores the historical roots of Methodism in Brazil, showing the impact that the arrival of the *confederados* had on establishing that religion there. In the second part, the author traces the support for the mission among the Americans in the Old South, and in the third part, he unravels some of the very important personal ties between the Methodists in Brazil and those in the United States.

James Dawsey picks up a theme present in chapters 4 and 5 and reminds us of the multiple personal connections that existed between the immigrants, their families and friends who remained in the South, and progressive Brazilians like Prudente de Moraes Barros, who promoted the adoption of elements of American culture. The establishment and success of Methodism in Brazil was conditioned by all three groups.

Conclusions

A notable contribution of this chapter to our understanding of the Southerners in Brazil is that it recognizes the important role that Annie Newman Ransom played in the story of Brazilian Methodism. Ransom helped found a major school and significantly affected other educational and religious institutions. Though she lived during a time when a woman's activities were restricted and though she died while still young, her influence was far-reaching. Church historians generally have underestimated the importance of the Norris community in the history of Brazilian Methodism, and many have consistently not recognized the key contributions that women like Annie Newman Ransom have made to the spread of Southern evangelical religion. Building upon the foundation laid by Bellona Smith in chapter 2, this chapter reminds us that women were full partners in the immigration to Brazil.

Cyrus Dawsey in chapter 8 examines an important element related to the preservation of the *confederados'* identity. His thesis is that the evolution of the particular site known as *Campo* was critical for the transfer of the heritage from one generation to the next. A similar location was not present in any of the failed colonies.

Dawsey first outlines the preconditions in the region of interior São Paulo and shows how the evolution of *Campo* was a response to particular needs of the Americans. The spatial distribution of the families is described, and the author shows how the location of *Campo* was influenced by the grouping of the Americans into clusters near the town of Santa Bárbara. Religious services were held at the site long before the construction of a church because *Campo* was centrally located with respect to the total community.

The essay goes on to describe the importance of the site, not only as a place of worship, but also as a community center. A compilation of early marriages shows that they most often occurred within the American population, and intercluster friendships and romances were usually established at *Campo*.

Finally, Dawsey outlines the continuing function of the site as a cultural shrine. It is the place where regular reunions are held and where the heritage is recalled. The basic contention of the chapter is that *Campo* was a very important element of cohesion to the original immigrants and their early descendants. It remains a significant asset to the current generation by contributing to the preservation of the *confederado's* unique identity in Brazil.

John Dawsey in chapter 9 looks at heretofore unexplored issues of identification and community self-awareness. The Americans have maintained a sense of identity and uniqueness within the larger Brazilian society, and Dawsey seeks to understand why and how this is so. The author examines two designations used by the descendants to describe themselves as a special group. The first is the tag "American." Dawsey notes that although the term was conferred on the group by outsiders, it was accepted by the immigrants. The reasons that Confederate exiles chose to accept this designation are complex. Motives included the Brazilian Republicans' support for and promotion of certain aspects of American culture and the success of the American plow as compared to the Brazilian and European tools used in the environs of Santa Bárbara.

While the descendants represented themselves in public as Americans, they also took steps to differentiate themselves from other Americans. Thus, they set limits to the group and defined Southern conditions for belonging to the community.

The second designation studied by John Dawsey is *confederado*. Here, the author is interested in how the descendants constructed their identities during the 1920s and 1930s. For various reasons, mainly economic, many of that generation stopped farming and took up work as interpreters and mid-level executives in English-speaking companies. Interestingly, these descendants chose to see themselves as Confederate workers, identifying themselves in such a way so as not to be confused with their American and British employers.

This chapter corrects the type of misinterpretation given by Jefferson's "American Colony in Brazil" and common among other writers of popular literature that see the *confederados* as unhappy rebels who tried to re-create the Old South in Brazil, but failed. The descendants do not feel confused or uncomfortable about their status as Brazilians. Rather, as John Dawsey points out, designations such as American and *confederado* have helped them secure their ethnic identity in that country. By alternately linking themselves with "Confederate" and "American" images and values, the community has sought to benefit from favorable connotations and associations.

In chapter 10, Michael Montgomery and Cecil Ataide Melo examine unique aspects of the English dialect used by the *confederados*. Though chapter 10 analyzes speech patterns of descendants living in Brazil, the major objective of the study is to understand aspects of the evolution of the language of their relatives who remained in North America. The preservation of Southern traits in distant Brazil, therefore, contributes to our knowledge of the recent linguistic history of the homeland of the original immigrants.

The use of English as a first language, the one learned by a child from its parents, is a vestige trait that has almost disappeared among the *confederados*. Most members of the younger generation grow up speaking Portuguese, their first exposure to English occurring when they tackle the public school curriculum requirements in foreign languages.

Montgomery and Melo recognize the historical importance of the *confederado* dialect spoken by a few of the descendants, for it is a window onto the language of the Civil War–era South. Unexposed to influence from the evolving North American English, the residents near Santa Bárbara maintained many of the nineteenth-century linguistic features that changed or disappeared over time in the United States.

This chapter, therefore, differs from the preceding sections of the book in that, though it examines an important element of the *confederado* culture, its real focus lies elsewhere. Viewed from the North American perspective, the primary goal of the study is to learn about ourselves; how does the spoken language of present-day Alabamians and Texans differ from that of their ancestors. In a sense, therefore, the saga of the *confederados* comes full circle. What begins in the early sections of this volume as a retelling of the century-old tale of adventure and exile, concludes in chapter 10 with a glimpse into the evolution of the contemporary language of the homeland left behind long ago. This is possible because a small group, living in a world that for years remained alien, doggedly preserved an important element of its imported culture.

The essays constituting the chapters described above trace different scholarly enquiries. In several places in the book, Cyrus and James Dawsey attempt to integrate the separate essays into the overall history of the initial migration and subsequent settlement in Brazil. The editors summarize aspects of the migration and provide background information that is related to the topics of the essays but not included elsewhere. These sections, therefore, help provide a context and story line for the book.

The book also includes a postscript written by Eugene Harter. In addition to being an author and a scholar, he is a descendant who grew up in Brazil. His reflections are laced with personal recollections and family stories that convey more than facts assembled from library documents. He possesses an insider's point of view, and his writing indicates pride in being part of the grand adventure.

Included at the end of the book is an annotated bibliography compiled by James M. Gravois and Elizabeth Weisbrod. The collection of citations includes references and notations for the most important primary and secondary sources, and the compilation will be an invaluable resource for anyone engaging in research on the topic.

C. B. Dawsey & J. M. Dawsey

Judith MacKnight Jones and Her Mother, Lizzie McAlpine MacKnight
(*Courtesy of Judith M. Jones, 1983*)

Most of the chapters, therefore, consider specific topics related to the migration and the persistence of the American settlement in Brazil. Some of the elements have been looked at before, but many have not. They represent new areas of study and may open major avenues for further investigation. In most cases the presented material expresses the first steps and not the final results of the research.

Though common themes emerge, this book draws few final conclusions. Its primary purpose is to present a snapshot of important ongoing scholarly study of the nineteenth-century immigration and settlement of the North Americans in Brazil. The press has frequently reported on the reunions at *Campo*, but presentations of serious scholarship have been rare. This volume should help fill the vacuum.

Judith M. Jones, who has labored perhaps more than anyone to preserve the story of the *confederados*, subtitled her book "A North American Epic under the Skies of Brazil." The epic adventure has continued for over a century, and the careful study of the events and players in this drama can shed light on processes that are significant to humans around the world. Migration, ethnic contact, diffusion, and cultural evolution are universal events, and the examination of the experiences of the *confederados* may help increase our understanding of similar groups elsewhere. The grand experiment launched from the Southern shores of a war-torn country in the mid 1860s may well continue to yield results that augment our knowledge of social behavior.

Postscript
Reflections of a *Confederado*

Eugene C. Harter

Some among the *confederados* know the stories, heard from the lips of their grandparents, recounting the long, hazardous voyage and the early adventures of arrival in a new homeland. Many descendants now speak only Portuguese, but some still use an English dialect much like the language of the original Confederate immigrants who left the Southern states over a century ago.[1]

Despite the problems of distance and language, there seems to be renewed interest in this story of Americans who left their native land, most of them never to return. Recently, just prior to his death, exile descendant Dr. James Jones, looking at the Confederate grounds in Americana and the new interest in the story, said: "I used to think that this place would go aground, but now there is hope."

Among the epic accounts preserved by the *confederado* community, none is more revered than the story of its founding and of the Norris family. The ink was barely dry on Lee's surrender documents. Only a few weeks after Appomattox, sixty-five-year-old William H. Norris and his son, Robert, headed for Brazil, where they cleared some acreage and established a successful farm. Good news travels fast, and within months other Confederates, also with agricultural know-how, bought land in the area.

The elder Norris lived to a ripe old age in Brazil, surrounded by his children and grandchildren. His son Robert, born in Brundridge, Alabama, eventually became a respected medical doctor in Americana. Dr. Norris, a dogged and patriotic soldier, had fought in thirty-seven battles and major engagements until he was made a prisoner by the Union army. He carried a bullet in his stomach and the scar of another bullet on his wrist.

Several stories recorded by Robert Norris's daughters, Kennie and Julia, were preserved within the *confederado* community, and today they are archived at the Museu da Imigração in Santa Bárbara. Kennie's lively account told of their happy and busy social life, and the abundance of fruits, vegetables, milk, and butter from the plantation. Their house was large, surrounded by a beautiful garden and arbor. Like many of their Confederate neighbors, the structure was built in the American style out of hardwood, located on 400 acres of land. The home, which was equipped with running water, had a large parlor for entertaining, an entire wall of bookshelves, and a fireplace to remove the evening chill. There was plenty of room to live in and to entertain the many sons and daughters of the medical doctor. It also had room to play for the forty-five grandchildren. Their servants and slaves were taught to speak English.

Discussions about the war were frequent. The girls' Uncle Henry and Uncle Clay, veterans of that bloody struggle, would tell Civil War stories as they churned the butter (there were six Norris brothers, all fought in the war, and all survived). One uncle told her, "We did not lose that war, Honey, we just wore ourselves plumb out whopping the damn Yankees."

The closest neighbors lived a mile from them, and others lived further away, but there was much visiting among the Confederates. According to Kennie Norris, "When one killed a hog, we would get a ham or a shoulder—and we shared things, loaned implements, tools, vehicles or whatever was needed."

The cultural life and recreation was described by Julia Norris, who wrote of picnics, dances, and community activities. Some of the young girls founded a society in which they entertained with games, literary discussions, and sewing gatherings.

Music abounded. John Domm cleared a space and erected a picnic ground and barbecue. The village brass band would be brought out, and the entire American colony would attend and spend the whole day. Community dances and musical sessions were frequent, with members of the group bringing their instruments. Many played the violin. A circulating library and a Masonic lodge were founded. There in faraway Brazil they tried to duplicate the way of life they remembered in the Confederate states.[2]

This author's mother, Maglin May Harris, born in 1899 in Americana, said that customs changed little during her years there (1899–1920), even well into the twentieth century. Mother (known to us as Mãe, in the Portuguese) remembered that attempts were made to keep ties with the United States. For example, several of the Brazilian Confederates were members of the United Daughters of the Confederacy, belonging to the "Cradle of the Confederacy" Chapter of Montgomery, Alabama, and they received the group's publications.

In her teens Mother was organist at the church. Following Sunday services, she and a group would take a portable organ to the local jail, where they would conduct additional services. My father was a retired U.S. diplomat, whose religious tastes required us to join the dignified Union (American) Church in the Copacabana section of Rio de Janeiro. From time to time, however, mother would take us to the rousing Brazilian Presbyterian services in that city's downtown section. There we would sing all the old Southern hymns, in Portuguese, of course.

The Confederate community was not of one mind; some attended church, and others did not. One family made a point of naming their children after well-known American atheists of the time. Others were critical of the energetic American missionary effort in Brazil.

Through the efforts of imported preachers, the church-energized Prohibition movement in the United States found roots in the Americana colony. Drinking was forbidden in many homes, but many Confederates and their offspring refused to "take the pledge."

Among the Confederate-Brazilian descendants, memory of the U.S. Civil War and its aftermath has dimmed, but at times the old feelings surface. Descendants show pride in their heritage. From time to time a "Forget, Hell!" sign appears among them, possibly in jest, possibly not. In 1986 the NBC "Today Show" telecast a short interview by host Bryant Gumbel of a Confederate descendant, Edward Carr, from Americana. In the discussion the descendant defended with pride the Confederate colony and his wish to stay in Brazil.

> Gumbel: "Americana was settled but it failed to thrive as other communities thrived, I mean the population now is dwindling just a little bit. Why?"
>
> Carr: "No! It is not dwindling, it's an up and coming community, very much so, not only because of the Americans, because of the textile industry that they started there. Americana is a thriving community."
>
> Gumbel: "You tried to make a go of cotton there and it didn't work?"
>
> Carr: "No! It did work, my ancestors lived off planting cotton and watermelons for many years. . . . "
>
> Gumbel: "You have been to the United States now on several occasions?"
>
> Carr: "Yes. I liked it very much, but I prefer to continue living in Brazil and to keep my family in Brazil."[3]

But few of the American citizens living in Brazil, and especially, few American government officials, shared the Southern pride of the *confederados*. Except for an occasional Texan or a political appointee, one seldom ran into Southerners in the senior levels of the U.S. career foreign service during my time in the corps (1966–82). Perhaps this has had its conse-

Postscript

quences. Though the war for Southern independence has been over for 127 years, the U.S. Department of State and its International Communication Agency still had trouble in defining the Confederate struggle in policy terms. Our embassy's policy at that time was to ignore the American Civil War as though it had never happened.

When I was a U.S. consul in Brazil (1970–73), I pointed out to our government that, seemingly oblivious to our self-interest, we had not shown recognition of the thousands of American-Confederate descendants living there. This contrasted with the British, French, and Italian embassies, which had close relations with their emigrant descendants, offering them travel and educational grants to visit their mother country and opening cultural offices and libraries in their Brazilian communities.

Americana had no such U.S. cultural office and library, though we had placed over a dozen in other cities in Brazil. I pointed out that the city of Americana, Brazil, was named after our country and we should acknowledge the courtesy. But to no avail. From time to time I would take groups of visiting Americans out to the Confederate grounds near Americana. One day a visitor from the U.S. South appeared, and through his press secretary, I invited him to join me at the Confederate grounds. His name was Jimmy Carter, and he later became president of the United States.

The visit to the *Campo,* with its cemetery and church, was an emotional discovery for Carter, his wife, Rosalynn, and their press secretary, Jodie Powell. It was also memorable for the several hundred Confederate descendants who, on hearing of his coming, turned out that day. They drew a large circle for his helicopter to land on and traced the word "Welcome" on the ground.

Carter seemed surprised. We conversed as we walked among the headstones (one was inscribed: "Private Jonathan Ellsworth, drummer boy of the First Arkansas Brigade"). I introduced him to some of the descendants, including my cousin Sra. Daisy Harris, and also Sr. Charles McFadden and Sra. Judith M. Jones, close friends of my mother's family. I recounted the history of the exiles and then asked Carter to address the crowd.

He spoke from the base of the Confederate monument that dominated the scene. As he talked, he looked carefully at the many faces surrounding him. They were Southern faces. He looked at the Confederate battle flag, perhaps contemplating its real, historic meaning.

His face showed happiness, not sadness. Yet he paused, and tears ran down his cheeks. Starting again, he told them he would never forget this scene and would tell Americans about it when he returned to his country.[4]

Georgia Governor (later U.S. President) Jimmy Carter at the Confederate Monument at Campo, Santa Bárbara (*Courtesy of Judith M. Jones*)

Jodie Powell also described the scene in his syndicated column written twelve years later:

> Jimmy Carter stood beneath the granite monument to say a few words to the crowd. As he spoke, I found a knot in my throat and tears beginning to trickle down my cheeks. Surprised and embarrassed, I looked up to see if anyone had noticed and discovered that Mrs. Carter was having the same problem. A moment later, her husband looked down at us and had to stop his speech to clear the lump in his own throat.
>
> None of us could explain exactly why Americana touched us so deeply. Part of it was the feeling that we had discovered a part of ourselves that we hardly knew existed.[5]

Notes

Introduction: The *Confederados*

1. The following essays were presented at the conference: chapter 3, "Migration of the McMullan Colonists and Evolution of the Colonies in Brazil," by William Griggs; chapter 4, "Relocating Family and Capital within the Nineteenth-Century Atlantic World Economy: The Brazilian Connection," by Laura Jarnagin; chapter 6, "Southern Religion and Émigrés to Brazil, 1865–1885," by Wayne Flynt; chapter 7, "Connections: The Southern Migrants and the Methodist Mission," by James Dawsey; and chapter 9, "Defining the American Descendants in Brazil," by John Dawsey.

2. Ballard Smith Dunn, *Brazil, the Home for Southerners; or, A Practical Account of What the Author, and Others, Who Visited That Country, for the Same Objects, Saw and Did While in That Empire* (New Orleans: Bloomfield and Steel, 1866); Daniel P. Kidder, *Sketches of Residence and Travels in Brazil, Embracing Historical and Geographical Notices of the Empire and Its Several Provinces,* 2 vols. (Philadelphia: Sorin & Ball, 1845); Lansford Warren Hastings, *The Emigrant's Guide to Brazil* (Mobile, 1867); Lawrence F. Hill, "Confederate Exiles to Brazil," *Hispanic American Historical Review* 7 (May 1927): 192–210. Hill also wrote "The Confederate Exodus to Latin America," a three-part series published in *Southwestern Historical Quarterly* 39. The parts have the following subtitles: I: "Romance and Strife," no. 2 (October 1935): 100–134; II: "Dixielands in South America," no. 3 (January 1936): 161–99; and III: "Confederates in Middle America," no. 4 (April 1936): 309–26. Hill's work was also published together as *The Confederate Exodus to Latin America* (Austin: Texas State Historical Association, 1936).

3. Mark Jefferson, "An American Colony in Brazil," *Geographical Review* 18 (1928): 226–31; Peter A. Brannon, "Southern Emigration to Brazil," *Alabama Historical Quarterly* 1 (Summer 1930): 74–95; (Fall 1930): 280–305; (Winter 1930): 467–88; Blanche Henry Clark Weaver, "Confederate Immigrants and Evangelical Churches in Brazil," *Journal of Southern History* 18 (1952): 446–68; and "Confederate Emigration to Brazil," *Journal of Southern History* 27 (1961): 33–53.

4. Desmond Holdridge, "Toledo: A Tropical Refugee Settlement in British Honduras," *Geographical Review* 30 (1940): 376–93; James E. Edmonds, "They've Gone—Back Home!" *Saturday Evening Post,* January 4, 1941, pp. 30, 33, 46–47; and José Arthur Rios, "Assimilation of Emigrants from the Old South in Brazil," *Social Forces* 26 (1947): 145–52.

5. Hamilton Basso, "The Last Confederate," *New Yorker,* November 21, 1953, pp. 143–61; Frank A. Knapp, Jr., "A New Source on the Confederate Exodus to Mexico: The Two Republics," *Journal of Southern History* 19 (1953): 364–73; William C. Nunn, *Escape from Reconstruction* (1956; reprint, Westport, Conn., Greenwood Press, 1974).

6. Alfred Jackson Hanna and Kathryn Abbey Hanna, *Confederate Exiles in Venezuela,* Confederate Centennial Studies, no. 15 (Tuscaloosa, Ala.: Confederate Pub-

lishing, 1960); Andrew F. Rolle, *The Lost Cause: The Confederate Exodus to Mexico* (Norman: University of Oklahoma Press, 1965); Julia L. Keyes, "Our Life, in Brazil," *Alabama Historical Quarterly* 28 (1966): 127–339; Douglas Grier, "Confederate Emigration to Brazil: 1865–1870" (Ph.D. diss., University of Michigan, 1968).

7. Judith MacKnight Jones, *Soldado descansa! Uma epopéia norte americana sob os céus do Brasil* (São Paulo: Jarde, 1967); Frank P. Goldman, *Os pioneiros americanos no Brasil: Educadores, sacerdotes, covos, e reis* (São Paulo: Livraria Pioneira Editora, 1972); Frank Cunningham, "The Lost Colony of the Confederacy," *American Mercury* 102 (1961): 33–38; Norma de Azevedo Guilhon, *Confederados em Santarém: Saga americana na amazônia* (Belém, Pará: Conselho de Cultura do Estado do Pará, 1979); David Afton Riker, *O último confederado na amazônia* (Manaus, Brazil: Imprensa Oficial do Estado de Amazonas, 1983).

8. Daniel E. Sutherland, "Looking for a Home: Louisiana Emigrants during the Civil War and Reconstruction," *Louisiana History* 21 (1980): 341–59; Sutherland, "Exiles, Emigrants, and Sojourners: The Post–Civil War Confederate Exodus in Perspective," *Civil War History* 31 (1985): 237–56; Sutherland, *The Confederate Carpetbaggers* (Baton Rouge: Louisiana State University Press, 1988); Betty Antunes de Oliveira, *Movimento de passageiros norte-americanos no porto do Rio de Janeiro* (Rio de Janeiro, 1981); David Gueiros Vieira, *O protestantismo, a maçonaria e a questão religiosa no Brasil* (Brasília: Editora Universidade de Brasília, 1980); Charles Willis Simmons, "Racist Americans in a Multi-Racial Society: Confederate Exiles in Brazil," *Journal of Negro History* 67 (1982): 34–39; Eugene C. Harter, *The Lost Colony of the Confederacy* (Jackson: University Press of Mississippi, 1985); Frank J. Merli, "Alternative to Appomattox: A Virginian's Vision of an Anglo-Confederate Colony on the Amazon, May, 1865," *Virginia Magazine of History and Biography* 94 (1986): 210–19; William Clark Griggs, *The Elusive Eden: Frank McMullan's Confederate Colony in Brazil* (Austin: University of Texas Press, 1987); Michael B. Montgomery and Cecil Ataide Melo, "The Phonology of the Lost Cause: The English of the Confederados in Brazil," *English World-Wide* 10 (1990): 195–216.

Chapter 1: Leaving

1. Jones, *Soldado descansa*, 44, 324.

2. Douglas French Forrest, *Odyssey in Gray: A Diary of Confederate Service, 1863–1865*, ed. William N. Still, Jr. (Richmond: Virginia State Library, 1979), Wednesday, May 17, 1865, p. 308; Saturday, May 20, 1865, p. 309; Thursday, May 25, 1865, p. 314.

3. Forrest, *Odyssey in Gray*, Tuesday, May 23, 1865, pp. 312–13; Wednesday, May 24, 1865, p. 313.

4. Forrest, *Odyssey in Gray*, Saturday, June 3, 1865, p. 317; Sunday, June 4, 1865, p. 317; Monday, June 5, 1865, p. 317.

5. Forrest, *Odyssey in Gray*, Saturday, June 3, 1865, p. 317; Sunday, June 4, 1865, p. 317; Monday, June 5, 1865, p. 317.

6. Sutherland, "Looking for a Home," 341.

7. George Eagleton, July 4–20, 1865, in Alden B. Pearson, Jr., "A Middle-Class, Border-State Family during the Civil War," *Civil War History* 22 (1976): 335.

8. Quoted in Sutherland, "Looking for a Home," 346.

9. Quoted in Hill, "The Confederate Exodus," I, 104.
10. Sutherland, *The Confederate Carpetbaggers.*
11. Hanna and Hanna, *Confederate Exiles in Venezuela,* 13.
12. Mary Elizabeth Massey, *Refugee Life in the Confederacy* (Baton Rouge: Louisiana State University Press, 1964), 240, 28–47.
13. Dan T. Carter, *When the War Was Over: The Failure of Self-Reconstruction in the South, 1865–1867* (Baton Rouge: Louisiana State University Press, 1985), 13–16.
14. Jones, *Soldado descansa,* 44.
15. Sutherland, "Exiles, Emigrants, and Sojourners," 239. The literature concerning the Brazilian attitude toward slavery at the time of Southern emigration is extensive. Important works include Magnus Mörner, ed., *Race and Class in Latin America* (New York: Columbia University Press, 1970); Robert Brent Toplin, *The Abolition of Slavery in Brazil* (New York: Atheneum, 1972); Robert Conrad, *The Destruction of Brazilian Slavery, 1850–1888* (Los Angeles: University of California Press, 1972); and Robert Edgar Conrad, *Children of God's Fire: A Documentary History of Black Slavery in Brazil* (Princeton: Princeton University Press, 1983).
16. Grier, "Confederate Emigration to Brazil," 115–16.
17. Quoted in Hill, "The Confederate Exodus," I, 115.
18. Dunn, *Brazil, the Home for Southerners,* 227–44.
19. Quoted in Hill, "The Confederate Exodus," I, 122–23.
20. Dunn, *Brazil, the Home for Southerners,* 142, 28, 48.
21. Holdridge, "Toledo," 379.
22. James C. Fletcher and Daniel P. Kidder, *Brazil and the Brazilians, Portrayed in Historical and Descriptive Sketches,* 9th ed. (London: Sampson Low, Marston, Searle, and Rivington, 1879).
23. Hanna and Hanna, *Confederate Exiles in Venezuela,* 36.
24. Grier, "Confederate Emigration to Brazil," 61.
25. Grier, "Confederate Emigration to Brazil," 72.
26. Grier, "Confederate Emigration to Brazil," 122.
27. Jones, *Soldado descansa,* 162.
28. Griggs, *The Elusive Eden,* 127.
29. Jones, *Soldado descansa,* 411; Goldman, *Os pioneiros americanos no Brasil,* 107.
30. Richard F. Burton, *Explorations of the Highlands of the Brazil* (1869; reprint, New York: Greenwood Press, 1969); Goldman, *Os pioneiros americanos no Brasil,* 10; Jones, *Soldado descansa,* 258.
31. Goldman, *Os pioneiros americanos no Brasil,* 10.
32. Julia Keyes, "Our Life, in Brazil."
33. Griggs, *The Elusive Eden,* 99.
34. Griggs, *The Elusive Eden,* 123.
35. The location of the Norris home is not clear, for Alabama included several communities named Spring Hill in 1865. None, however, was located in Dallas County, the area represented by Norris in the state legislature during the 1840s.

Chapter 2: The Journey

1. James McFadden Gaston, *Hunting a Home in Brazil: The Agricultural Resources and Other Characteristics of the Country, also, the Manners and Customs of the Inhabitants*

(Philadelphia: King & Baird, 1867); John Codman, *Ten Months in Brazil* (New York, 1872); Hasting Charles Dent, *A Year in Brazil* (London, 1886).

2. Edwin Ney McMullan, "Texans Established Colony in Brazil Just after Civil War," *Farm News* (Dallas), January 25, 1916; Eugene C. Smith, "Sailing Down to Rio in 1866–67," *Brazilian American* (Rio de Janeiro), March 9, 1931.

3. Sarah Bellona Smith Ferguson, "Emigrating to Brazil," *Farm and Ranch* (Dallas), December 2 and 16, 1916; January 13 and 20, 1917; and "The American Colonies Emigrating to Brazil," *Times of Brazil* (São Paulo), December 18, 24, and 31, 1936.

4. Emergrating

5. For-word

6. my childhood's memories

7. Judith MacKnight Jones gives the correct spelling as Mac Mullan; William Griggs, as McMullan; and Lawrence Hill, as McMullen.

8. Merriwether

9. Ballars

10. "Lizzie Land"

11. Tarvers. The leader of the Rio Doce colony was actually Col. Charles G. Gunter (see Hill, "The Confederate Exodus," II, 178–79).

12. 'Rio Docy'

13. Villa

14. . . . impressions given to the regarding . . .

15. confederat

16. The original has no quotation marks.

17. Rio de Pexia

18. Guanhanha

19. Ariado

20. *Captão* Martins

21. Navaro

22. old fashoned

23. pic-nic

24. travelling

25. curry

26. when

27. enrout

28. Huston

29. delapidated

30. John Coss

31. white sailed

32. When

33. Quillen

34. Dier

35. 2 hundred

36. shors

37. breakes

38. rops

39. them

40. self
41. on to
42. dont
43. sleevs
44. climed
45. discribe
46. som
47. fortunit
48. appeard
49. Cubian
50. Steemer
51. piccaninies
52. playin
53. stiring
54. old style
55. emaginable
56. *tresty*
57. Cubians
58. emprisoned
59. intensly
60. awfull
61. bearly
62. seven masted
63. ten cent
64. suffies
65. sharred
66. was
67. confederat
68. masters
69. we having
70. Calven
71. and
72. plesent
73. Don
74. imeegration
75. intrest
76. those
77. remem
78. Seewrites
79. proceeded
80. followered
81. forsight
82. develope
83. is
84. powful
85. principle
86. Maryion

87. ascent
88. befor
89. Norfork
90. Calven
91. juce
92. molases
93. driping
94. Racliff
95. Wingutten
96. The most
97. till
98. Dire
99. Franks
100. Moor
101. Franks
102. commendible
103. monts
104. commisary
105. McMullens
106. colony's
107. Ribeiro
108. colonies
109. Bowens
110. whil
111. Eugen
112. Portugese
113. rout
114. mean time
115. planed
116. Jesuits
117. ma
118. Agupé
119. first-time
120. effeges
121. battle ships
122. fire works
123. in
124. box like
125. embroided
126. bate
127. make shift
128. acomodating
129. uncermoniously
130. maned
131. threatened
132. drgged
133. . . . people were yet housed up.

134. rought
135. mean time
136. comaradas
137. past
138. anoyed
139. boys
140. en route
141. Wengetten
142. Xiriria. The town's modern name is Eldorado Paulista.
143. nights
144. *onces*
145. fashin
146. esconcened
147. Bowens
148. The good church people of New Yorks gift of two boxes of . . .
149. principly
150. cours
151. Quillen
152. vallies
153. McMullens
154. ever
155. rout
156. litterally
157. fatal
158. Stanleys
159. empted
160. us
161. angel
162. The text cannot be deciphered.
163. orang
164. Crowey
165. Crowey
166. oposite
167. crowey
168. . . . before us and came / to an old Brazilian house, Name—Carmargo.
169. alowed
170. feather bed
171. empted
172. Crowy
173. roca
174. sugar cane
175. This was worth approximately twenty-five dollars at the time.
176. exilent
177. lean to
178. They they
179. 2ed
180. began

181. mean time
182. sugar cane
183. *tatues*
184. oncas
185. to
186. untill
187. probably *Ficus religiosa*
188. sea coast
189. Peruibe
190. superentendent
191. oncas
192. monkes
193. over head
194. neighbours
195. Crowey
196. Piruibe
197. out side
198. morter
199. horizentle
200. . . . hand and each roller . . .
201. The text cannot be deciphered.
202. de
203. . . . and called them our sweetcakes.
204. substuted
205. is
206. not
207. potatos
208. porvilia
209. pictur
210. tucana
211. anvel
212. poor-whip-will
213. acquaintence
214. The text cannot be deciphered.
215. its self
216. The text cannot be deciphered.
217. recolections
218. besides
219. omited
220. old fashuned
221. songes
222. Pilgrims Progress
223. asperation
224. *onçes*
225. till
226. Saks
227. mountain side

228. till
229. spell bound
230. opertunity
231. which
232. . . . small stream above us about half a mile above us.
233. morter
234. abanden
235. *raca*
236. pastur
237. *farva*
238. Marsine
239. *comarado*
240. Marsine
241. *matto*
242. *pysadas*
243. bear
244. some how
245. mountans
246. it
247. *Peruibie*
248. *Jundiahy*
249. *Reboncas*
250. well built
251. discription
252. moevabiles
253. apacked
254. . . . for cash and bring him away . . .
255. . . . did and first settled on . . .
256. Arche
257. mountans
258. wast
259. Pruibe
260. *Conceicão*
261. Cooks
262. Hanny
263. mountans
264. burried
265. and
266. figuers
267. *lanca-perfume*
268. four footed
269. . . . sea monster the back bone joints some one had set them on end . . .
270. The text is difficult to decipher.
271. climed
272. bear footed
273. ignorent
274. forengner

275. riden
276. *Jundiahy*
277. *Jundiahy*
278. *Fazenda de Bocudo*
279. tire some
280. muls
281. portugese
282. cart men and mule tears
283. day
284. rout
285. whizzin
286. air ships
287. toilling
288. cart man
289. barefooted also as well . . .
290. *cabrauva. Myrocarpus frondosus.*
291. extending
292. *taquera*
293. down hill
294. *laranga*
295. horse back
296. stirup
297. was
298. it
299. buck board
300. travling
301. white washed
302. floord
303. bed rooms
304. and
305. negros
306. English man
307. morter
308. *fagoes*
309. and
310. *marcella.* Probably *Achyrocline satureoides.*
311. ever
312. foreigeners

Chapter 3: Settling

1. Sarah Bellona Smith Ferguson, "Emigrating to Brazil in 1866–67," unpublished ms., 1935, Blanche Henry Clark Weaver Papers, in possession of William Clark Griggs, Houston, Texas.

2. Griggs, *The Elusive Eden*, 4–5; Ferguson, "The American Colonies" (December 18, 1936), 41.

3. Griggs, *The Elusive Eden*, 4–5.

4. Ferguson, "The American Colonies" (December 18), 41; Ferguson, "Emigrating to Brazil" (1935), 3.

5. Ferguson, "Emigrating to Brazil" (1935), 2–3.

6. See chapter 2 above.

7. Griggs, *The Elusive Eden*, 32.

8. See chapter 2 above.

9. A. J. Hanna, *Flight into Oblivion* (reprint; Bloomington: Indiana University Press, 1959), 244.

10. "Champ Ferguson," *Harper's Weekly*, September 23, 1865, p. 593.

11. Hanna, *Flight into Oblivion*, viii.

12. Griggs, *The Elusive Eden*, 12; Grier, "Confederate Emigration to Brazil," 19.

13. Rolle, *The Lost Cause*, 18.

14. Hill, *The Confederate Exodus to Latin America*, 90.

15. Antunes de Oliveira, *Movimento de passageiros norte-americanos*, 1, 3; Hill, *The Confederate Exodus*, 39–40.

16. Gaston, *Hunting a Home in Brazil*, 5; Antunes de Oliveira, *Movimento de passageiros norte-americanos*, 5.

17. Gaston, *Hunting a Home in Brazil*, 42–43.

18. "Joseph Long Minchin," manuscript transcribed by Mame Almira Minchen, ca. 1935, Weaver Papers.

19. Hill, *The Confederate Exodus*, 27–28; Gaston, *Hunting a Home in Brazil*, 151–225; Antunes de Oliveira, *Movimento de passageiros norte-americanos*, 11.

20. Antunes de Oliveira, *Movimento de passageiros norte-americanos*, 7.

21. Dunn, *Brazil, the Home for Southerners*.

22. Dunn, *Brazil, the Home for Southerners*, 105–51.

23. Dunn, *Brazil, the Home for Southerners*, 47, 48.

24. Antunes de Oliveira, *Movimento de passageiros norte-americanos*, 39; Hill, *The Confederate Exodus*, 42–44; Eliza Kerr Shippey, "When Americans Were Emigrants," *Kansas City Star*, June 16, 1912, p. 4.

25. Shippey, "When Americans Were Emigrants," 4; Goldman, *Os pioneiros americanos no Brasil*, 21–32.

26. Dunn, *Brazil, the Home for Southerners*, 227; Hill, *The Confederate Exodus*, 29; Antunes de Oliveira, *Movimento de passageiros norte-americanos*, 10–11.

27. Antunes de Oliveira, *Movimento de passageiros norte-americanos*, 9; Harold B. Simpson, *Hill County [Texas] Trilogy* (Hillsboro, Tex.: Hill College Press, 1896), 52, 59; William C. Pool, "The Battle of Dove Creek," *Southwestern Historical Quarterly* 53 (April 1950): 367–85; Griggs, *The Elusive Eden*, 20.

28. Dunn, *Brazil, the Home for Southerners*, 152–79.

29. Griggs, *The Elusive Eden*, 43–54; Ferguson, "The American Colonies" (December 18), 18–41; (December 24), 14–15; (December 31), 20–21.

30. Griggs, *The Elusive Eden*, 56–63; Edwin Ney McMullan, "Texans Established Colony in Brazil," 2. See the personal account in chapter 2.

31. Griggs, *The Elusive Eden*, 76–78.

32. Griggs, *The Elusive Eden*, 79–107.

33. Antunes de Oliveira, *Movimento de passageiros norte-americanos*, 12–31; Griggs, *The Elusive Eden*, 19; Brannon, "Southern Emigration to Brazil," 74–95.

34. Hill, *The Confederate Exodus*, 56–59.

35. Hill, *The Confederate Exodus*, 64–65.
36. Antunes de Oliveira, *Movimento de passageiros norte-americanos*, 10–11; Dunn, *Brazil, the Home for Southerners*, 237.
37. "Emma Broadnax," manuscript transcribed by Mame Almira Minchen, 1935, Weaver Papers; Hill, "Confederate Exiles in Brazil," 192–210.
38. Lansford Warren Hastings, *The Emigrant's Guide to Oregon and California* (reprint, Princeton: Princeton University Press, 1932), xii–xxii; Charles Kelly, *Salt Desert Trails: A History of the Hastings Cutoff and Other Early Trails Which Crossed the Great Salt Desert Seeking a Shorter Road to California* (Salt Lake City: Western Printing, 1930), 15–19; George R. Stewart, *The California Trail: An Epic with Many Heroes* (New York: McGraw-Hill, 1962), 182–83.
39. "Shipwreck of a Brazilian Colony," *New Orleans Daily Crescent*, January 29, 1867, p. 2.
40. Hastings, *The Emigrant's Guide to Brazil*, 1–2.
41. Hastings, *The Emigrant's Guide to Brazil*, 12, 191–98.
42. Griggs, *The Elusive Eden*, 18.
43. Griggs, *The Elusive Eden*, 122–23.

Chapter 4: Fitting In

1. For a complete treatment of the modern world-system theory, see the numerous works of Immanuel Wallerstein, most notably his three-volume work *The Modern World-System*; vol. 1: *Capitalist Agriculture and the Origins of the European World-Economy in the Sixteenth Century*; vol. 2: *Mercantilism and the Consolidation of the European World-Economy, 1600–1750*; and vol. 3: *The Second Era of Great Expansion of the Capitalist World-Economy, 1730s–1840s*, Studies in Social Discontinuity (New York: Academic Press, 1974–89). For a short examination of how the *confederados* related directly to worldwide developments, see Ana Maria dos Santos, "Os benvindos confederados: Colonização e modernização no Brasil Imperial (1865–1870)," in *Sociedade brasileira de pesquisa historica, anais da VII reunião* (São Paulo, 1988), 115–18.
2. Immanuel Wallerstein, *Geopolitics and Geoculture: Essays on the Changing World-System*, Studies in Modern Capitalism/Etudes sur le capitalisme moderne (Cambridge: Cambridge University Press; Paris: Editions de la Maison des Sciences de l'Homme, 1991), 38.
3. There are two subtypes of peripheral areas: the periphery and the semi-periphery, the latter displaying a combination of characteristics of the core and the more extreme peripheral areas (Wallerstein, *The Modern World-System* 1:349–50).
4. Wallerstein, *The Modern World-System 3*, chap. 4.
5. Historians generally use the term "bourgeois" to refer to urban dwellers and "gentry" to refer to landed rural elites. Unfortunately, there is no term to refer to the phenomenon of family alliances that intentionally include individuals from both categories and exist specifically for the purpose of enhancing social and economic success based on the best of both worlds. Wallerstein argues that capitalist gentry farmers are in essence bourgeois in their mentality. Here, we will opt to use the awkward term "bourgeois/gentry" as a means of reinforcing the presence of the combination of urban- and rural-based occupations and mentalities in the communities under study. For various treatments of the term "bourgeois," including

distinctions between it and "aristocracy," see Wallerstein, *The Modern World-System* 2; Lawrence Stone, *The Crisis of the Aristocracy, 1558–1641*, abridged ed. (London: Oxford University Press, 1967); Fernand Braudel, *Civilization and Capitalism, 15th–18th Century*; vol. 3: *The Perspective of the World*, trans. Siân Reynolds (New York: Harper & Row, 1984); and Peter Gay, *The Bourgeois Experience: Victoria to Freud*; vol. 1: *Education of the Senses* (New York: Oxford University Press, 1984).

6. A. C. Tavares Bastos, *Os males do presente e as esperanças do futuro*, preface by Cassiano Tavares Bastos, introduction by José Honório Rodrigues, 2d ed., Brasiliana, vol. 151 (São Paulo: Companhia Editora Nacional, 1976), 63n–64n. It is unclear from Tavares Bastos's notations whether the figure of $500–$1,000 was per person or per family. For Gunter's assets, see C. G. Gunter to W. A. Gunter, December 21, 1865, Gunter-Poellnitz Papers, Southern Historical Collection, University of North Carolina Library, Chapel Hill (hereinafter cited as SHC/UNC). Tavares Bastos puts the value of Gunter's first harvest (in 1867) at 40:000$000 (Brazilian *milreis*); using the average exchange rate of that year at 1$000 equal to US$0.49, this figure amounts to roughly US$19,600.00.

7. J. D. Porter to John D. Templeton, July 5, 1867, James Denford Porter Papers, Virginia Historical Society, Richmond (hereinafter cited as VHA).

8. The Brazilian constitution of the time stipulated that other religions would be tolerated, but with the understanding that Roman Catholicism was the religion of the country (Vieira, *O protestantismo*, 247).

9. See, for example, Harris Gunter to Brother, August 24, 1866; Harris Gunter to Brother, November 6, 1866; and R. W. [?] M. Eachin [McEachin] to Will, November 23, 1866, Gunter-Poellnitz Papers.

10. J. D. Porter to John D. Templeton, July 5, 1867, Porter Papers.

11. For accounts of the reception given to the various advance agents, see, for example, Weaver, "Confederate Emigration to Brazil," 36–42 and 45; Grier, "Confederate Emigration to Brazil," 38. See C. G. Gunter to W. A. Gunter, December 21, 1865, Gunter-Poellnitz Papers, for Charles Grandison Gunter's meeting with the minister of agriculture.

12. See, for example, Weaver, "Confederate Emigration to Brazil," 33–35.

13. Kidder, *Sketches of Residence and Travels in Brazil*; James C. Fletcher, *International Relations with Brazil: Proceedings on the Reception of H. E. Senhor d'Azambuja, Envoy Extraordinary and Minister Plenipotential from Brazil . . . with Remarks of Rev. James C. Fletcher* (New York: John W. Amerman, 1865); and James C. Fletcher and Daniel P. Kidder, *Brazil and the Brazilians, Portrayed in Historical and Descriptive Sketches* (Philadelphia: Childs and Peterson, 1857), which went through several editions between 1857 and 1866.

14. Weaver, "Confederate Emigration to Brazil," 44; Grier, "Confederate Emigration to Brazil," 50.

15. With thanks to Theda Skocpol, whose seminal work *States and Social Revolution: A Comparative Analysis of France, Russia, and China* (Cambridge: Cambridge University Press, 1979), 15–16, critiques those theories of revolution which accept the premise that revolutions are the result of the emergence of a deliberate effort toward effecting that particular outcome. While her own theory of revolution successfully challenges the validity of such a "purposeful" image for revolution, the concept proves to be useful in the context of the Southern migration to Brazil.

16. R. L. [Robert Lewis] Dabney to Brother, January 27, 1866, Dabney Family Papers, VHS.

17. As reported in R. L. Dabney to Brother, 1872 [?], Dabney Family Papers.

18. As reported in R. L. Dabney to Brother, 1872 [?], Dabney Family Papers.

19. See, for example, Weaver, "Confederate Emigration to Brazil," 50–53; and Hill, "Confederate Exiles to Brazil," 197.

20. On the presence of a hegemonic bourgeoisie class in the antebellum South, see F. N. Boney, *Southerners All* (Macon, Ga.: Mercer University Press, 1984), 98–99 and 117.

21. At least 40 percent of the Alabamians who migrated to Brazil can readily be identified as being connected to the Broad River group, either directly or by marriage. Further research into marriages and genealogies would probably reveal a significantly higher percentage. The surnames associated with this 40 percent are Anderson, Berney, Boyle, Broadnax, Brown, Bryan, Campbell, Carr, Daniel, Davis DeYampert, Emerson, Ezelle, Fenley, Gaston, Gunter, Hall, Hardie, Harris, Judkins, McDade, McIntyre, Mathews, Miller, Mitchell, Moore, Norris, Russell, Smith, Storrs, Strong, Taylor, Thomas, Thompson, Townsend, Weissinger, Whitaker, and Yancey. See George Rockingham Gilmer, *Sketches of Some of the First Settlers of Upper Georgia, of the Cherokees, and the Author* (Americus, Ga.: Americus Book, 1926); Clanton Ware Williams, *The Early History of Montgomery and Incidentally of the State of Alabama*, ed. W. Stanley Hoole and Addie S. Hoole (University, Ala.: Confederate Publishing, 1979); and J. Mills Thornton III, *Politics and Power in a Slave Society: Alabama, 1800–1860* (Baton Rouge: Louisiana State University Press, 1978), 8–10.

22. Thornton, *Politics and Power*, 10.

23. Charles Grandison Gunter to William A. Gunter, August 23, 1866, Gunter-Poellnitz Papers; "Articles of Agreement of the Florida Emigration Society," undated, and Edward McCrady L'Engle to I. P. Bouse, June 6, 1865 [?], Edward McCrady L'Engle Papers, SHC/UNC. Gaston's wife was the former Susan Brumby, daughter of Richard Trapier Brumby; see Grier, "Confederate Emigration to Brazil," 35. The information that Brumby served as Gaston's agent in Georgia is found in "Letter from Brazil," *Montgomery Weekly Advertiser*, October 29, 1867.

24. Thornton, *Politics and Power*, 26; although Thornton treats the Yanceyite movement throughout this work, chapter 6 is particularly useful in this regard.

25. Grier, "Confederate Emigration to Brazil," 55; Orville Vernon Burton, *In My Father's House Are Many Mansions: Family and Community in Edgefield, South Carolina* (Chapel Hill: University of North Carolina Press, 1985), 66; Julia Norris Jones, "Reminiscences of the Confederates in Brazil," typewritten manuscript, 1951, p. 1, Tutweiler Southern Collection, Birmingham Public Library, Birmingham, Alabama; and Goldman, *Os pioneiros americanos no Brasil*, 107–17.

26. Lucy Judkins Durr, "Brazilian Recollections," typescript copy, n.d., Tutwiler Southern Collection, Birmingham (Ala.) Public Library; *The Story of Alabama: A History of the State*, vols. 4 and 5: *Personal and Family History* (New York: Lewis Historical Publishing, 1949), 4:388; Richardson Dougall and Mary Patricia Chapman, *United States Chiefs of Mission, 1778–1973 (Complete to 31 March 1973)* (Washington, D.C.: U.S. Government Printing Office, 1973), 17; *The National Cyclopedia of American Biography*, 63 vols. (Ann Arbor: University Microfilms, 1967), 10:150–51; and "The Hardies: Descendants of John Hardie and Mary Meade Hall Hardie," Hardie Papers, SHC/UNC.

27. See Charles H. Brown, *Agents of Manifest Destiny: The Life and Times of the Filibusters* (Chapel Hill: University of North Carolina Press, 1980), for a fuller treatment of this subject.

28. For various biographical treatments of Tavares Bastos, see Vieira, *O protestantismo*, 95–100; José Honório Rodrigues, introduction to Tavares Bastos, *Os males do presente*, 9–14; and Augusto Victorino Alves Sacramento Blake, *Diccionario bibliographico brazileiro*, 7 vols. (1883–1902; reprint, Rio de Janeiro: Apex Gráfica e Editora for the Conselho Federal de Cultura, 1970), 1:370–71.

29. Vieira, *O protestantismo*.

30. Rodrigues, introduction to *Os males do presente*, 9–11.

31. Grier, "Confederate Emigration to Brazil," 73; Rodrigues, introduction to *Os males do presente*, 11. Tavares Bastos was born in 1839 and died at age thirty-six in 1875.

32. Vieira, *O protestantismo*, 83 and 87. The dates of Fletcher's service in this capacity were July 1852 to October 1853.

33. Ibid. The boyhood friend and personal adviser of Dom Pedro II was Luís Pedreira do Couto Ferraz, the Visconde do Bom Retiro; see Eul-Soo Pang, *In Pursuit of Honor and Power: Noblemen of the Southern Cross in Nineteenth-Century Brazil* (Tuscaloosa: University of Alabama Press, 1988), 209 and 246.

34. Rodrigues, introduction to *Os males do presente*, 12.

35. For Fletcher's movements back and forth between Brazil and the United States, see Vieira, *O protestantismo*. Members of merchant communities typically exhibited a high degree of mobility among the various port cities in which their businesses were located. For an example of a family whose members moved among Rio, Santos, Baltimore, Philadelphia, New York, Liverpool, London, and Oporto, among other cities, see the Wright-May-Thom and Wright collections of the Maryland Historical Society Library, Baltimore.

36. Robert E. Lee to Robert W. Lewis, Jr., April 6, 1866, Robert Edward Lee Letterbook, 1865–1866, pp. 126–28, Lee Family Papers, VHS.

37. Weaver, "Confederate Emigration to Brazil," 39; Thomas McAdory Owen, *History of Alabama and Dictionary of Alabama Biography*, introduction by Milo B. Howard, Jr., 4 vols. (Spartanburg, S.C.: Reprint Company, 1978), 4:1820; *The Story of Alabama* 4:387. On the linkage between the Presbyterians and Freemasonry, see Vieira, *O protestantismo*, 289–91.

38. Vieira, *O protestantismo*, 225n.

39. Weaver, "Confederate Emigration to Brazil," 45–46; and Tavares Bastos, *Os males do presente*, 63n.

40. Weaver, "Confederate Emigration to Brazil," 41–42.

41. Vieira, *O protestantismo*, 42.

42. Blake, *Diccionario bibliographico brazileiro* 4:237–41.

43. J. D. Porter to John D. Templeton, July 5, 1867, Porter Papers.

44. *Organizações e programas ministeriais: Regime parlamentar no império*, 2d ed. (Rio: Ministério da Justiça e Negócios Interiores and Arquivo Nacional, 1962), 447–48; Rodrigues, introduction to *Os males do presente*, 11.

45. Blake, *Diccionario bibliographico brazileiro* 5:50.

46. Alves Motta Sobrinho, *A civilização do café (1820–1920)*, 3d ed. (São Paulo: Editora Brasiliense, 1978), 67. Caetano Furquim de Almeida was the son-in-law of the Barão de Vassouras, Francisco José Teixeira Leite. See Affonso de E. Taunay,

"Uma irmandade de grandes cafesistas e civilizadores os Teixeira Leite: Nascimento, vida, e morte de Vassouras," in *O café no segundo centenário de sua introdução no Brasil,* 2 vols. (Rio: Departamento Nacional do Café, 1934), 2:48; Pang, *In Pursuit of Honor and Power,* 97–98; and Alberto Ribeiro Lamego, *O homem e a serra: Setores da evolução fluminense* IV, 2d ed., Biblioteca Geográfica Brasileira, ser. A, no. 8 (Rio: Instituto Brasileiro de Geografia e Estatística, Conselho Nacional de Geografia, 1963), 340.

47. Vieira, *O protestantismo,* 87.

48. Vieira, *O protestantismo,* 223–24.

49. Pang, *In Pursuit of Honor and Power,* 136.

50. Pang, *In Pursuit of Honor and Power,* 123.

51. On the modernization of the sugar industry in Brazil in the 1870s, see, for example, Eul-Soo Pang, "Modernization and Slavocracy in Nineteenth-Century Brazil," *Journal of Interdisciplinary History* 9, no. 4 (Spring 1979): 667–88. On the McCords' friendship with the Carneiro da Silvas, see João José Carneiro da Silva to Anne E. MacCord, May 22, 1879, Mrs. Russell McCord Papers, SHC/UNC.

52. Vieira, *O protestantismo,* 215–16. Quintino Bocaiuva's close friend Manuel Batista da Cruz Tamandaré was married to the daughter of the Barão de Sousa Queirós. The Sousa Queirós clan was part of an extensive kinship network that included such other prominent São Paulo and Rio de Janeiro clans as the Sousa Barroses, the Silva Prados, the Sousa Aranhas, and the Monteiro de Barroses. See Pang, *In Pursuit of Honor and Power,* 136.

53. Affonso de E. Taunay, *História do café no Brasil,* vol. 8: *No Brasil imperial, 1872–1889,* tomo VI (Rio: Departamento Nacional do Café, 1939), 248–49.

54. Vieira, *O protestantismo,* 262.

55. For the Silva Prados' classification as gentry, see Pang, *In Pursuit of Honor and Power,* 124. For the Jones-Norris connection to the Monteiro de Barros clan, see Frederico de Barros Brotero, *A família Monteiro de Barros* (São Paulo, 1951), 59–61; Gueiros, *O protestantismo,* 234n, refers to Newton Benaton as Nathan's nephew. The name also appears as "Bennaton."

56. Alberto's great-grandfather was George Rudge, who was a partner in the company as of the early 1840s (William H. De Courcy Wright Documents, June 28, 1843, Wright-May-Thom Collection).

57. Vieira, *O protestantismo,* p. 262.

58. Wallerstein, *The Modern World-System* 3:22.

59. See *Diário do Rio de Janeiro,* August 15, 1860, for reference to a planters' organization in Campos; and June 5 and 16, September 17, October 15, and November 14, 1861, for the Sociedade Círculo Agrícola de São José da Cacaria. In particular, it was the Sousa Breves clan of Rio Province, which was intermarried with the Monteiro de Barroses and the Silva Prados of São Paulo, whose members were instrumental in the founding and administration of the Cacaria society.

Chapter 5: The Heritage

1. Grier, "Confederate Emigration to Brazil," 178.

2. See chapter 2.

3. Rev. W. C. Emerson, *The Missionary* 5 (1872): 188.

4. Maria José F. de Araujo Ribeiro and Melquesedec Ferreira, *Americana e sua história* (Americana, São Paulo: Prefeitura Municipal, 1992), 3.

5. Ribeiro and Ferreira, *Americana e sua história*, 4.

6. Ribeiro and Ferreira, *Americana e sua história*, 7–8.

7. Hugh Clarence Tucker, *The Bible in Brazil: Colporter Experiences* (New York: Young People's Missionary Movement of the United States and Canada, 1902), 254.

8. Griggs, *The Elusive Eden*, 116; Jones, *Soldado descansa*, 322.

9. Jones, *Soldado descansa*, 352.

10. *The Missionary* 4 (1871): 17, 81, 132; 5 (1872): 72, 99.

11. *The Missionary* 5 (1872): 10, 141.

12. Griggs, *The Elusive Eden*, 117.

13. Jones, *Soldado descansa*, 339, 311.

14. *The Missionary* 4 (1871): 132.

15. José Arthur Rios, "A imigração dos confederados norte-americanos no Brasil," *Revista de emigração e colonização*, September 1948 and December–January 1949.

16. Zilmar Ziller Marcos, "The Influence of the American Colonists on the Development of Brazilian Agriculture and Education" (Paper delivered at the conference Fried Chicken under the Southern Cross: American Migration to Brazil after the Civil War, Auburn University, Auburn, Alabama, July 17–18, 1992).

17. Weaver, "Confederate Immigrants and Evangelical Churches in Brazil," 447.

18. Grier, "Confederate Emigration to Brazil," 179–82.

19. Jones, *Soldado descansa*, 188–89, 190.

20. Weaver, "Confederate Immigrants and Evangelical Churches in Brazil," 447.

21. Weaver, "Confederate Immigrants and Evangelical Churches in Brazil," 449.

22. Goldman, *Os pioneiros americanos no Brazil,* 158.

23. Weaver, "Confederate Immigrants and Evangelical Churches in Brazil," 449.

24. Weaver, "Confederate Immigrants and Evangelical Churches in Brazil," 454.

25. Weaver, "Confederate Immigrants and Evangelical Churches in Brazil," 457.

26. For a history of the early years of the Presbyterian church in Brazil, see Robert Leonard Mcintire, *Portrait of Half a Century: Fifty Years of Presbyterianism in Brazil (1859–1910)*, Sondeos no. 46 (Cuernavaca: CIDOC, 1969). Chapter 4 concerns Simonton.

27. Samuel R. Gammon, *The Evangelical Invasion of Brazil; or, A Half Century of Evangelical Missions in the Land of the Southern Cross* (Richmond: Presbyterian Committee of Publication, 1910), 111.

28. *The Missionary* 1 (1868): 100; Duncan A. Reily, *História documental do protestantismo no Brasil* (São Paulo: ASTE, 1984), 110.

29. Reily, *História documental do protestantismo*, 116, 155 n. 229.

30. Weaver, "Confederate Immigrants and Evangelical Churches in Brazil," 455 n. 18; Ernest Trice Thompson, *Presbyterians in the South*; vol. 2: *1861–1890* (Richmond: John Knox Press, 1973), 110–11.

31. *The Missionary* 1 (1868): 100–101.

32. *The Missionary* 2 (1869): 19–26, 24; 1 (1868): 122; 2 (1869): 24.

33. *The Missionary* 2 (1869): 25.

34. *The Missionary* 2 (1869): 25–26.

35. *The Missionary* 2 (1869): 24.

36. *The Missionary* 2 (1869): 113, 119, 145, 181.

37. *The Missionary* 3 (1870): 3.
38. *The Missionary* 3 (1870): 3.
39. *The Missionary* 3 (1870): 49, 149, 129, 181.
40. *The Missionary* 4 (1871): 163, 3–6, 132–33; 5 (1872): 6, 97.
41. *The Missionary* 3 (1870): 181–82, 99.
42. *The Missionary* 4 (1871): 17–18; 5 (1872): 7, 19, 34.
43. *The Missionary* 3 (1870): 182.
44. *The Missionary* 5 (1872): 20.
45. *The Missionary* 5 (1872): 23–24.
46. *The Missionary* 3 (1870): 149, 182.
47. Jones, *Soldado descansa*, 215.
48. *The Missionary* 3 (1870): 149; 4 (1871): 18.
49. *The Missionary* 3 (1870): 181.
50. *The Missionary* 4 (1871): 163; 5 (1872): 19, 140.
51. *The Missionary* 4 (1871): 163, 114.
52. *The Missionary* 5 (1872): 41; 4 (1871): 113.
53. *The Missionary* 4 (1871): 114–15.
54. *The Missionary* 5 (1872): 19, 23, 25–26.
55. *The Missionary* 5 (1872): 26.
56. *The Missionary* 5 (1872): 25.
57. *The Missionary* 5 (1872): 130.
58. Jones, *Soldado descansa*, 232.
59. Weaver, "Confederate Immigrants and Evangelical Churches in Brazil," 454; Grier, "Confederate Emigration to Brazil," 180.
60. *The Missionary* 5 (1872): 142.
61. *The Missionary* 5 (1872): 142. In fact, at the second meeting of the presbytery, held June 13, 1872, Emerson was granted permission to unite with the Presbytery of Tombecbee. He was also directed to present a report to the General Assembly on the state of religion in Brazil.
62. *The Missionary* 5 (1872): 21–22.
63. *The Missionary* 3 (1870): 3.
64. Jones, *Soldado descansa*, 218.
65. Jones, *Soldado descansa*, 218.
66. *The Missionary* 4 (1871): 163–64.
67. Tucker, *The Bible in Brazil*, 244.
68. Thompson, *Presbyterians in the South*, 302.
69. Weaver, "Confederate Immigrants and Evangelical Churches in Brazil," 458–59.
70. McIntire, *Portrait of Half a Century*, 7/52.
71. Gaston, *Hunting a Home in Brazil*, 270–71; Goldman, *Os pioneiros americanos no Brazil*, 159.
72. Jones, *Soldado descansa*, 328.
73. Jones, *Soldado descansa*, 328.
74. Jones, *Soldado descansa*, 328.
75. Goldman, *Os pioneiros americanos no Brazil*, 168.
76. Goldman, *Os pioneiros americanos no Brazil*, 168.
77. Jones, *Soldado descansa*, 307.

78. Jones, *Soldado descansa*, 261.
79. Goldman, *Os pioneiros americanos no Brazil*, 169.
80. Goldman, *Os pioneiros americanos no Brazil*, 168.
81. Jones, *Soldado descansa*, 215, 220.
82. Jones, *Soldado descansa*, 243.

Chapter 6: The Baptists

1. Quoted in Ulrich B. Phillips, *Life and Labor in the Old South* (Boston: Little, Brown, 1929), 340–41.
2. W. B. Cooper to Gov. Lewis E. Parsons, August 8, 1865, in "Destitution" file, Gov. Lewis E. Parsons Official Files, Alabama State Archives, Montgomery.
3. Report by Probate Judge Jackson Gardner of Bibb County, November 18, 1865; Moses M. Guise to Gov. Robert M. Patton, February 1866; Louis Wyeth to Governor Patton, April 2, 1866; Rev. J. J. Grace to Governor Patton, April 20, 1866; J. L. Sheffield to Governor Patton, September 17, 1866; Benjamin F. Porter to Governor Patton, October 2, 1866; S. S. Anderson to Governor Patton, June 13, 1867; all in "Destitution" file in Gov. Robert M. Patton Official Files, Alabama State Archives. There are dozens of such letters from every part of the state from spring 1865 through 1867.
4. L. M. Stiff et al. to Gov. Lewis E. Parsons, August 6, 1865, "Destitution" file, Parsons Official Files.
5. Resolution, March 19, 1866, in "Destitution" file, Parsons Official Files.
6. S. K. McSpadden to Gov. Robert M. Patton, September 21 and October 19, 1866; both in "Destitution" file, Parsons Official Files.
7. Robert A. Gilmour, "The Other Emancipation: Studies in the Society and Economy of Alabama Whites during Reconstruction" (Ph.D. diss., Johns Hopkins University, 1972), 42–53, 124, 129–33.
8. Quoted in William B. Hesseltine and David L. Smiley, *The South in American History* (Englewood Cliffs, N.J.: Prentice-Hall, 1964), 419.
9. E. Merton Coulter, *The South during Reconstruction, 1865–1877* (Baton Rouge: Louisiana State University Press, 1947), 184. Estimates of the number of immigrants are generally unreliable for a variety of reasons.
10. Quoted in H. A. Tupper, *The Foreign Missions of the Southern Baptist Convention* (Richmond: Foreign Mission Board of the Southern Baptist Convention, 1880), 10.
11. Tupper, *The Foreign Missions of the Southern Baptist Convention*, 10.
12. Tupper, *The Foreign Missions of the Southern Baptist Convention*, 11.
13. Tupper, *The Foreign Missions of the Southern Baptist Convention*, 12.
14. Tupper, *The Foreign Missions of the Southern Baptist Convention*, 3, 13.
15. E. H. Quillin Biography, in E. H. Quillin File, Foreign Mission Board Papers, Southern Baptist Historical Archives, Nashville.
16. B. H. Carroll to Dr. H. A. Tupper, November 19, 1880, Quillin File, Foreign Mission Board Papers.
17. E. H. Quillin to Dr. H. A. Tupper, July 12, and December 28, 1880, Quillin File, Foreign Mission Board Papers.
18. B. P. Thomas to Dr. H. A. Tupper, April 26, 1886, Quillin File, Foreign Mission Board Papers.

19. E. H. Quillin to Dr. H. A. Tupper, December 28, 1880; ms. for proposed "Santa Barbara Mission School"; in Quillin File, Foreign Mission Board Papers.

20. E. H. Quillin to Dr. H. A. Tupper, March 20, 1881, Quillin File, Foreign Mission Board Papers.

21. B. P. Thomas to Dr. H. A. Tupper, April 26, 1886; Warden G. Whitaker to Foreign Mission Board, May 10, 1886; Quillin File, Foreign Mission Board Papers.

22. Rufus C. Burleson to Dr. H. A. Tupper, December 20, 1884, January 27 and June 26, 1885; B. H. Carroll to Dr. H. A. Tupper, January 27, 1885; E. A. Puthuff File, Foreign Mission Board Papers.

23. Charles D. Daniel to Dr. H. A. Tupper, February 11 and 19, March 16, and May 31, 1886; March 31, April 4, September 24, October 11, and December 24, 1887; March 2 and 29, 1888; Daniel to T. P. Bell, July 28 and 30, August 7, October 1, 1888; Daniel to Tupper, August 2, September 9, December 12, 1889; January 12, 1890, all in Daniel File, Foreign Mission Board Papers.

24. E. A. Puthuff to Dr. H. A. Tupper, January 10, 1888, Puthuff File, Foreign Mission Board Papers.

25. Charles D. Daniel to Dr. H. A. Tupper, January 12, 1890, Daniel File, Foreign Mission Board Papers.

26. "The Pernambuco Field," February 28, 1948; ms. in Daniel File, Foreign Mission Board Papers.

27. Avery Hamilton Reid, *Baptists in Alabama: Their Organization and Witness* (Montgomery: Alabama Baptist State Convention, 1967), 566–69.

28. Oscar Handlin, "The Immigrant and American Politics," in *Foreign Influences in American Life*, ed. David F. Bowers (Princeton: Princeton University Press, 1944), 91.

29. Tupper, *The Foreign Missions of the Southern Baptist Convention*, 13–14.

30. Tupper, *The Foreign Missions of the Southern Baptist Convention*, 14.

Chapter 7: The Methodists

1. Duncan A. Reily, *Metodismo brasileiro e wesleyano* (São Bernardo do Campo, S.P.: Imprensa Metodista, 1981), 227.

2. The beginning of Methodism in Pará is often credited to Bishop William Taylor (1880) and Rev. Justus H. Nelson (1888–95). But Southern colonists had settled in Belém as early as 1866 and in Santarém as early as 1867. One of the early immigrants was Dr. Joseph Pitts, whose father actually was the first Methodist preacher sent to Brazil. Another immigrant was Rev. Richard T. Herrington, who preached among the colonists in Pará until his death in 1894. See José Gonçalves Salvador, *História do metodismo no Brasil*, vol. 1 (São Bernardo do Campo, S.P.: Imprensa Metodista, 1982), 88–96. Also see *Apologista Cristão Brasileiro* 26 (1890): 7.

3. Methodist work in Amazonas began in 1887 in Manaus with Justus Nelson and a companion by the name of Carver. But in 1892 the work was strengthened by the arrival of the Reverend Frank R. Spaulding, most certainly a descendant of the Reverend Justin Spaulding.

4. When J. J. Ransom of the Methodist Episcopal Church, South, traveled to Rio Grande do Sul in 1877, he discovered that a Methodist from Montevideo, Mr. João da Costa Correia, had already been active distributing Bibles in the area. Later Correia transferred his church affiliation from the Methodist Episcopal Church to

the Methodist Episcopal Church, South (John J. Ransom, *Annual Reports* of 1877 and 1878, General Archives of the Board of Missions of the United Methodist Church, pp. 106–24).

5. W. J. Townsend, H. B. Workman, and George Eayrs, eds., *A New History of Methodism*, vol. 2 (Nashville: Publishing House of the Methodist Episcopal Church, South, 1906), 197.

6. The others were the missions in China, Japan, Korea, and Mexico.

7. Townsend, Workman, and Eayrs, *A New History*, 197.

8. Although still flushed with optimism, James Cannon begins to present a more balanced view: "No small degree of success has attended the ministry of the Church. In 1906 the membership was reported as being over five thousand, and in 1919 the Foreign Secretary reported to the Board of Missions on Brazil: 'The work in this field has been wonderfully successful. There are twice as many converts in the Church in Brazil as in the other South American countries combined—more than in Mexico, more communicants in proportion to the population than in China. It is the only Latin American country where there is found a native Church with a strong and entirely independent native leadership.' Yet, after a period of substantial growth, a period of slow progress was manifested, a point beyond which it seemed to be impossible to carry the evangelistic or educational work of the Church" (James Cannon III, *History of Southern Methodist Missions* [Nashville: Cokesbury Press, 1926], 189).

9. The number of missionaries and church members was culled from J. L. Kennedy's *Cincoenta annos de methodismo no Brasil* (São Paulo: Imprensa Metodista, 1928), 20–101; population figure from Thomas W. Merrick and Douglas H. Graham, *Population and Economic Development in Brazil: 1800 to the Present* (Baltimore: Johns Hopkins University Press, 1969), 31, 46.

10. Kennedy, *Cincoenta annos de methodismo*, 101.

11. Kennedy, *Cincoenta annos de methodismo*, 422, 424.

12. For histories of Methodism in Brazil, see Kennedy, *Cincoenta annos de methodismo*; Isnard Rocha, *Histórias da história do metodismo no Brasil* (São Bernardo do Campo, S.P.: Imprensa Metodista, 1967); Rocha, *Pioneiros e bandeirantes do metodismo no Brasil* (São Bernardo do Campo, S.P.: Imprensa Metodista, 1967); Eula K. Long, *Do meu velho baú metodista* (São Paulo: Junta Geral de Educaçaõ Cristã, 1968); and Salvador, *História do metodismo no Brasil.*

13. Bishop Andrew, who was born in Wilkes County, Georgia, and died in Mobile, Alabama, is perhaps most often remembered today as the catalyst to the Plan of Separation of 1844, which divided American Methodism into its Northern and Southern branches.

14. The early Methodist works of Pitts and Kidder, in particular, were important precursors to the post–Civil War migration of Southerners to Brazil. As already mentioned, Pitts's son was himself a colonist to Santarém, having sailed from Mobile and prospered (Jones, *Soldado descansa*, 122–23). Daniel Kidder collaborated with J. C. Fletcher on a book called *Brazil and the Brazilians* that proved very important to the immigration effort. The first four editions of the book appeared in 1857, 1866, 1867, and 1868 (Jones, *Soldado descansa*, 57–60).

15. Jones, *Soldado descansa*, 110. Newman hints of the same in a letter written in 1869; see *Nashville Christian Advocate*, December 11, 1869.

16. "Em 1866, um numero consideravel de sulistas, que tinham soffrido prejui-

zos enormes em consequencia dessa conflagração, resolveu emigrar para o Brasil. O Rev. Junius E. Newman, que antes era homen de certa fortuna, tendo perdido tudo que possuia durante essa guerra, precisava de alguma forma restabelecer os seus haveres. Vendo muitos dos seus amigos e patricios partirem para uma terra longinqua e estrangeira, resolveu acompanhá-los, especialmente animado pela esperança de poder auxiliar na popaganda [*sic*] do Evangelho na 'Terra de Santa Cruz', pelos canaes da Egreja Methodista" (Kennedy, *Cincoenta annos de methodismo*, 16). Jones, *Soldado descansa*, 47, 204, relates the case of another family of immigrants, the Carltons, who went to Brazil after seeing their house and goods destroyed by Sherman's army. Richard and Cynthia Carlton were two of the founding members of Newman's Methodist Church in Santa Barbara.

17. Jones, *Soldado descansa*, 101–10.

18. Isnard Rocha assumes that Newman went to Rio to continue Kidder's work (*Histórias da história do metodismo*, 40–41).

19. Jones, *Soldado descansa*, 42, 64, 226–27.

20. Jones, *Soldado descansa*, 110.

21. For a firsthand account of migration to Rio Doce, failure, and return to Alabama, see Julia L. Keyes, "Our Life, in Brazil," 129–339.

22. Jones, *Soldado descansa*, 109.

23. Rocha, *Histórias da história do metodismo*, 40–43; Rocha, *Pioneiros e bandeirantes*, 33–35.

24. *Nashville Christian Advocate*, December 11, 1869.

25. *Nashville Christian Advocate*, August 5, 1871.

26. *Nashville Christian Advocate*, June 12, 1875; Salvador, *História do metodismo no Brasil*, 59; Jones, *Soldado descansa*, 217, lists more than fifty members, but that was an aggregate roll. The founding members were Junius and Mary Newman, A. I. and Sarah Smith, Richard and Cynthia Carlton, Mr. and Mrs. T. D. Smith, and Leonor Smith.

27. *Nashville Christian Advocate*, June 12, 1875.

28. *Nashville Christian Advocate*, August 5, 1871.

29. *Nashville Christian Advocate*, June 12, 1875.

30. *Nashville Christian Advocate*, June 12, 1875.

31. *Nashville Christian Advocate*, June 26, 1875.

32. *Nashville Christian Advocate*, July 3, 1875.

33. *Nashville Christian Advocate*, July 17, 1875.

34. *Nashville Christian Advocate*, August 7, 1875.

35. *Nashville Christian Advocate*, August 7, 1875.

36. *Nashville Christian Advocate*, August 7, 1875.

37. *Nashville Christian Advocate*, December 18, 1875.

38. For a history, see Mrs. F. A. Butler, *History of the Woman's Foreign Missionary Society* (Nashville and Dallas: Publishing House of the M. E. Church, South, 1904), 36–131.

39. *Nashville Christian Advocate*, October 9, 1875. See also Butler, *History of the Woman's Foreign Missionary Society*, 74.

40. *Nashville Christian Advocate*, December 25, 1875.

41. "Newman organizou o 'circuito da Santa Bárbara' entre sulistas que emigraram para o Brasil depois de derrotados na guerra civil. Sob sua insistência, a

IMES enviou John James Ransom como missionário oficial, visando o trabalho entre a população brasileira. Ransom esteve no Brasil por dez anos (1876–86), período em que, sob sua direção, o metodismo tomou sua forma característica. Ransom determinou que a sede da Missão Metodista fosse o Rio de Janeiro onde, em janeiro de 1879, ele iniciou a pregação em inglês e português. A data da organização da primeira igreja é desconhecida, mas segundo o relato de Ransom já havia 'dezenove membros, ingleses e brasileiros' no final daquele ano. No segundo domingo de novembro de 1878, Ransom recebeu o ex-sacerdote católico romano Antônio Teixeira d'Albuquerque, sem rebatizá-lo. Ransom lutou pela fundação do primeiro educandário metodista (em Piracicaba, São Paulo, setembro de 1881). Desde sua chegada ao Brasil, interessou-se pela tradução de obras metodistas para o português. Uma das mais significativas dessas obras, embora pouco conhecida, é o *Compêndio da Igreja Metodista Episcopal*, publicada em 1878" (Reily, *História documental do protestantismo*, 88–89).

42. Jones, *Soldado descansa*, 241 (author's translation).

43. Jones, *Soldado descansa*, 232.

44. *Nashville Christian Advocate*, September 25, 1880.

45. By all accounts Ransom became a true force in Methodist publishing in Brazil.

46. Kennedy, *Cincoenta annos de methodismo*, 422, 424.

47. Jones, *Soldado descansa*, 261.

48. Jones, *Soldado descansa*, 232. Dom Pedro visited the school two more times.

49. Jones, *Soldado descansa*, 261.

50. Butler, *History of the Woman's Foreign Missionary Society*, 106.

51. *Nashville Christian Advocate*, September 25, 1880.

52. Butler, *History of the Woman's Foreign Missionary Society*, 74.

53. Butler, *History of the Woman's Foreign Missionary Society*, 81.

54. *Nashville Christian Advocate*, September 25, 1880. Jones, *Soldado descansa*, 22, points out that twenty of the colonists married Protestant preachers.

55. Salvador, *História do metodismo no Brasil*, 107.

56. The appropriation that the Woman's Missionary Society had made in 1880 had been reserved (after Collégio Newman closed) for the next outgoing missionary (Butler, *History of the Woman's Foreign Missionary Society*, 83). See also Kennedy, *Cincoenta annos de methodismo*, 319.

57. Cannon, *History of Southern Methodist Missions*, 197.

58. Butler, *History of the Woman's Foreign Missionary Society*, 112–13.

59. As late as 1914, it was still the custom of new Methodist missionaries to Brazil to preach at Igreja do Campo of the American colonists (Paul Eugene Buyers, *Autobiografia de Paul Eugene Buyers* [São Paulo: Imprensa Metodista, 1952], 160). Oftentimes, it was the missionary's first sermon in the new country. And as late as the 1950s, it was still the practice to send new missionaries to the American school in Campinas to learn Portuguese.

60. Kennedy, *Cincoenta annos de methodismo*, 339 (author's translation).

61. For history, see Kennedy, *Cincoenta annos de methodismo*, 331–47.

62. Kennedy, *Cincoenta annos de methodismo*, 321 (author's translation).

63. The article written by Bishop Arthur J. Moore of the Methodist Episcopal Church, South, "Methodism's World Parish," illustrates this view (in *Methodism*, ed.

William K. Anderson [Nashville: Methodist Publishing House, 1947]). "Christianity was intended to be, and of necessity is, a missionary religion. To take away its world view, to steal away its missionary passion, is to rob it of its character and leave it something other than its true self" (p. 206). "Wesley declared that there were two things of chief importance for Methodism. The first was its intention; the second was its mission" (p. 209). "For more than two centuries Methodism has been characterized by a triumphant missionary aggressiveness. It has followed the vision of the eternal Christ to whom all continents, tongues, and races belong. Year after year and generation after generation, in spite of war, paganism, and disappointment, it had carried the banner of Christ's Kingdom of love and righteousness, freedom and humanity, into the world of sin and selfishness, oppression and wrong" (p. 210). See also Charles Claude Selecman, *The Methodist Primer* (Nashville: Tidings, 1950), 51.

64. Anderson, *Methodism*, 210.

65. "O objectivo deste livro," according to Kennedy, "é registrar em forma permanente os planos, os feitos, os actos, os conseguimentos da Egreja Methodista Brasileira durante os 50 annos de sua existencia na terra do Cruzeiro do Sul" (*Cincoenta annos de methodismo*, introduction).

Chapter 8: A Community Center

1. Jefferson, "An American Colony," 226–31.

2. Jefferson, "An American Colony," 230–31.

3. Richard F. Burton, *Explorations of the Highlands of Brazil: With a Full Account of the Gold and Diamond Mines*, vol. 1. (London: Tinsley Brothers, 1869), 5; Goldman, *Os pioneiros americanos no Brasil*, 10; Jones, *Soldado descansa*, 258. In 1869 Presbyterian missionary Rev. Nash Morton stated that 350 Americans had settled in the area twenty miles beyond Campinas (the region around Santa Bárbara) (*The Missionary* 2 [1869]: 24).

4. See the discussion in Griggs, *The Elusive Eden*, 117. The Santarém colony is thoroughly described in Guilhon, *Confederados em Santarém*.

5. The migration of Americans to Brazil and other areas during the period following the Civil War has been described by many authors. Among the most notable sources on the movement to Brazil are Brannon, "Southern Emigration to Brazil," 74–95; Goldman, *Os pioneiros americanos no Brasil*; Grier, *Confederate Emigration to Brazil*; Griggs, *The Elusive Eden*; Harter, *The Lost Colony of the Confederacy*; Hill, "Confederate Exiles to Brazil," 192–210; Hill, *The Confederate Exodus to Latin America*; Jones, *Soldado descansa*; Rios, "Assimilation of Emigrants," 145–52; and Weaver, "Confederate Emigration to Brazil," 51–53.

6. Ribeiro and Ferreira, *Americana e sua história*, 2; Griggs, *The Elusive Eden*, 19.

7. Jones, *Soldado descansa*, 162, mentions the lack of communication between Norris and Estação's most prominent Brazilian, Antonio Bueno Rangel.

8. Goldman, *Os pioneiros americanos no Brasil*, 145; Jones, *Soldado descansa*, 150, 168, 339, 352.

9. See the discussion by Laura Jarnagin in chapter 4.

10. See the discussion by Laura Jarnagin in chapter 4 and John Dawsey in chapter 9.

11. Jesse Bianco, *Americana* (São Paulo: Focus, 1975), 7–9. The present museum at the Salto Grande *fazenda* near the city of Americana houses a substantial collection of historical items from the periods prior to the arrival of the Americans.

12. Kennie Norris, *Notes*, Norris collection at the Museu da Imigração, Santa Bárbara. The Machadinho *fazenda* included land taken from a *sesmaria* (a large grant to crown favorites by the Portuguese king) that had belonged to Manoel Alves Machado and later to Domingos da Costa Machado. Another portion of the Machadinho estate was purchased by Antonio Bueno Rangel, whose son, Basílio Bueno Rangel, sold sections to a friend named Inácio Correia Pacheco. Bueno Rangel and Correia Pacheco developed residential lots after the railroad was opened in 1875, and they, not the Americans, are officially credited with founding the city of Americana (Ribeiro and Ferreira, *Americana e sua história*, 1–2).

13. Goldman, *Os pioneiros americanos no Brasil*, 107–17; Jones, *Soldado descansa*, 411–14; both sources rely on a list compiled by immigrant Henry Steagall.

14. Unfortunately, very little access to property deeds and maps was available to the author. Information on the initial location of the holdings of the major families has been obtained primarily from secondary sources. The most valuable of these was Jones, *Soldado descansa*. Jones's book is a rich, though at times unstructured and confusing, compendium of the events associated with the Americans in the region around Santa Bárbara. The locational references in the book are sometimes specific, as is the identification of Alfred I. Smith's home at the present site of a sugar refinery that is plainly marked on current maps (Jones, *Soldado descansa*, 23). Usually, however, the references are more general. Families are said to have moved to property adjacent to someone who lived at a known location, but no mention is made regarding the shape of the holding or the side of adjacency. Most often, location information is provided by unspecific phrases such as "near to" or "in the neighborhood of," so an absolute identification of a site is impossible. Because certainty of the exact location is not available for over half of the families, the names are identified by community clusters. All of the names presented in the text have been unambiguously identified with the indicated community cluster. Confirmation of many of the sitings was obtained from conversations with descendants.

15. Jones, *Soldado descansa*, 152.

16. In 1890 the city of "Distrito de Paz da Vila Americana" was incorporated, and in 1938 the name was shortened to Americana (Bianco, *Americana*, 9, 11, 13).

17. Griggs, *The Elusive Eden*, 19; Jones, *Soldado descansa*, 149–52.

18. Jones, *Soldado descansa*, 152.

19. Jones, *Soldado descansa*, 152.

20. Jones, *Soldado descansa*, 152, 181.

21. Malcolm Bolim, *A mappa de sítio Machadinho* (Campinas, 1875); Jones, *Soldado descansa*, 181, 182, 203, 204.

22. Jones, *Soldado descansa*, 204, 221.

23. Bolim, *A mappa de sítio Machadinho*; Jones, *Soldado descansa*, 205.

24. Jones, *Soldado descansa*, 203, 204; Guilherme (William) Pyles Creek presently flows into the Quilombo through the northwest section of Americana (Estação).

25. Jones, *Soldado descansa*, 281.

26. Jones, *Soldado descansa*, 152, 185.

27. Jones, *Soldado descansa*, 227.

28. Jones, *Soldado descansa*, 166, 185.

29. Jones, *Soldado descansa*, 166, 176, 185, 186. The Steagall list (cited by Goldman, *Os pioneiros americanos no Brasil*, 109, and Jones, *Soldado descansa*, 412) shows Widow Ruth Priscilla Holland in the town of Tatuí, about 100 kilometers to the southwest. Jones, *Soldado descansa*, 166, locates her at Retiro, near Santa Bárbara. She may have moved to Tatuí in 1870, when Rev. William Emerson relocated to that city (see n. 45).

30. Jones, *Soldado descansa*, 185, 186, 213–15, 245.

31. Jones, *Soldado descansa*, 251; Kennedy, *Cincoenta annos de methodismo*, 16.

32. Griggs, *The Elusive Eden*, 119; Jones, *Soldado descansa*, 167.

33. Goldman, *Os pioneiros americanos no Brasil*, 116; Jones, *Soldado descansa*, 182.

34. Jones, *Soldado descansa*, 183.

35. Jones, *Soldado descansa*, 184, 185, 328.

36. Jones, *Soldado descansa*, 23.

37. Quoting Frank McMullan correspondence, Griggs places Quillin at Estação (*The Elusive Eden*, 112). Jones identifies the location as Campo (*Soldado descansa*, 222). Quillin may have moved from Estação to Campo, or a locational error may have resulted from confusion between the mailing address (Estação) and the residential location (Campo).

38. Jones, *Soldado descansa*, 183.

39. Jones, *Soldado descansa*, 183.

40. Jones, *Soldado descansa*, 183–84.

41. Jones, *Soldado descansa*, 185–86.

42. Jones, *Soldado descansa*, 205.

43. Jones, *Soldado descansa*, 177, 186, 221.

44. Jones, *Soldado descansa*, 264.

45. Jones, *Soldado descansa*, 191; Thompson lists Emerson's date of death as 1875 (*Presbyterians in the South*, 111), while Griggs indicates 1873 (*The Elusive Eden*, 128). In 1870 the Reverend Edward Lane preached at Emerson's house, which he stated to be thirty miles from Campinas and near the home of the Reverend James Baird (*The Missionary*, 3 [1870]: 3). In 1870, therefore, he still resided in Santa Bárbara, probably in the Campo cluster (near Baird). A letter to the United States in December 1872 indicated that he had relocated to Tatuí, about 100 kilometers from Santa Bárbara (*The Missionary* 5 [1872]: 187). Why he and others, including Priscilla Holland, went to Tatuí remains a mystery.

46. Jones, *Soldado descansa*, 284.

47. Jones, *Soldado descansa*, 325.

48. Jones, *Soldado descansa*, 202.

49. Jones, *Soldado descansa*, 285. The Santa Bárbara congregation included thirty-two members, and the Estação church had twelve (*Southern Baptist Convention 1881 Annual*).

50. Jones, *Soldado descansa*, 215; Thompson, *Presbyterians in the South*, 111.

51. See n. 45.

52. A quote from Newman's daughter, Mary Newman Carr, in Kennedy, *Cincoenta annos de methodismo*, 17.

53. See chapter 2.

54. Jones, *Soldado descansa*, 216–17.
55. Jones, *Soldado descansa*, 217. The source does not indicate if the referred location was the Campo general area or the *Campo* compound at the cemetery.
56. Newman letter to the *Nashville Christian Advocate*, June 12, 1875.
57. See n. 24.
58. Jones, *Soldado descansa*, 249.
59. Jones, *Soldado descansa*, 327.
60. See nn. 52 and 53.
61. See nn. 52 and 53.
62. Jones, *Soldado descansa*, 224.
63. Jones, *Soldado descansa*, 246.
64. Jones, *Soldado descansa*, 215, 268.
65. Jones, *Soldado descansa*, 249.
66. *The Missionary* 3 (1870): 149.
67. Goldman, *Os pioneiros americanos no Brasil*, 174; Jones, *Soldado descansa*, 297, 402.
68. Jones, *Soldado descansa*, 328.
69. Kennedy, *Cincoenta annos de methodismo*, 77.
70. Jones, *Soldado descansa*, 295.
71. Jones, *Soldado descansa*, 325.
72. The genealogies do not contain dates, so they provide no clues about when the unions took place. Marriages may have preceded the settlement in the Santa Bárbara area (as when William Norris arrived with married daughters and sons-in-law). Or first-generation unions may have involved children not yet born at the time of arrival. Later birth dates would probably correlate positively with marriages to Brazilians and Americans outside the Santa Bárbara group. The genealogical information for some of the families identified in the text and location information about others listed in the genealogies were not available. Other families, such as the Bookwalters, who arrived after the initial settlement, were also not included.
73. Jones, *Soldado descansa*, 402.
74. Jones, *Soldado descansa*, 22; Kennedy, *Cincoenta annos de methodismo*, 77.
75. Bianco, *Americana*, 19.
76. Bianco, *Americana*, 19.
77. Goldman, *Os pioneiros americanos no Brasil*, 174.

Chapter 9: Constructing Identity

1. Of course Marajoara Indians might be just as surprised to find some of their own creations in middle-class homes in São Paulo, Atlanta, or New York.
2. Griggs, *The Elusive Eden*, 146.
3. The *Campo* (country) cemetery is located in the countryside, surrounded by sugarcane fields, ten miles from both Americana and Santa Bárbara. These two cities are located one hundred miles from São Paulo, Brazil's largest city. A reunion at a cemetery is particularly intriguing to Brazilians, with their Roman Catholic and Iberian backgrounds.
4. Indeed, visitors from the United States often react with sadness or pathos when visiting the cemetery. Judith MacKnight Jones related how an Alabama sena-

tor was led to tears when visting the cemetery. Harter told of the deep sadness which Jimmy Carter experienced as a result of his visit. Elihu Root was reported to have been deeply moved by the sight of Confederate families at the Americana railroad station in 1906.

5. As Geertz remarked, in this type of theater, actors are also the spectators (Clifford Geertz, *A interpretação das culturas* [Rio de Janeiro: Zahar, 1978], 316).

6. Goldman discussed the composition of the groups (*Os pioneiros americanos no Brasil*, 33).

7. Madan Sarup, *An Introductory Guide to Post-Structuralism and Postmodernism* (Athens: University of Georiga Press, 1989), 35.

8. Ibid., 35–36.

9. See the following three works by Manuela Carneiro da Cunha: *Negros, estrangeiros: Os escravos libertos e sua volta à Africa* (São Paulo: Brasiliense, 1985); "Etnicidade: Da cultura residual mas irredutivel," in *Antropologia do Brasil: Mito, história, etnicidade* (São Paulo: Brasiliense, 1986); and "Religião, comércio, e etnicidade: Uma interpretação preliminar do catolicismo brasileiro em lagos no século XIX," in *Antropologia do Brasil.*

10. Abner Cohen, *Custom and Politics in Urban Africa* (London: Routledge and Kegan Paul, 1969).

11. See Eunice Durham, "A dinâmica cultural na sociedade moderna," *Ensaios de opiniao* 2 no. 2 (1977): 32–35.

12. Goldman, *Os pioneiros americanos no Brasil*, 140 (the author's translation).

13. Harter, *The Lost Colony*, 34.

14. "In the United States, it was once widely believed that the only good psychiatrists were those with Viennese accents. Similarly, many Brazilians came to believe that a dentist almost had to be an American to be effective. Margaret Meade's colleague, Gilberto Freyre . . . wrote: 'The American dentist became an institution. Even an Englishman like Dr. Rawlinson of Recife, styled himself an "American" dentist'" (Harter, *The Lost Colony*, 72).

15. Harter, *The Lost Colony*, 88.

16. Jones, *Soldado descansa*, 46.

17. Daniel Carr DeMuzio, "Confederate Descendants in Brazil," *Confederate Veteran*, July–August 1991, p. 18.

18. Jones, *Soldado descansa*, 269.

19. Harter, *The Lost Colony*, 90.

20. Jones, *Soldado descansa*, 324.

21. Jones, *Soldado descansa*, 161.

22. Harter, *The Lost Colony*, 70.

23. Harter, *The Lost Colony*, 69.

24. Goldman, *Os pioneiros americanos no Brasil*, 70; Harter, *The Lost Colony*, 15; Jones, *Soldado descansa*, 54.

25. Ana Maria de Siqueira Costa, "O destino (não) manifesto: Os imigrantes norte-americanos no Brasil" (Ph.D. diss., University of São Paulo, 1985), 141.

26. Cited by Zuleica de Castro Coimbra Mesquita, "Educação metodista: Uma questão não resolvida" (Master's thesis, Universidade Metodista de Piracicaba, 1991), 197.

27. Vianna Moog, *Bandeirantes and Pioneers* (New York: George Braziller, 1964).

28. See the excellent discussion by Thomas Skidmore, *Preto no branco: Raça e nacionalidade no pensamento brasileiro*, trans. Raul de Sá Barbosa (Rio de Janeiro: Paz e Terra, 1989).

29. Harter, *The Lost Colony*, 55.

30. However, some of the São Paulo Republicans wanted states' rights in order to prevent abolition. See Conrad, *The Destruction of Brazilian Slavery*.

31. Jones, *Soldado descansa*, 290.

32. Siqueira Costa, "O destino (não) manifesto," 193.

33. Jones, *Soldado descansa*, 177; Griggs, *The Elusive Eden*, 116; Goldman, *Os pioneiros americanos no Brasil*, 144.

34. Goldman, *Os pioneiros americanos no Brasil*, 144.

35. Siqueira Costa, "O destino (não) manifesto," 179.

36. The Fazenda Modelo was later transformed into the University of São Paulo's Escola de Agronomia "Luiz de Queiroz," one of the outstanding agronomy schools of Latin America (Jones, *Soldado descansa*, 253).

37. Jones, *Soldado descansa*, 348.

38. Cited by Griggs, *The Elusive Eden*, 117.

39. Jones, *Soldado descansa*, 370.

40. Jones, *Soldado descansa*, 401.

41. Jones, *Soldado descansa*, 358.

42. Jones, *Soldado descansa*, 338.

43. Jones, *Soldado descansa*, 365.

44. Goldman, *Os pioneiros americanos no Brasil*, 33.

45. Goldman, *Os pioneiros americanos no Brasil*, 153.

46. Griggs, *The Elusive Eden*, 116.

47. Goldman, *Os pioneiros americanos no Brasil*, 144–45.

48. Jones, *Soldado descansa*, 344, 393.

49. Goldman, *Os pioneiros americanos no Brasil*, 155. Rev. Ballard Smith Dunn, who organized the colony of Lizzieland, presented himself as, and was thought to have been, a Virginian. Goldman (p. 31) presents evidence showing that Dunn was actually from New York and had worn a Yankee uniform at least once in his life.

50. Goldman, *Os pioneiros americanos no Brasil*, 14.

51. Goldman, *Os pioneiros americanos no Brasil*, 14.

52. Siqueira Costa, "O destino (não) manifesto," 177.

53. Jones, *Soldado descansa*, 232.

54. Jones, *Soldado descansa*, 161.

55. Jones, *Soldado descansa*, 338.

56. Jones, *Soldado descansa*, 340.

57. Jones, *Soldado descansa*, 249.

58. Harter, *The Lost Colony*, 75.

59. Jones, *Soldado descansa*, 18.

60. Skidmore, *Preto no branco*, 164–226.

61. Goldman, *Os pioneiros americanos no Brasil*, 155.

62. Goldman, *Os pioneiros americanos no Brasil*, 156.

63. Jones, *Soldado descansa*, 389.

64. Jefferson, "An American Colony," 231; Harter, *The Lost Colony*, 105.

65. Jones, *Soldado descansa*, 24, 389.

66. Harter, *The Lost Colony*, 77.
67. Jones, *Soldado descansa*, 400.
68. Harter, *The Lost Colony*, 74.
69. Siqueira Costa, "O destino (não) manifesto," 165.
70. Jones, *Soldado descansa*, 404.
71. Harter, *The Lost Colony*, x.
72. Harter, *The Lost Colony*, 30 (emphasis added).
73. Harter, *The Lost Colony*, 109–11.
74. Harter, *The Lost Colony*, 111–12.
75. Harter, *The Lost Colony*, 112.
76. Harter, *The Lost Colony*, 109–10.
77. Goldman, *Os pioneiros americanos no Brasil*, 47; Jones, *Soldado descansa*, 124. "There is no doubt regarding the validity of Hill's hypothesis [in *Confederate Exodus to Latin America*], according to which the migratory movement to Brazil had a definite relation to an earlier period of migratory movements inside the United States (still the case of 'Manifest Destiny')" (Goldman, *Os pioneiros americanos no Brasil*, 47).
78. Siqueira Costa, "O destino (não) manifesto," 125.
79. Griggs, *The Elusive Eden*, 2.
80. Cited by Jones, *Soldado descansa*, 143–44.
81. Jones, *Soldado descansa*, 145.
82. There are several indications that the Constitutional Revolution of 1932 continues to be an important moment in memories of descendants. One of the gravesites at the *Campo* cemetery bears the inscription "Once a rebel, twice a rebel, and forever a rebel." The "twice a rebel" is a reference to the 1932 revolution. During this year, the state of São Paulo, which, along with Minas Gerais and Rio de Janeiro, had played a dominant political role during the First Republic, entered into rebellion in order to restore the "Old Republic." Some descendants of Santa Bárbara settlers signaled their support of rebellion by means of Confederate symbols. Evidently, the movement had deep resonance among people with an American or Confederate Civil War heritage. There was much to draw on from the Confederate cultural trunk. Nonetheless, some of the signs may have been inverted. In 1932 São Paulo was well on the way to becoming the center of Brazil's industrial power. In the context of the 1932 Constitutional Revolution, Confederate symbols may have been used not in order to differentiate descendants from outside Americans competing for similar jobs but to distinguish Confederate descendants from other Brazilians and to establish firmly the former as allies of the Paulista secessionist elites.
The Fraternidade Descendencia Americana (Fraternity of American Descendancy) was formed on December 4, 1954. The statutes define members as the descendants of the old United States colony. Harter, perhaps worried about what the reader might think, inserts parenthetically, "Confederate" colony (*The Lost Colony*, 125). The fraternity was thus created during the aftermath of World War II and of Getulio Vargas's second term in office.
Judith MacKight Jones published her book *Soldado descansa* in 1967, three years after Brazilian generals overthrew the nationalist and left-leaning government of João Goulart. This period would be characterized by an increased presence of U.S. interests in Brazil. Frank P. Goldman published his book *Os pioneiros americanos no*

Brasil in 1972, during the period of the so-called Brazilian economic miracle, which was largely financed by North American capital. *The Lost Colony of the Confederacy,* by Eugene C. Harter, was published in 1985. It marked a significant break with the ways in which Jones and Goldman were constructing the identity of the descendants. The late 1970s, like the late 1920s, witnessed increasing economic troubles accompanied by criticism of the role of the United States in Brazil. While writing about the 1920s and 1930s, Harter indirectly interpreted his immediate Brazilian and American setting. Recent developments might indicate further transformations. In 1987 the city of Santa Bárbara created the Museum of Immigration. The inaugural exposition, which continues to be the only one inside the museum, is called "Americans in Brazil." Outside the building, exposed to the weather, a "temporary exposition" concerning "Negro heritage" has been on display. In April 1992 the city of Americana organized the first regular bus tours, which include a visit to the American cemetery.

83. In the documents concerning the history of these people, much evidence would encourage us to support trends in social sciences to speak much of racism and little of race. Just as it is certain that Brazilian authorities and some abolitionists encouraged immigration of American and European white people as a way of "purifying the Brazilian race," it is also certain that many settlers came to Brazil because they were looking for a place where slavery still existed (Jones, *Soldado descansa,* 89; Goldman, *Os pioneiros americanos no Brasil,* 10; Harter, *The Lost Colony,* 37; Griggs, *The Elusive Eden,* 15; Siqueira Costa, "O destino [não] manifesto," 15). When Gaston proposed that the Brazilian Empire encourage immigration of American former slaves because of their superior technical knowledge of cotton production, authorities did not approve (Goldman, *Os pioneiros americanos no Brasil,* 121). Not only did the hypothesis of the presence of former slaves represent a potential threat as "bad" examples for those still in slavery, but this hypothesis was contrary to another, that Brazilian "progress" depended also on "purifying the race." Whatever the technical qualifications of former slaves, abolitionists themselves were interested in substituting African labor with white American or European labor.

Some in the United States looked toward Latin America, and Amazonia specifically, as a place where Negroes might be sent following abolition, thereby allowing America to remain "pure." Hastings, who organized the Confederate colony near Santarém, was active in these schemes (Siqueira Costa, "O destino [não] manifesto," 125). As for the Santa Bárbara settlers themselves, Jones and other authors offer much evidence which could be pursued. A slave was lynched by settlers whose identity was kept secret (Jones, *Soldado descansa,* 224). When a pro-abolitionist senator was assassinated in 1888, Santa Bárbara settlers were the first to be suspected (Harter, *The Lost Colony,* 55). During the period in which the rattlesnake watermelons planted by settlers were prohibited from being sold by authorities, who suspected that they might be causing yellow fever, settlers called on the American consul. Jones says that "they prepared a big reception then gulped [*engolir em seco*]. The consul was black" (*Soldado descansa,* 311).

The authors themselves made comments which could be analyzed. The following are excerpts from Jones, *Soldado descansa*: The slaves "were like large children and as such they were treated. They never had any idea of what they were worth, nor of the price of their work. They belonged to their owners who provided all things for them, including the family name, which they used" (p. 44). "From one day to the next the slaves were freed. Like birds which were let out of the cage, they left without direction, drunken by freedom. They gathered in bands going from one place to the other practicing all sorts of disorder. Three and a half million men and women, many of whom had recently arrived from African jungles. . . . Nobody told the blacks that freedom brings responsibility. After a time, some of them remembered the good plate of food which they could have at the owner's house, and returned, but the majority just wandered. The enemy incited them to robbery and disrespect. When white women began to be molested the situation got out of control and indignation came to a peak" (p. 50).

Harter wrote from the perspective of a *confederado* who equates Brazilian-style friendship and "mixture" among races with racial equality. Commenting on the marriage between a white woman and a black man within the group of American descendants in 1920, Harter stated: "There was no outcry—none. The man, after all, was an American. . . . The Americans, like their Brazilian neighbors, had learned how to change a person from black to white" (*The Lost Colony,* 117). Harter took this transformation of black into white as a demonstration of racial equality (contrary to Skidmore's thesis about Brazilian racism presented in 1989 in his book *Preto no branco* [Black into white]).

Goldman said in regard to the Fraternidade Descendencia Americana: "There is a tenuous (in truth very tenuous!) and almost imperceptible 'color line' at the cemetery" (*Os pioneiros americanos no Brasil,* 174). Whatever this "color line" might look like, it appears that outsiders may help reinforce it. In April 1992 an editor from *Parade Magazine* organized a group of descendants who were meeting at the cemetery in order to take some photos. He organized them according to shades of skin color, to the delight of those with melanin deficiency. Also, the caretakers of the cemetery are a black family which lives in a wooden house within cemetery grounds. Is this family being used as another diacritical sign, serving to differentiate these descendants from other Brazilian groups?

84. John Domm was a Dutchman who has been called a fellow Texan. Horace Lane was a Yankee from Maine who, according to unofficial reports, was a Southerner. Dunn from New York presented himself as a Confederate. Franz Muller, a German, was oftentimes considered an American. His name is given as Miller by some. There were other cases. The Vaughan family, one of the main groups among the Americans, descended directly from Seminole Indians. They were called black Americans.

Harter told of the taboo among American descendants against marrying Brazilians. In 1920 the daughter of a prominent white American family provoked initial conceptual disorder by marrying a respected black American of the community. In the end, according to Harter, the couple was warmly accepted. After all, said Harter, both were American.

One of the success stories of the descendants is that of Steve Watson (called Watson by Harter, Wesson by Jones, and Wasson by Griggs). He had come to Brazil with his former owner, Judge Dyer, and Dyer's nephew, Columbus Watson, whose name Steve would later adopt. They started a sawmill in the Juquiá Valley. The business was doing well until a storm sank their boat. The judge and nephew gave up, leaving the mill and sunken boat with the former slave. Steve Watson, who had learned the Portuguese language, rebuilt the business and, according to our sources, became very rich. Jones speaks of him as a "legendary figure" (*Soldado descansa*, 127). According to Griggs, the former slave "always held he was a true American" (*The Elusive Eden*, 127). Many Brazilian families with the name of Vassão still live in the region (Harter, *The Lost Colony*, 55).

85. The hardest evidence I found refers to rumors surrounding the assassination of a pro-abolition senator in 1888.

86. Griggs, *The Elusive Eden*, 146.

87. Harter, *The Lost Colony*, 70.

Chapter 10: The Language

1. An earlier version of this chapter was published as "The Phonology of the Lost Cause," *English World-Wide* 10 (1990): 195–216, copyright © John Benjamins Publishing Co., used by permission. The authors are grateful to the Mississippi Authority for Educational Television, particularly to Roy E. Duncan, director of production, for permission to use the excerpts of interviews with American speakers (conducted in the 1970s) that were used in *The Last Confederates*, a half-hour television documentary produced in 1984 by MAET with the assistance of Eugene C. Harter. They wish to thank Eugene Harter for supplying personal information about the speakers interviewed on the program. They are also grateful to Guy Bailey and Crawford Feagin for helpful comments on an earlier draft of this chapter. Any errors of transcription from the telecast or of categorization of the data analyzed in this paper are the authors' alone.

2. Raven I. McDavid, Jr., "The Dialects of American English," in *The Structure of American English*, ed. W. Nelson Francis (New York: Ronald, 1958), 480–543.

3. Eugene C. Harter, personal correspondence.

4. For a more technical linguistic statement and analysis of these features, see Montgomery and Melo, "The Phonology of the Lost Cause," 195–216. See also Hans Kurath and Raven I. McDavid, Jr., *Pronunciation of English in the Atlantic States* (Ann Arbor: University of Michigan Press, 1961); Charles-James N. Bailey, *English Phonetic Transcription* (Dallas: Summer Institute of Linguistics, 1985); McDavid, "The Dialects of American English."

5. James B. McMillan and Michael B. Montgomery, eds., *Annotated Bibliography of Southern American English* (Tuscaloosa: University of Alabama Press, 1989).

6. George Philip Krapp, *The English Language in America*, 2 vols. (New York: Unger, 1925), 2:25; Edward A. Stephenson, "The Beginnings of the Loss of the Post-Vocalic /r/ in North Carolina," *Journal of English Linguistics* 2 (1968): 69.

7. Lindsay Benjamin Crane, Jr., "Social Stratification of English among White Speakers in Tuscaloosa, Alabama" (Ph.D. diss.: University of Massachusetts, 1973), 49.

8. Crawford Feagin and Guy Bailey, "The Restoration of R in Southern States English" (Paper delivered at the Southeastern Conference on Linguistics, Washington, D.C., 1988).

9. In a recent paper based on interviews with a number of Americana residents, Guy Bailey and Clyde Smith found "r" occurring most often after the central vowel [a], next most often after back vowels, and least after front vowels ("Southern American English in Brazil, No?" *SECOL Review* 16 [1992]: 71–89). This pattern also differs significantly from that found in Feagin and Bailey, "The Restoration of R."

10. Kurath and McDavid, *Pronunciation of English*, 109.

11. Norman E. Eliason, *Tarheel Talk: An Historical Study of the English Language in North Carolina to 1860* (Chapel Hill: University of North Carolina Press, 1956); Krapp, *The English Language in America.*

12. Guy Bailey, "Some Phonological Changes in Southern American English" (Paper delivered at the Fortieth Annual Meeting of the Southeastern Conference on Linguistics, Norfolk, Va., 1989); Crane, "Social Stratification of English."

13. James W. Hartmann, "Guide to Pronunciation," in *Dictionary of American Regional English*, ed. Frederic G. Cassidy (Cambridge: Harvard University Press, Belknap Press, 1985), liv.

14. Krapp, *The English Language in America* 2:213ff.

15. Eliason, *Tarheel Talk*, 212.

16. Charles-James N. Bailey, "The Patterning of Sonorant Gemination in English Lects," in *Language Use and the Uses of Language*, ed. Roger W. Shuy and Anna Shnukal (Washington, D.C.: Georgetown University Press, 1980), 1–11.

17. Crawford Feagin, "A Closer Look at the Southern Drawl: Variation Taken to Extremes," in *Variation in Language NWAV-XV at Stanford*, ed. Keith M. Denning et al. (Stanford, Calif.: Stanford University Department of Linguistics, 1987), 137.

18. Claude Merton Wise, "Southern American Dialect," *American Speech* 8, no. 2 (1933): 37–43.

19. Crawford Feagin (personal communication) suggests that "the situation of a TV interview would evaporate any drawl that [the] informants might have had" and that the women informants who were schoolteachers would have an additional reason for avoiding the drawl. Only further fieldwork that records the speech of Americana residents in less formal contexts can reveal the influence of these factors.

20. Vivian Brown, "Evolution of a Sound Change in Tennessee" (Paper delivered at the Fortieth Annual Meeting of the Southeastern Conference on Linguistics, Norfolk, Va., 1989), 15.

21. Eliason, *Tarheel Talk*; Krapp, *The English Language in America* 2:96.

22. Raymond K. O'Cain, "A Diachronic View of the Speech of Charleston, South Carolina," in *Papers in Language Variation: SAMLA-ADS Collection*, ed. David L. Shores and Carole P. Hines (Tuscaloosa: University of Alabama Press, 1977), 139.

23. Charles Reagan Wilson, "History," in *Encyclopedia of Southern Culture*, ed. Charles R. Wilson and William Ferris (Chapel Hill: University of North Carolina Press, 1989), 590.

24. Raven I. McDavid, Jr., "Changing Patterns of Southern Dialects," in *Essays in Honor of Claude M. Wise*, ed. Arthur J. Bronstein et al. (Hannibal, Mo.: Standard, 1970), 226.

25. McDavid, "Changing Patterns of Southern Dialects," 227.

26. Bailey and Smith, "Southern American English," 71–89.

Chapter 11: Conclusions

1. Hill, "Confederate Exiles to Brazil," 192–93.
2. Hill, "The Confederate Exodus," I, 100–134.
3. See his three works "Looking for a Home"; "Exiles, Emigrants, and Sojourners"; and *The Confederate Carpetbaggers.*
4. Weaver, "Confederate Immigrants and Evangelical Churches in Brazil," 446–68.
5. Goldman, *Os pioneiros americanos no Brasil.*
6. Keyes, "Our Life, in Brazil," 127–339.
7. Rios, "Assimilation of Emigrants," 145–52.
8. Rios, "Assimilation of Emigrants," 151.
9. Rios, "Assimilation of Emigrants," 151.
10. Rios, "Assimilation of Emigrants," 149.
11. Michael Ryan, "A Continent Away, Confederates Flourish," *Parade Magazine,* September 6, 1992, pp. 14–16.

Postscript: Reflections of a *Confederado*

1. Montgomery and Melo, "Phonology of the Lost Cause," 200.
2. Julia Norris and Kennie Norris, unpublished mss., 1951, 1958, Milton Norris Adams Papers, Americana, Brazil.
3. "Today Show," NBC Television, February 1986, discussion between Senhor Edward Carr and the program's host, Bryant Gumbel.
4. Jimmy Carter to Eugene Harter, May 2, 1972; September 23, 1985; December 9, 1985.
5. Jody Powell, syndicated column "Confederacy's Old Times Are Not Forgotten in Brazil," appearing in the *Marietta* (Ga.) *Daily Journal* and many other American newspapers, January 28, 1986.

Annotated Bibliography

James M. Gravois and Elizabeth J. Weisbrod

The purpose here is to bring together, with brief annotations, most of the sources readily available at large libraries and through interlibrary loan. The authors based their selections on the excellent bibliography compiled by William Clark Griggs (listed below), as well as the notes of other researchers in this field. Important collections of papers and archives which the authors did not review are listed at the end of this chapter. The term *confederados* refers to those Southerners who moved to Brazil after the Civil War, as well as to their descendants.

Primary Sources—Books

Burton, Richard F. *Explorations of the Highlands of the Brazil.* 1869. Reprint. New York: Greenwood Press, 1969.

This two-volume work by a famous adventurer and anthropologist relates his observations during a five-month journey down Brazil's Rio São Francisco. Of interest is his claim that 2,700 Southerners had already arrived in Brazil by the beginning of 1868. Also, his detailed descriptions of gold and diamond mining suggest the strike-it-rich attractions of Brazil.

Dunn, Ballard S. *Brazil, the Home for Southerners; or, A Practical Account of What the Author, and Others, Who Visited That Country, for the Same Objects, Saw and Did While in That Empire.* New Orleans: Bloomfield & Steel, 1866.

Dunn's book ranks with Gaston's and Hastings's books as a bugle call to Southerners. This Episcopal minister and Confederate veteran visited Brazil soon after the Civil War to determine the feasibility of emigration there. He states his belief that postwar conditions in the South are unacceptable, disputes arguments that Brazil provides little economic opportunity for Southerners, and describes the area of land ("Lizzieland") which he has picked out for a colony. He includes descriptions of the Brazilian government, tables of weather information, copies of letters and reports which favorably discuss economic prospects in Brazil (including one report by Dr. Gaston and one by Maj. Robert Merriwether), a condensation of a book on Brazilian social customs, documentation of Brazil's international trade over a ten-year period, and a fold-out map of Brazil. He announces within the book that he will be leading a colony of settlers from New Orleans the following spring and asks that anyone interested get in touch with him. (Afterward, he did indeed found a colony at Lizzieland but abandoned the project sometime later.) The book includes an engraved portrait of the author.

Fletcher, James C., and Daniel P. Kidder. *Brazil and the Brazilians, Portrayed in Historical and Descriptive Sketches.* 9th ed. London: Sampson Low, Marston, Searle, and Rivington, 1879.

This is an updated edition of *Sketches of Residence and Travels in Brazil,* originally written by Kidder alone and published in 1845. The book combines history, current facts, and travel observations to produce an encyclopedic view of Brazil in the mid-nineteenth century. The first edition demonstrates that information about Brazil was available to potential émigrés well before the Civil War, and the fact that it was updated so many times indicates its popularity. However, one searches in vain for any references to the *confederados* in this 1879 edition, which seems surprising, since there are several references to other colonizers of Brazil, mostly Swiss and Germans. This handsome book includes 150 engravings and numerous appendixes giving a variety of information about Brazil.

Gaston, James McFadden. *Hunting a Home in Brazil.* Philadelphia, 1867.

Gaston, a South Carolina doctor, arrived in Rio in September 1865 with the express purpose of scouting Brazil for possibilities of settlement by former Confederates. He spent about six months there before concluding that "people in Brazil [are] capable of appreciating the Southern character and ready to extend a cordial greeting to all who come." He writes in a wonderfully eloquent nineteenth-century style, detailing many aspects of Brazilian life. He describes the weather, the streets and monuments of Rio, the types of produce in the marketplace, and the many varieties of coffee. In a diary format, he recounts his day-to-day experiences, commenting on Brazilian Catholicism, clothing styles of the upper class, and dining customs. More important, he describes his meetings with Brazilian officials, his talks with American and European settlers, and his studies of crops and agricultural lands, all of which lead him to conclude that Southerners could indeed make a new beginning in Brazil.

Hastings, Lansford Warren. *The Emigrant's Guide to Brazil.* Mobile, 1867.

Not only did Hastings write this book, but he also led a colony to Brazil. Unfortunately, the authors of this bibliography failed to obtain a copy, as it seems to be a very rare book. Based on contemporary accounts, however, it had an important impact on the movement in favor of emigration to Brazil. Any researcher who can find a copy will likely be well rewarded. Hastings also wrote *The Emigrant's Guide to Oregon and California,* which is readily available.

Herndon, William Lewis, and Lardner Gibbon. *Exploration of the Valley of the Amazon.* Washington, D.C.: Robert Armstrong, Public Printer, 1853.

This two-volume work was published before the Civil War, but its discussions of crops and minerals may well have contributed to Southern interest in Brazil after the war. The book contains numerous engravings of ethnographic interest.

Annotated Bibliography

Keyes, Julia L. "Our Life, in Brazil." *Alabama Historical Quarterly* 28, nos. 3–4 (Fall and Winter 1966): 127–339.

Although not a book, this account of the Keyes's family life in Brazil from 1867 to 1870 is included here because of its length. The story uses extracts from the diaries of her children and letters of her husband. It discusses the emigrants' daily life in Brazil, the emigrants' encounters with the native Brazilians, and other events during their stay in Brazil. It concludes with the family's return to Montgomery.

Primary Sources—Short Articles

"The American Emigrants in Brazil." *New York Herald*, July 7, 1867.

A special correspondent summarizes the plight of Southerners who have moved to Brazil. He points out that some 300 men, women, and children have arrived monthly for the preceding six months. Most of these, he claims, are destitute. Only the folks who brought down a lot of money are doing well. He catalogs the migration's problems as poor organization; undeveloped land; lack of tools, seed, and shelter; poor transportation; hostile Brazilians; and unhealthy climate.

Barnsley, George Scarsborough. "Foreign Colonization in Brazil: The American (and English) Attempt at Colonization in Brazil—1866–7." *Brazilian American* (Rio de Janeiro), March 10, 1928.

Barnsley wrote his account of the McMullan group's voyage to Brazil a few years after his arrival in Brazil. Although Barnsley includes an analysis of why so many American and British settlements in Brazil failed, the article is primarily a colorful description of the nearly disastrous trip from Galveston to Rio de Janeiro. Refreshing because of its humor and sharp depictions of his fellow passengers, Barnsley's version provides a less-than-romantic account of the emigrant experience in Brazil.

Brannon, Peter A. "Southern Emigration to Brazil: Embodying the Diary of Jennie R. Keyes, Montgomery, Alabama." *Alabama Historical Quarterly* 1, no. 2 (Summer 1930): 74–95; no. 3 (Fall 1930): [280]–305; no. 4 (Winter 1930): [467]–488.

The first part includes an overview of Southern emigration to Brazil and gives genealogical information on some of the leaders in the movement. It concludes with part of Julia Keyes's diary. She emigrated from Montgomery and left with her family on the Steamship *Marmion* for Brazil in 1867 and returned to Alabama in 1870. She was the mother of Jennie Rutledge Keyes, author of the diary that appears in the following two articles. Jennie R. Keyes, around fifteen years old at the time the diary was written, gives an account of her family's time in Brazil. She writes about daily life in the American settlements. The diary was not reproduced completely, breaking off in 1869.

Crist, Sara. "With Alabama Emigres in Brazil—1867–70." *Montgomery Advertiser*, August 4, 1940.

This short article contains excerpts from Jenny Rutledge Keyes's diary.

"The Emigration from the South to Brazil Destined to Prove a Success." *New Orleans Times*, February 10, 1867.

An unnamed writer for this newspaper argues that much has been written in the press to discourage Southerners from going to Brazil. This writer tries to show that these accounts are false and recommends that his readers believe the writings of Ballard Dunn, Dr. Gaston, and others, who promote the enterprise.

Foster, Josephine. "Letter from Brazil." *New Orleans Times*, April 26, 1868.

Writing from Lake Juparanã, in the province of Espírito Santo, Foster makes the case that Brazil is an excellent place to live for those who are willing to work. She feels that many starry-eyed Southerners returned to their homeland because they did not want to perform the necessary manual labor. She includes some details about meeting the Keyes family of Alabama down in Brazil.

"From Brazil." *New Orleans Daily Picayune*, March 8, 1866.

This is a paraphrased summary of a letter from Mr. M. S. Swain, who migrated to a plantation on the Bay of Paranaguá. He points out that a number of migrants had arrived from Missouri, with more expected. He describes the agricultural prospects as questionable for cotton but excellent for sugar and coffee, pointing out that sugarcane is much cheaper to produce in Brazil than in Louisiana. All in all, he makes the prospect of migration sound quite appealing.

"Letter from Brazil." *Mobile Daily Register*, November 17, 1869.

Excerpts from a letter from a woman living in Santarém. Her letter reports that her husband is successfully farming and that their life is going well in Brazil. Her only complaint is lack of schools, churches, and society. She includes the prices of basic supplies. The letter is dated September 27, 1869, and signed N.F.W.

"Letter from Brazil." *New Orleans Times*, November 9, 1867.

A migrant from Louisiana, who reached Pará, Brazil, in August 1867, echoes the complaints of the *New York Herald* story above. He speaks of the lack of roads and scarcity of water outside of the valleys and laments that "there is no such thing as cornbread known." Although he describes the method of planting cacao trees, he is already thinking of moving on to Jamaica. He saves his sharpest criticism for the "speculating men who are endeavoring to establish colonies. . . . The manner in which these gentlemen colonists have deceived the people is worse than criminal."

Annotated Bibliography

McMullan, Frank. "Brazil Still Alive!" *New Orleans Times,* January 24, 1867.

McMullan writes this "circular" from Galveston in January 1867 to warn Southerners of the difficulties he has had arranging passage to Brazil through a dishonest agent in New Orleans. But he is still optimistic. He invites any "honorable" Southerners to join him in Brazil in the future.

Meridian Gazette, March 30, June 30, July 4, July 28, and September 14, 1867; June 22, 1869.

This Mississippi newspaper printed a number of letters and articles by and about locals who had emigrated to Brazil. Rev. W. C. Emerson, a Presbyterian minister, moved to Rio and published the *Brazil Emigration Reporter,* devoted to commerce, agriculture, and emigration. His son, Frank, traveled back to Mississippi in September 1867 to sell subscriptions to the paper. A less optimistic view of emigration was contained in a letter from John H. Evans, who returned from Brazil and lectured in towns throughout eastern Mississippi to publicize the hazards of emigrating to Brazil. Another Mississippian, R. W. Wiggins, wrote a letter to the *Gazette* in 1869 in which he chronicled his failure to save his cotton crop from the "army worm" of Campinas and asked for money to return to Meridian.

Montgomery Advertiser, August 8, 1867.

A short article reprinted "from one of the leading journals of Rio." It reports the arrival of more former Confederate planters and mentions the great successes that the earlier emigrants have already achieved in farming.

"The Old South That Went South." *United Daughters of the Confederacy Magazine,* May 1948, p. 2.

A short article reprinted from the *Times-Picayune* interviewing Mrs. Virginia Carlton Fenley, one of the original settlers in Vila Americana. Mrs. Fenley, eighty-eight years old at the time of the interview, discusses her life in Brazil and the reasons for her family's emigration to Brazil.

"Return of the Confederate Colonists from Brazil." *Talladega Watchtower,* August 11, 1869.

A report on the returned Confederate emigrants. The article relates that Dr. George W. McDade, of Montgomery, Alabama, along with several of the other colonists, returned to the United States after an unsuccessful attempt at planting. The account asserts that the emigrants are satisfied to be back in the United States and would not try a second migration to Brazil.

"The Self-exiled Southerners." *New York Times,* May 21, 1871.

A correspondent writing from Rio de Janeiro claims that the Confederate colonists are having a miserable time in Brazil. Many are destitute and would return to the United States if only they could afford the passage.

"Shall Southerners Emigrate to Brazil?" *Debow's Review*, July 1866.

This lengthy article is taken from the report of Robert Merriwether and H. A. Shaw, who arrived in Brazil in November 1865. Their purpose was to explore the country with the object of possible migration by their fellow South Carolinians. They give a fairly detailed summary of agricultural prospects, crop varieties, land costs, and fertility of soil. They point out the difficulties of a foreign language, the "mixed class" of the population, and the lack of transportation and education facilities. Still, they give hortatory particulars of how to emigrate to Brazil. "There is a spontaneous movement of the whole Empire to open wide its arms for the men of enterprise and labor of all nations who have a mind to seek the grandest theatre for the exercise of their energies and the display of their genius ever presented on the face of the green earth."

Shippey, Eliza Kerr. "When Americans Were Emigrants." *Kansas City Star*, June 16, 1912, p. 4.

An account of Mrs. Shippey's experiences in Brazil. She and her family, who were a part of the group led by Ballard Dunn, returned to the United States a few years after arriving in Brazil. The article gives a short overview of the reasons for Confederate emigration, some of her impressions of Brazilian life, and the reasons for her family's departure from Brazil.

Secondary Sources—Major Studies

This category includes books and articles showing evidence of significant research into this topic.

Bullied, James Alan. *The Confederate Exodus to Brazil.* Ann Arbor, Mich.: University Microfilms, 1971.

This master's thesis, written at California State College, Fullerton, in 1971, gives an overview of the Confederate emigration to Brazil. Bullied's analysis includes the reasons for Southern emigration to Brazil, the planning involved in the emigration, the reasons for the failure of the Confederate colonies, and brief overviews of five colonies. The thesis concludes with a discussion of some of the inconsistencies between the colonists' perceptions of Brazil before arriving and the realities of Brazilian life.

Goldman, Frank P. *Os pioneiros americanos no Brasil: Educadores, sacerdotes, covos, e reis.* Translated by Olivia Krähenbühl. São Paulo: Livraria Pioneira Editora, 1972.

Goldman was a native American who lived in Brazil and taught at Brazilian universities for many years. Although he wrote this book in English, only the Portuguese translation seems to be still available. This is a general account of the Confederate movement to Brazil, with particular emphasis on the educational and missionary activities of the emigrants. In one chapter, he gathers together several lists of *confederados* and other Americans who moved to different parts of Brazil during the four decades after the Civil War. This is of par-

Annotated Bibliography

ticular use to genealogical researchers. The book has good footnotes, but no bibliography.

Grier, Douglas Audenreid. *Confederate Emigration to Brazil, 1865–1870.* Ann Arbor, Mich.: University Microfilms, 1969.

This doctoral dissertation, directed by Professor Charles Gibson at the University of Michigan, is a well-researched study of the subject. Grier covers such basic points as the motivation to emigrate by frustrated former rebels; the romanticism versus the reality of emigration; the choice of Brazil over other locales; a study of the type of people who actually emigrated, as opposed to those who talked about, wrote about, and promoted emigration; and a fairly detailed account of the Brazilian experiences of former Confederates Rev. Ballard Dunn (whom Grier detests), Frank McMullan, Dr. James Gaston, Lansford Hastings, William Norris, and others. Grier discusses the economic experiences of the various colonists and their sometimes-difficult relationships with the Brazilian people. He briefly traces the survival of the colonies up to about 1890 and completes the work with an analysis of their influence on Brazilian life, especially in agriculture, education, and religion. Grier rates this influence as far greater than would be expected from such a small number of individuals. Genealogists and other researchers can make use of the appendix, which attempts to name as many emigrants as possible who went to the various colonies in Brazil. Excellent footnotes and a bibliography are included.

Griggs, William Clark. *The Elusive Eden: Frank McMullan's Confederate Colony in Brazil.* Austin: University of Texas Press, 1987.

While concentrating on only one of the Confederate colonies in Brazil, Griggs nevertheless presents probably the single most detailed study of the *confederados*. He focuses on the efforts of Frank McMullan of Texas to plan, organize, and personally lead the foundation of a colony in the interior of São Paulo State. It is a story of one disappointment after another, but this points to the determination of these latter-day pilgrims. Griggs concludes that those who joined up with other Americans in the Santa Bárbara colony had the best chance for success. He explains the gold-mine dreams of some of the colonists but also shows the contributions to agriculture made by those who were willing to work the tropical soil. Griggs includes three appendixes listing the family names of those in the McMullan colony and a collection of photos. His endnotes are excellent, and his bibliography is probably the best source of information for those who wish to begin research into this subject.

Guilhon, Norma de Azevedo. *Confederados em Santarém: Saga americana na amazônia.* 2d ed. Rio de Janeiro: Presença, 1987.

A history of the Confederate emigrants in Santarém. The first part of the work gives a history of the emigration to Santarém, while the second part consists of family histories of the Santarém emigrants. Photographs and family trees of the emigrants are included.

Harmon, George D. *Confederate Migrations to Mexico.* Bethlehem, Pa.: Lehigh University Publications, 1938. Reprinted from *Hispanic American Historical Review* 17, no. 4 (November 1937).

As its name indicates, this twenty-eight-page study concerns itself with Confederates in Mexico during the Maximilian years. However, it casts light on the general motivations and difficulties of expatriation projects of this period and points out that the Brazilian migrations were far better organized than those to Mexico. The study includes footnotes, but no bibliography.

Harter, Eugene C. *The Lost Colony of the Confederacy.* Jackson: University Press of Mississippi, 1985.

This book holds a special distinction among writings in English on this topic. Harter not only has studied the *confederados* but also is a direct descendant. His experiences growing up in Brazil, related in this book, give an extra air of authority to this study. He has gathered first-person knowledge of what some *confederados* (many of his relatives and friends) were doing at the beginning of this century, where they lived, their occupations, and their involvement in Brazilian affairs, particularly the São Paulo rebellion of 1932. Harter gives a good summary of the various colonization schemes and their outcome, with the greatest attention to the colony that became the town of Americana. In addition, he touches on such subjects as Protestantism in Brazil, racial attitudes in Brazil and the United States, and Elihu Root's visit to Americana in 1906. Possibly because of the writer's dependence on oral tradition, this book is not documented in a scholarly manner. Nevertheless, he includes a useful appendix of family names of *confederados*, photos, and a map of principal colonies.

Hill, Lawrence F. "Confederate Exiles to Brazil." *Hispanic American Historical Review* 7 (May 1927): 192–210.

Professor Hill deserves credit for doing some of the very first serious scholarly research into this topic. This article discusses conditions in the South following the war and the reasons for the emigration. It includes details on several of the settlements, including Santarém, Espírito Santo, São Paulo, and Santa Bárbara (Vila Americana).

Hill, Lawrence F. *The Confederate Exodus to Latin America.* Austin: Texas State Historical Association, 1936. Also published in *Southwestern Historical Quarterly* 39, no. 2 (October 1935): 100–134; no. 3 (January 1936): 161–99; and no. 4 (April 1936): 309–26.

Hill provides an overview of the Confederate emigration to Brazil as well as other Latin American countries. He discusses the influence of different publications about Latin America that appeared in the South before and after the war, and the conditions in the South that led many Confederates to consider emigration. A substantial part of the work concerns the settlements in Brazil. Hill traces the fate of the major communities from their departure from the United States to the establishment of colonies and to the eventual return of many of the settlers to the United States.

Annotated Bibliography

James, Edwin S. "The Last Confederates Live in Brazil." Rock Hill, S.C., 1991.

This ninety-five-page typed manuscript, subtitled "A Lecture," is housed in the South Caroliniana Library in Columbia, South Carolina. James was born in Portugal, later married into the family of Dr. James Gaston of Brazilian emigration fame, and lived in Brazil for many years. He first began to hear of this migration at the start of World War II and researched it over the years as a hobby in both Brazil and the United States. He is the first to admit that he is not a scholar or historian, but his personal contacts with some of the scholars who have written about the subject, such as Frank Goldman, and his attempts to talk to descendants in Brazil and in the American South give some authority to his work. Although this is a respectable project on his part, it does not appear to break any new ground; it is, however, a good overview of much of the previously published material. Nevertheless, he gives a good account of how an amateur historian attempts to separate fact from fiction, especially when considering the oral evidence of family descendants.

Jefferson, Mark. "An American Colony in Brazil." *Geographical Review* 18, no. 2 (April 1928): 226–31.

This article is especially interesting because it is an early study of this subject by a geographer. The history of the Vila Americana group is recounted from its founding until 1928, including its agricultural innovations, such as the plow and better-tasting watermelons. The author asserts that the emigrants "were apt to become Brazilianized, as they put it, which seems to mean lazy, shiftless, and content to get along on little. The colony is not expected to endure." The article includes pictures of American houses in Vila Americana.

Jones, Judith MacKnight. *Soldado descansa! Uma epopéia norte americana sob os céus do Brasil.* São Paulo: Jarde, 1967.

Probably more than any other single living person, Judith MacKnight Jones has labored to tell the story of the *confederados*. She has been interviewed many times, has opened a historical museum in Americana dedicated to the *confederados*, and published this book over a quarter century ago. Like other writers on this topic, she summarizes the motivations of the emigrants and tells the story of the various colonies, with the emphasis on Americana. She divides her tale into decades of activity, tracing the *confederado* story through the 1870s, 1880s, 1890s, 1900s, and then on to 1924. She makes a strong case for the cultural influence of the *confederados* on Brazilian life. These influences included farm implements, the kerosene lamp, a type of trolley, schools, Protestant missionary activity, butter production, silk weaving, and the successful cultivation of "dry land" rice, upland cotton, Georgia watermelons, pecans, and Australian eucalyptus. While this book lacks index, notes, and bibliography desired by the scholar, the genealogist who does not read Portuguese can make use of numerous family trees she has compiled, the breakdown by state and year of colonists arriving from 1866 to 1902, and the diagrams showing the location of different families in 1875. The book includes many useful photos.

Nunn, W. C. *Escape from Reconstruction.* 1956. Reprint. Westport, Conn.: Green-wood Press, 1974.

Nunn's book deals entirely with the migration to Mexico. Nevertheless, its descriptions of the motivations of exiles and their difficulties in a strange land often parallel the experiences of those Confederates who went to Brazil. He includes endnotes, a bibliography, and an appendix listing names and home states of Confederates who went to Mexico.

Riker, David Afton. *O último confederado na amazonia.* Manaus, Brazil: Imprensa Oficial do Estado de Amazonas, 1983.

Writing in Portuguese, this Brazilian author has compiled a biography of his father, David Bowman Riker, the last of the original migrants from the Confederacy. Born in 1861, he came to Santarém soon after the Civil War and lived out his life in Brazil, finally dying in 1954 at the age of ninety-two. The ninety-three-page text includes photographs and is followed by a family tree that details the Brazilian descendants of Riker through 1983. An important appendix is the photocopy of Riker's memoirs in eighteen pages of handwritten English, done at the age of ninety. Also included is a Portuguese translation of the 1941 *Saturday Evening Post* article (see below).

Rios, José Arthur. "Assimilation of Emigrants from the Old South in Brazil." *Social Forces* 26, no. 2 (December 1947): 145–52.

This article, a sociological study of emigration, focuses on the assimilation and acculturation of the Southern emigrants in Brazil. It discusses the differences in agriculture, housing, diet, and social culture between the Southerners and Brazilians and how the two cultures influenced each other.

Rolle, Andrew F. *The Lost Cause: The Confederate Exodus to Mexico.* Norman: University of Oklahoma Press, 1965.

Professor Rolle concentrates on migration into Mexico but inevitably covers the motivations of all Confederates who chose to leave rather than reunite with the North. Rolle discusses the return of various exiles years later and the general topic of expatriation. He includes an appendix on exiles to Brazil and other countries, as well as a lengthy bibliography.

Weaver, Blanche Henry Clark. "Confederate Emigration to Brazil." *Journal of Southern History* 27, no. 1 (February 1961): 33–53.

This article and the following one should receive special attention because of the author's long research into the phenomenon of *confederados* in Brazil. This article overviews the Confederate emigration, covering the period immediately following the Civil War to 1871 and discussing the Brazilian emigration policies that encouraged and enabled many Southerners and other Americans to emigrate after the war. Several pamphlets and books that were used for information on Brazil by Southerners are examined, as are the efforts of the

American and Brazilian governments to deal with the colonies that failed, and the attempts of the American officials in Brazil to return some of the colonists to the United States.

Weaver, Blanche Henry Clark. "Confederate Immigrants and Evangelical Churches in Brazil." *Journal of Southern History* 18, no. 4 (November 1952): 446–68.

This second Weaver article, predating the first, discusses the influence of the Southern emigrants on missionary work in Brazil. The author alleges that because of the Southern emigration, the Methodist, Presbyterian, and Southern Baptist denominations established missionary activity in Brazil.

Werlich, David P. *Admiral of the Amazon: John Randolph Tucker, His Confederate Colleagues, and Peru.* Charlottesville: University Press of Virginia, 1990.

Werlich tells the fascinating story of a former Confederate naval officer who was commissioned in the combined navies of Chile and Peru after the Civil War. He spent several years in Iquitos, Peru, on the Amazon River, where he established his headquarters for his main occupation, the command of the Hydrographic Commission of the Amazon. In this role, he encountered some of the Confederates who had emigrated to Brazil. However, this book is primarily the biography of an individual former Confederate who emigrated to the Peruvian Amazon, rather than a study of the phenomenon of Confederate emigration. His attempts to run a Southern-style plantation at Iquitos will sound familiar to those who read of similar activities among the emigrants in Brazil. The author includes excellent notes, bibliography, and index. The bulk of his research was carried out at archives in Peru, Chile, and the United States.

Secondary Sources—Articles

The articles in this section are mostly of the popular variety, with little original research. Nevertheless, their number indicates the fascination with this topic in the popular media.

"Americana, Brazil, Residents Trace Confederate Heritage." *Lubbock Avalanche-Journal,* April 21, 1978.

A short piece about the emigrants, based on an interview with Judith Mac-Knight Jones. It describes some of the emigrants and their descendants.

Basso, Hamilton. "The Last Confederate." In *A Quota of Seaweed: Persons and Places in Brazil, Spain, Honduras, Jamaica, Tahiti, and Samoa,* pp. 99–132. Garden City, N.Y.: Doubleday, 1960. Originally published in *New Yorker,* November 21, 1953.

A *New Yorker* article about Robert Pyles, a descendant of several Confederate immigrant families. The article discusses Mr. Pyles's life in Brazil and the history of some of the Confederate emigrants. He is a descendant of William and Robert Norris and Judson Pyles, who settled close to Vila Americana.

Clark, Elmer T. "A Pilgrimage to Brazil." *World Outlook*, May 1942, pp. 6–8.

The author, a delegate to the General Conference of the Methodist Church in Brazil, made a pilgrimage to Americana to visit the site of the Confederate colony. He interviewed Mrs. Anna Bookwalter, then the only living original colonist, at her home on the former Norris plantation. The article also discusses the beginnings of the Methodist church in Brazil by the Reverend Junius E. Newman and its development by the Reverend John J. Ransom. The article includes three pictures.

Cunningham, Frank. "The Lost Colony of the Confederacy." *American Mercury* 93 (July 1961): 33–38.

This short article decries the sad failure of the Santarém colony. Cunningham bases this article on a report in the mid-1930s by Northwestern University geography professor Dr. W. H. Haas, who claimed to have visited the remnants of the Confederate migration and found the 350-odd descendants living in great poverty. Haas found one very elderly woman who spoke perfect English and could remember her antebellum home. It is unclear if the Haas report was ever published.

Davis, William C. "Confederate Exiles." *American History Illustrated* 5 (June 1970): 31–43.

This article discusses the different areas of the world to which the Confederates emigrated. It includes a short section on Brazil and gives several reasons why Brazil was an appealing destination for the emigrants and why most of the colonies failed.

"Dixie City in Brazil." *Ebony*, November 1966, pp. 89–94.

This short article about Americana is based on interviews with Dr. Jim Jones and his wife, Judith MacKnight Jones. The article reviews the history of Americana and the Confederate emigrants in Brazil and interviews Dr. and Mrs. Jones about their attitudes toward race in Brazil and the United States. It includes pictures of Americana.

Edmonds, James E. "They've Gone—Back Home!" *Saturday Evening Post*, January 4, 1941, pp. 30–47.

Edmonds writes charmingly, though perhaps disparagingly, of David B. Riker, a descendant of Charleston emigrants. Riker remained in the Santarém area around 1940, living beside a jungle river in a house with an American eagle painted on it. He still spoke English, though his children did not. The title of this piece refers to Riker's two oldest sons, who had moved to Detroit

Annotated Bibliography

and gotten jobs with the Ford Motor Company. The article includes photos of a house and of some descendants.

Garner, Phil. "Jimmy Carter in Latin America." *Atlanta Journal and Constitution (Sunday Magazine)*, June 11, 1972, pp. 12–18.

An account of Jimmy and Rosalyn Carter's trip to Latin America. While in Brazil, Carter visited the descendants of the emigrants and laid the cornerstone of the Confederate Museum in Americana. The article includes Carter's impressions of the descendants.

Geyer, Georgie Anne. "Descendants of Confederacy Mark 100th Year of Rebellion against U.S." *Times-Picayune*, February 6, 1966.

Geyer reports on her visit to Americana, Brazil, in 1966. She points out that the few descendants are split into two groups. "The first group has to its credit a textile industry, a university, innumerable doctors and dentists, the first radio station in São Paulo, and many missionaries. . . . The wayward blood of the other group can be found in the Brazilian hill(s), in the red-headed, blue-eyed Caboclos (hillbillies) south of São Paulo." A brief summary of the Norris expedition is included.

Jones, M. "The Southern Confederacy in South America." *United Daughters of the Confederacy Magazine*, October 1948, pp. 28–32.

An article summarizing the emigration to Brazil. The author focuses on the colony at Santa Bárbara, quoting from several articles written by the colonists. The author reports on several of the descendants still living in Vila Americana in 1942, including Mrs. Anna Bookwalter.

Kepp, Michael. "Rebel Refugees Picked Brazil, Home of Cotton and Slaves." *Atlanta Journal/Atlanta Constitution*, August 2, 1992, p. M4. Reprinted from the *London Observer*.

Kepp apparently attended one of the reunions of the Fraternidade Descendencia Americana, which celebrated the 125th anniversary of the migration in November 1991. This short article quotes several of the *confederados*, including Charlotte Ferguson Costarelli, Sydney Mills, Claude McFadden, and Judith MacKnight Jones. Interestingly, Kepp puts the number of Confederate refugees who moved to Brazil at 3,500. The article includes a photo of the gravestone of Col. William Norris (1800–1893).

Lee, Henry. "Brazil's Dixie Fades." *Dallas Morning News*, January 3, 1966, pp. 11–12A.

Lee recounts his visit to Americana in 1965 with a brief history of the Norris colony. He traces the story to the 1960s through conversations with Norris's descendants, the Jones family, named for Dr. Cicero Jones of Troy, Alabama, who joined the colony in the 1890s. A map shows the location of Americana in Brazil.

McDowell, Edwin. "The Confederate Outpost in Brazil." *Wall Street Journal*, August 22, 1975, p. 11.

A report on the descendants of the Confederate emigrants. Based on interviews with Judith MacKnight Jones and her husband, Dr. James R. Jones, the article traces the history of the former Confederates in Brazil. The author concludes that the most lasting Confederate contribution may be to literacy, citing that Americana has one of the lowest illiteracy rates in Brazil, the ratio of schools to pupils is several times above average, and the city has a large library (by Brazilian standards).

Ross, Madeline Dane, and Fred Kerner. "Stars and Bars along the Amazon." *Reporter*, September 18, 1958, pp. 34–36.

A report on some of the descendants of the original emigrants, especially Mrs. William Terrell and Mrs. Julia Jones. The article gives a general history of the Confederate emigration and describes life among the settlers.

Ryan, Michael. "A Continent Away, Confederates Flourish." *Parade Magazine*, September 6, 1992, pp. 14–16.

Ryan bases this article on recent attendance at one of the frequent reunions of *confederados* held in Americana, as well as long discussions with Judith Jones. He includes a discussion with anthropologist John Dawsey, who notes the remarkable double allegiance of the *confederados*: "I am Brazilian, and I am Southern." Noteworthy is Ryan's claim that as many as 20,000 Southerners may have emigrated to Brazil, with only 30 percent returning to the United States. This article gives a good feel for the current culture of *confederados* in Brazil but does not reflect serious historical study. It includes two photos.

Smith, A. M. "Still in Exile, Sixty-One Years after War." *Detroit News*, January 6, 1929.

Smith, a correspondent for the *Detroit News*, visited the remnants of the Confederate colony of Santarém, Brazil, in the fall of 1928. His main source of information was George "Clem" Jennings, who had left Nashville for Brazil in 1867 at the age of sixteen. Now over seventy-five years old, Jennings looked back on the migration as "the foolishest thing a man could do." He felt that the colonists had been misled by false promises of easy living in Brazil. In his own case, he put the blame on General Dobbins, who led a group of migrants, including Jennings and his family, from Mobile to Santarém. The article traces the life of Jennings, his adaptation to the new country, and a description of Santarém in 1928. Besides Jennings, survivors in 1928 were from the Vaughan and Pitts families of Nashville and the Riker family of Charleston, South Carolina. The article includes eight photographs.

Annotated Bibliography

Wiley, Bell I. "Confederate Exiles in Brazil." *Civil War Times Illustrated* 15, no. 9 (January 1977): 22–32.

Wiley has written frequently on the Civil War. This article followed a 1973 visit to Americana, Brazil, where he interviewed Judith MacKnight Jones. He gives a good account of the influences on Confederates who moved to Brazil, including the writings of Matthew Fontaine Maury, Daniel Parrish Kidder, W. W. Wood, Ballard Dunn, and L. Warren Hastings. Wiley summarizes the experiences of each emigrant colony in Brazil, with special emphasis on the Keyes family and the Norris colony at Americana, both originating from Alabama. He gives the Confederates credit for influencing Brazilian society through agriculture, education, and religion. Wiley puts the number of émigrés to Brazil at between 2,500 and 4,000 and concludes that only 20 percent remained permanently—figures that are open to debate. The article includes one map and twelve photos and prints.

Williams, Frederick G., and Roberta S. Rohwedder. "Brazil's Confederate Exiles: Where Are They Now?" *California Intermountain News*, March 1, 1973, pp. 2ff.; March 22, 1973, pp. 5ff.; April 5, 1973, pp. 3ff.

This is an interesting genealogical study of the family of Elijah H. Quillin, an emigrant from Texas who settled in Iguape. He was a Baptist minister and worked to establish the Baptist mission in Santa Bárbara. The article, co-authored by a great-granddaughter of Quillin, traces his descendants through the fourth generation. By the 1950s, many of the descendants had emigrated to the United States. The authors point out the interesting sidelight that of Quillin's approximately one hundred descendants, around half have become Mormons, most of the remainder are Catholics, and only a few have retained the Baptist faith.

General Studies Which Relate to the *Confederados*

Bryant, Solena V. *Brazil.* World Bibliographical Series. Santa Barbara, Calif.: Clio Press, 1985.

This is a general bibliography which will be of use to anyone interested in finding sources relating to any background topic on Brazil, though not specifically on Confederate emigration. It includes a good index and a map of Brazil.

Crabtree, A. R. *Baptists in Brazil.* Rio de Janeiro: Baptist Publishing House of Brazil, 1953.

A historical overview of Baptist missionary work in Brazil, written by a long-time Baptist missionary. Although most of the book is concerned with the mission's work with Brazilians, a few pages (pp. 31–40) describe the American colony in Brazil and its role in attracting the first Baptist missionaries.

Hill, Lawrence F., ed. *Brazil.* United Nations Series. Berkeley: University of California Press, 1947.

Professor Hill has gathered together a collection of chapters written by various Brazil scholars. Arthur Ramos, in a chapter on immigration, fails to mention the *confederados* (probably because they made up such a tiny group when compared with Italians, Germans, Portuguese and Spanish immigrants). In contrast, Manoel Filho makes quite clear the importance of American influences on Brazil's educational system. He points out that Methodist, Baptist, Presbyterian, and Episcopalian missionaries founded schools and colleges that had a beneficial effect on Brazilian educational methods. He fails to make any connection, however, between these schools and the *confederados*.

Hill, Lawrence F. *Diplomatic Relations between the United States and Brazil.* 1932. Reprint. New York: AMS Press, 1971.

In this book-length discussion of Brazilian-American relations from 1808 to 1930, Hill devotes one chapter to the *confederados*, since their existence resulted in certain diplomatic discussions between Rio and Washington, often concerning U.S. citizenship or return migration to the United States. The majority of the chapter discusses each of the settlements and their success or failure. Hill puts the number of emigrants at between 3,000 and 4,000 and makes two interesting points. He wonders why these people would move to a nation that had large numbers of black freedmen of full citizenship if one of their reasons for flight was repugnance at abolition in the South. Also, he points out that many of the *confederados* rejected Brazilian citizenship for the first thirty years or so because they felt more secure with American citizenship.

Kelsey, Vera. *Seven Keys to Brazil.* New York: Funk & Wagnalls, 1940.

In a brief discussion of the *confederados*, Kelsey claims that only about one-third of 3,000 emigrants remained in Brazil. She suggests they might have done better if they had all settled in the same area but admits that Vila Americana thrived during the decades after the Civil War. She implies that many of those who did not stay may have been disillusioned by finding Brazil a paradise that demanded hard work and persistence.

Kennedy, James L. *Cincoenta annos de methodismo no Brasil.* São Paulo: Imprensa Methodista, 1928.

Although this is a general history of the Methodist church in Brazil from the late nineteenth century through the early twentieth century, Kennedy makes plain the important role played by the *confederados*. Specifically, he mentions the preaching of Rev. Junius Newman at Vila Americana in 1869 and the beginnings of the Methodist school in Piracicaba, which was connected with the Southerners and their descendants. The book includes photos of the *Campo* church and the first building at Piracicaba College, as well as numerous photos of Methodist missionaries and their congregations in Brazil.

Annotated Bibliography

Kottak, Conrad Phillip. *Prime-Time Society: An Anthropological Analysis of Television and Culture.* Wadsworth Modern Anthropology Library. Belmont, Calif.: Wadsworth Publishing, 1990.

An anthropological study of the effects of television on Brazil and Brazilians. Using six field sites, television and Brazil's cultural values are compared. One of the field sites selected was the Americana–Santa Bárbara area, chosen in order to study Brazilians with an American cultural heritage. Among other findings, the study links the *confederados'* tradition of literacy and reading to their views on television. The respondents gave some of the most negative evaluations of television and its effects. The author, linking these findings to a tradition of literacy, concludes that the "value of print is expressed through hostility toward television."

Levine, Robert M. *Brazil, 1822–1930: An Annotated Bibliography for Social Historians.* New York: Garland Publishing, 1983.

This work and its successor, *Brazil since 1930,* will prove tremendously valuable to the scholar who wants to find sources on a wide variety of Brazilian topics. Levine includes an introductory guide to reference works on Brazil, as well as separate sections dealing with history, politics, economics, society, and culture. About half of the references are to works in English, with the bulk of the balance being in Portuguese. A few important sources in Spanish, French, and German are included. The book includes both a subject index and an author index.

Levine, Robert M. *Historical Dictionary of Brazil.* Metuchen, N.J.: Scarecrow Press, 1979.

This is another valuable contribution from Levine. Rather than a strictly politico-historical dictionary of terms, this is a far-reaching cultural approach to Brazil which includes information on slang, music, sports, women, and popular culture. The book includes a seventy-page bibliography of pertinent works in English only.

McIntire, Robert Leonard. *Portrait of Half a Century: Fifty Years of Presbyterianism in Brazil (1859–1910).* Sondeos no. 46. Cuernavaca, Mexico: CIDOC, 1969.

In this general history of the first fifty years of Presbyterianism in Brazil, McIntire discusses the roles played by the Southern colonists urging the Presbyterian Church, U.S., to send missionaries to Brazil. McIntire also includes a section concerning the Santa Bárbara church and the founding of Colégio Internacional in Campinas. The book includes a full bibliography through 1959.

Moog, Vianna. *Bandeirantes and Pioneers.* Translated from the Portuguese by L. L. Barrett. New York: George Braziller, 1964.

The writer, a member of the Brazilian Academy of Letters, attempts in this book to explain how the United States has achieved so much economic success while Brazil, seemingly an equal, has not. Within this large discussion, he frequently mentions the Confederate emigrants who made their way to Brazil. He argues that these *confederados* had a distinctly American approach to earning a living and that they had great impact as farmers, innovators, and educators. He disputes the often-repeated charge that these emigrants failed to make a go of colonization in Brazil.

Poppino, Rollie E. *Brazil, the Land and People.* 2d ed. New York: Oxford University Press, 1973.

This well-written overview of Brazil contains a lengthy chapter on immigration but only a brief mention of the *confederados*. Poppino says that about 4,000 "disgruntled Southerners" emigrated to Brazil by 1872, but except for Vila Americana, the colonies failed, and most settlers returned home.

Schurz, William Lytle. *Brazil, the Infinite Country.* New York: E. P. Dutton, 1961.

Schurz calculates the Confederate emigrants at about 3,000 and dismisses the colony at Santarém as a failure. But he recognizes the success of those farmers who settled Vila Americana and points out the fame of Southerners who practiced medicine and dentistry in São Paulo and Rio de Janeiro.

Papers and Archives

Durr, Lucy Judkins. "Brazilian Recollections." N.d. Unpublished typescript in Durr Family Papers, Alabama State Archives, Montgomery. 23 pages.

Born just months before Appomattox, Lucy Judkins Durr emigrated to Brazil with her family in 1868 and stayed less than three years. She wrote this charming reminiscence many years after the events. Considering her extreme youth while in Brazil, it is reasonable to suppose that her "memories" were colored over the years by listening to Brazilian stories from her parents. She even mentions that she had access to the Keyes diary to help her get dates straight. (Her family and the Keyes family interacted a great deal while in Brazil.) She says that her grandfather abandoned The Bluff, the family plantation near Tuskegee, Alabama, which had over 500 slaves at the start of the Civil War, in order to start fresh in Brazil. He purchased Fazenda du Bangu, a plantation twenty-five miles from Rio for $30,000 in gold in 1868. The sale included 30,000 acres, 90 slaves, 125 head of cattle, and a furnished plantation house containing thirty rooms. In spite of successful production of rum, coffee, sugar, corn, and manioc, the Judkinses remained in Brazil only until 1871. Durr examines the question of why so few Confederate emigrants remained in Brazil. She confesses to being too young at the time to know the motivations of her elders. Nevertheless, she posits the theory that cultural differences and homesickness probably were the main reasons. She gives an amusing account of her grandfather's frustration at not learning Portuguese (although she herself easily learned "negro Portuguese" from her slave playmates). In addition, she believes that the pending abolition of slavery in Brazil led her family to return home. Internal evidence suggests that she wrote this account sometime after 1930. She died in 1959 at the age of ninety-four.

The following collections will be of great use to the serious researcher but were not available to the authors of this bibliography.

Archives of the Brazilian Institute of History and Geography, Rio de Janeiro.
Archives of the State of São Paulo, São Paulo.
Barnsley, George S. Papers. Southern Historical Collection, University of North Carolina, Chapel Hill.
Barnsley, Godfrey. Papers. Manuscript Department, William R. Perkins Library, Duke University, Durham, N.C.
Barnsley, Godfrey. Papers. Robert W. Woodruff Library for Advanced Studies, Emory University, Atlanta.
Barnsley, Godfrey. Papers. Tennessee State Library and Archives, Knoxville.
Barnsley, Godfrey. Papers. University of Georgia Library, Athens.
Fayssoux, Callender Irvine. Collection of William Walker Papers, Latin American Library, Tulane University, New Orleans.
McKenzie College Papers. Perkins Theological Seminary Library, Southern Methodist University, Dallas.
National Archives of Brazil, Rio de Janeiro.
United States, National Archives. Papers Relating to Clearance of Ships at New Orleans, Record Group 36, Washington, D.C.
Weaver, Blanche Henry Clark. Papers. In possession of William Clark Griggs, Houston.
Works Progress Administration. Survey of Federal Archives in Louisiana: Passenger Lists Taken from the Manifests of the Customs Service, Port of New Orleans, 1864–1867. Bound Volume, 1941. Louisiana Collection, Library, Tulane University, New Orleans.
Xavier, Jose Hygino, Accountant of the Plantation of São Paulo. Accounting Report on Surveys of Public Lands Designated for American Emigrants, March 5, 1867. Archives of the State of São Paulo, São Paulo.

In addition, we recommend perusal of collections in the various state archives, state and county historical societies, as well as special collections maintained by large public libraries and universities throughout the South.

Contributors

MICHAEL L. CONNIFF serves as Professor of History and codirector of the Institute for Latin American Studies at Auburn University. He has written and edited a number of books on Latin America, including *Urban Politics in Brazil* (1981) and *Modern Brazil* (1989). He is currently writing broad treatments of Latin American history and Africans in the Americas, plus editing a volume on populism in the region.

CYRUS B. DAWSEY is chairman and Professor of the Department of Geography and codirector of the Institute for Latin American Studies at Auburn University. He has published over forty professional articles and reviews on a wide range of topics, including Latin American cultural and economic geography, computer cartography, and geographic education.

JAMES M. DAWSEY, until recently, the Alumni Professor of religious studies at Auburn University, is currently the Dean of the Faculty at Emory and Henry College. Born in Spartanburg, South Carolina, he obtained his Ph.D. in New Testament Studies in 1983 from Emory University. He is the author of *The Lukan Voice: Confusion and Irony in the Gospel of Luke,* and the coauthor of *From Wasteland to Promised Land: Liberation Theology for a Post-Marxist World.*

JOHN C. DAWSEY has published several important papers on anthropological topics in Brazil. In addition to his work on the cultural identity of the *Confederados,* he has conducted extensive research related to the *boias frias* sugarcane workers in the Piracicaba area. A Ph.D. graduate from Emory University, he is a member of the faculty at the Methodist University of Piracicaba and the University of São Paulo in Brazil.

The personal background of Cyrus (Sonny), James, and John Dawsey is tied to the history of the *Confederados.* They and their sister, Suzanne, grew up in the interior of the state of São Paulo in the household of Cy and Marshlea who were missionaries of the Methodist Church. Cy was born in Brazil (as was John), and he was the son of Cyrus, Sr., who also was a missionary and a bishop of the Methodist Church. Cyrus, Sr., arrived in Brazil in 1914, and he preached his first sermon at the Campo chapel of the Americans. For several years the family lived in Americana, and friendships with the descendants of the early adventurers have been maintained over the years.

WAYNE FLYNT is Distinguished University Professor in the History Department at Auburn University. Author of eight books, the best known is *Poor But Proud: Alabama's Poor Whites* (1989), which won the Lillian Smith Award, the Alabama Library Association Award for Non-Fiction, the James F. Sulzby, Jr., Award of the Alabama Historical Association, and the *Choice* Outstanding Academic Book for 1990–91 award.

267

JAMES M. GRAVOIS serves as reference librarian in the Microforms and Documents Department of Auburn University Libraries. As a high-school social studies teacher, he was the recipient of a National Fellowship for Independent Study in the Humanities in 1988. His research topic was *Conquistadors and Mystics: The Paradox of Sixteenth-Century Spain.*

WILLIAM C. GRIGGS is the president of Southwest Museum Services in Houston, Texas, an international corporation that designs and builds interpretive exhibits. A Fulbright Scholar who has served as executive director of two of Texas's most important museums, Griggs taught museum management in Rio de Janeiro to Brazilian museum professionals. He is the author of *The Elusive Eden: Frank McMullan's Confederate Colony in Brazil* (1987), and a recently completed work entitled *Parson Henry Renfro: Free Thinking on the Texas Frontier* (1994), both of which were published by the University of Texas Press.

EUGENE C. HARTER, writer, journalist and career diplomat in the United States Senior Foreign Service is author of *Boilerplating America: The Hidden Newspaper* (1991) and *The Lost Colony of the Confederacy* (1985), named companion book to the PBS documentary *The Last Confederates.* He has lectured and published in the fields of journalism, communications, and American history both in the U.S. and Latin America.

LAURA JARNAGIN (PANG) is the director of the Latin American Center and an associate professor of history and Latin American studies at Colorado School of Mines where her efforts focus on internationalizing engineering education. The author of articles on such issues as the environment and nonrenewable natural resources in Latin America, she is also a consultant to private corporations and Latin American governments on these same matters. She continues to research nineteenth-century Brazilian socioeconomic history and is the co-author of several articles on contemporary Brazil for *Current History.*

CECIL ATAIDE MELO is Senior Teaching Associate in the English Programs for Internationals at the University of South Carolina, Columbia. He is also a doctoral student in the Linguistics Program at USC.

MICHAEL B. MONTGOMERY is Professor of English and Linguistics at the University of South Carolina. He has edited five books on the English language in the American South, including *Language Variety in the South: Perspectives in Black and White* (with Guy Bailey) and *Annotated Bibliography of Southern American English* (with James B. McMillan). He was Consulting Editor for Language for the *Encyclopedia of Southern Culture.* At present he is investigating the influence of Scotch-Irish immigrants on the language of the South.

ELIZABETH J. WEISBROD is Humanities/Music Cataloger at the Ralph Brown Draughon Library at Auburn University. Her research is in the area of information science.

Index

Index